# Power and Progress

# Power and Progress
Joseph Ibn Kaspi and the Meaning of History

Alexander Green

Cover art modified from commons.wikimedia.org/wiki/file:Braunschweiger Quadriga.

Published by State University of New York Press, Albany

© 2019 State University of New York

All rights reserved

No part of this book may be used or reproduced in any manner whatsoever without written permission. No part of this book may be stored in a retrieval system or transmitted in any form or by any means including electronic, electrostatic, magnetic tape, mechanical, photocopying, recording, or otherwise without the prior permission in writing of the publisher.

For information, contact State University of New York Press, Albany, NY
www.sunypress.edu

Library of Congress Cataloging-in-Publication Data

Names: Green, Alexander, (Writer on Jewish philosophy) author.
Title: Power and progress : Joseph Ibn Kaspi and the meaning of history / Alexander Green.
Description: Albany : State University of New York, [2019] | Includes bibliographical references and index.
Identifiers: LCCN 2018046841 | ISBN 9781438476032 (hardcover) | ISBN 9781438476025 (pbk.) | ISBN 9781438476049 (ebook)
Subjects: LCSH: Caspi, Joseph, approximately 1280–approximately 1340. | Jewish philosophy. | Philosophy, Medieval. | History—Philosophy.
Classification: LCC B759.C374 G74 2019 | DDC 901—dc23
LC record available at https://lccn.loc.gov/2018046841

10 9 8 7 6 5 4 3 2 1

*In Memory of my Grandfather*
*Patrick Hart Green (1922–2014)*
*A Proud Canadian Jew*

# Contents

| | |
|---|---|
| Preface | ix |
| Acknowledgments | xv |
| Abbreviations | xvii |
| Introduction | 1 |
| Chapter 1  History as Power and Competition | 13 |
| Chapter 2  History as the Progressive Revelation of the Divine Chariot | 55 |
| Chapter 3  The Pedagogical Structure of the Hebrew Bible | 107 |
| Conclusion | 145 |
| Notes | 149 |
| Bibliography | 191 |
| Index | 205 |

# Preface

This work is a continuation of a study of the ethical and political thought of medieval Jewish philosophers after Maimonides that I began in my last book, *The Virtue Ethics of Levi Gersonides*. The thesis of this book is that Ibn Kaspi develops a two-tiered philosophy of history in his interpretation of the Hebrew Bible, building on Maimonides's philosophy of history; he does so by radicalizing the competitive strength of nations on the political level and combines it with the progressive movement of the knowledge of the divine chariot on the intellectual level. The first model represents the endless competition of states and empires driven by a lust for power and glory, and the second model signifies a cumulative historical process of coming to know and then slowly spreading the knowledge of the nature of the divine chariot, an allegory for the nature and structure of existence. In understanding the medieval philosophical roots of modern approaches to Jewish history and life, it is possible to mitigate the conflict in modern Jewish thought between power and progress seeing that they are not separate political programs, but dependent on one another. For as Ibn Kaspi argues, power needs progress and progress needs power. To our great surprise, a sophisticated and nuanced view of history was possible for some thinkers in the Middle Ages.

One of the central premises of modern Jewish thought is that Judaism is not static, but influenced by history. Some think it is becoming more ethically universalistic or rationally scientific throughout its history. Others attribute this to its involvement in the endless and secular competition between nations that are driven by the forces of power politics. The competition between these two historical narratives can be said to define Jewish modernity. On one side are the nineteenth-century enlightenment scholars of academic Jewish Studies (*Wissenschaft des Judentums*) who sought to create a model of Judaism that idealized its rational elements at the expense of its magic, mysticism, superstition, and particularism, describing a historical process in which Judaism was constantly moving toward greater universalism and rationality. On the other side are the nineteenth- and twentieth-century Zionist leaders and academics who saw Jews suffering, over the course of their history in the Middle Ages, due to their living in exile under Christian and Islamic kingdoms. This second group, they concluded, instead of relying passively on God's help, must assert themselves by reestablishing their own state. The other, progressive, narrative is focused on political emancipation. It attempted to adapt Judaism to fit into modern European nation-states, turning Jews into integrated members of modern liberal societies. The second narrative crystallized into Zionism. It attempted to divorce Judaism from the modern European liberal nation-state and transform Jews into an independent sovereign people with their own nation. Both of these models understand "history" as referring to a discernible pattern and law underlying particular and contingent events over time, but they disagree about the nature of this pattern and the character of that law.

Among the advocates of the first, progressive, model are German Jewish scholars such as Leopold Zunz (1794–1886), the founder of academic Jewish Studies; Abraham Geiger (1810–1874), the founder of reform Judaism; and Heinrich Graetz (1817–1891), the first author of a comprehensive modern history of the Jewish people. They all build on Hegel's model of history as different stages in the development of reason or spirit. Of course, they all reject Hegel's characterization of Judaism as a merely adolescent or preparatory stage, but differ on how Jewish history should be viewed as a development reflective of this process. Zunz lays out a program for academic Jewish Studies, working to revise as well as reconceptualize the tradition in order to prepare Jews for political emancipation. He writes that scholars must "recognize and distinguish among the old and useful, the obsolete and harmful, the new and desirable, we must embark upon a considerable study of the people and its political and moral history."[2] Zunz sharply criticizes the Rabbis as being ignorant, arrogant, and fanatical, thus setting the stage for a reformation of the tradition. Geiger took Zunz's emancipated ideal for Judaism as being the most developed stage to date in a progressively evolving history of Judaism. He divided Jewish history into four stages. The first stage is revelation during the biblical era; the second stage is tradition as it developed from the completion of the Bible to the completion of the Talmud; the third stage is legalism, the "toilsome preoccupation with the heritage as it then stood" lasting until the middle of the eighteenth century; and the fourth stage is liberation, the period of modern enlightenment in which Judaism can express its universalistic essence. The third stage is the most problematic for Geiger, because he saw Jewish law as a historical construct meant to separate Jews from their surrounding society. Now that Jews can be integrated in a more universalistic and scientific culture, he argued, they should abandon the practices that withheld or prevented their integration.³ One of Geiger's critics, Heinrich Graetz, focused on the tension between Judaism understood as a developing liberal religion and Judaism understood as a national entity. He, too, thought Judaism had undergone a four-stage process of historical development, but differed somewhat as to the stages. His first stage is from the Bible to the First Temple; the second stage is from the establishment of the second commonwealth to the destruction of the Second Temple in 70 CE; the third stage is from the Medieval period to the eighteenth century; and the fourth stage is enlightened emancipation and the science of Judaism.⁴

Among the advocates of the second, competitive, and power-based model of Jewish history are notable Israeli scholars such as Isaac Baer (1888–1980), Yehezkel Kaufmann (1889–1963) and Ben-Zion Dinur (1884–1973). The Hebrew term "the negation of the diaspora" (*shlilat ha-galut*) expresses the Zionist critique of the emancipation and enlightenment ideal of history as progressing toward integration and assimilation for Jews in European societies.⁵ Each of these three scholars makes the problem of exile central to their thought and each published a book on this theme. Baer's book *Galut* (*Exile*, published originally in 1947) narrates a history of the concept of exile in Jewish thought since the destruction of the Second Temple, arguing that while it has been a central tenet of Judaism over the last thousand years, the ideal has always been for Jewish sovereign rule. He states this eloquently in writing that "the Galut has returned to its starting point. It remains what it always was: political servitude, which must be completely abolished."⁶ Similarly for Baer, the Holocaust has only confirmed this problem and made this imperative even greater. Kaufmann in his book, *Exile and Alienation*, proposes a "law" that it is impossible for a nation that is removed from its land to exist as a collective for more than a generation or two. The pull to assimilation is too great. The survival of the Jews is an exception to this rule.⁷ Taking this approach even further, Dinur, in *Israel in its Land* and *Israel in Exile*, developed this into an alternative historical method, which has been referred to as "Palestinocentric" in arguing that the Jewish connection to their ancestral land is the main driving force in Jewish history. Here he explicitly rejects the *Wissenschaft* historical narrative for its describing Jewish history as the result of solely external factors and defining Judaism in only religious-spiritual rather than national-historical terms.[8]

Both narratives of Jewish history have clear practical goals, whether they be emancipation and assimilation or restoring national sovereignty. Both approaches are valuable for their noble ideals, but they are also weakened by limiting history to a single teleological narrative. This problem is sharply criticized by Gershom Scholem (1897–1982), the founder of the modern academic study of Jewish mysticism and a keen observer of modern Jewish history and the philosophy of history more generally. While Scholem believes in both the Zionist and the progressive *Wissenschaft* models of history, he is also a critic of both.[9] Scholem's article "Reflections on Modern Jewish Studies," is his challenge to the first group, the progressive and assimilationist German *Wissenschaft* scholars. He argues there that their understanding of Jewish history is driven by apologetics and ignores the demonic.[10] Scholem refers polemically to their project as "grotesque" and perceives it as originating in the liberal Romantic Movement in Germany.[11] He critiques them for presenting an idealized picture of Jewish tradition that ignores its demonic side while grossly and dogmatically simplifying the historical forces that shaped it. As Scholem sees it, their "original sin" is the "removal of the pointedly irrational and of demonic enthusiasms from Jewish history, through an exaggerated emphasis upon the theological and the spiritual."[12] But in ignoring the demonic, he implies that they become demonic themselves! This is why he refers to these scholars as having a "demonic side" and as being "truly demonic figures." Scholem's charge is that in attempting to present an idealized, rational portrait of Judaism and by burying its irrational elements, they mistakenly believe that if they cling to the high-mindedness of the liberal, romantic view of humanity, the ideal can thereby be willed into existence. In falsely supposing one can destroy the demonic, Scholem argues, one is merely encouraging the irrational and the demonic to reappear in other guises.[13] He sees this mistake as going back to the medieval Jewish philosophers who (in his reading) attempted to liberate Judaism from its mythology, the source of the irrational and demonic. Instead of succeeding, this merely encouraged a more uncontrollable mythology to arise in the kabbalah.[14] Scholem expands upon this in *Major Trends in Jewish Mysticism* where he contrasts the medieval philosophers and kabbalists:

> Philosophy ignored these fears, out of whose substance man wove myths, and in turning its back upon the primitive side of man's existence, it paid a high price in losing touch with him altogether. For it is cold comfort to those who are plagued by genuine fear and sorrow to be told that their troubles are but the workings of their own imagination. . . . Philosophy came dangerously near to losing the living God; Kabbalism, which set out to preserve Him, to blaze a new and glorious trail to Him, encountered mythology on its way and was tempted to lose itself in its labyrinth.[15]

Scholem concluded that this attempt by *Wissenschaft* scholars to present Judaism as progressively rational and universal, while ignoring irrational forces, such as the transformation of anti-Semitism from a theological to a racial phenomenon, is also the source of one of the great myths in German Judaism, the existence of a German-Jewish dialogue.[16]

Scholem aims his critique of the second group's narrative of history, which sees power and survival as the sole determining factors, at Zionist nationalists, who were followers of Ze'ev Jabotinsky.[17] Scholem viewed such a worldview as equally dangerous. Whereas the *Wissenschaft* scholars highlighted the higher universalism and ignored the demonic irrationalism, the nationalists glorified the lower human impulses of desire and glory, while neglecting to provide a more noble vision or ideal to guide us (this is my rewording of Scholem's point). This is why, in his youth, Scholem joined Brit Shalom, a Zionist movement that sought the establishment of a bi-national state where Jews and Arabs would have equal rights, and rejected Revisionist Zionism that focused on Jewish sovereignty on all of Mandatory Palestine. He wrote that

> if the dream of Zionism is numbers and borders and if we can't exist without them, then Zionism will fail . . .The Zionist movement has still not freed itself from the reactionary and imperialistic image that not only the Revisionists had given it. . . .[18]

In denying a positive worldly and non-apocalyptic vision that transcends power, he argues, the demonic irrational forces will project itself as an apocalyptic ideal. He sees a constant danger that a secular political project that harnesses messianism for pragmatic ends, will end up being engulfed by it.[19] In other words, if secular politics does not craft a more moderate "messianism" as the end goal of historical striving, he fears that a more radical and wild messianism will take its place. This, I surmise, is what Scholem is intimating in the statement near the end of his life, "The power that Zionism connected itself with, in its victories, was the visible and aggressive force. Zionism has forgotten to connect with the hidden, oppressed force that is due to reveal itself in the coming future."[20]

The relationship between these two narratives of history is not simply a product of the modern era, for they had already been developed within medieval Judaism by interpreters of the medieval Jewish philosopher, Moses Maimonides. The most notable of these interpreters, Joseph Ibn Kaspi, argued that the narratives of both power and progress are essential parts of the Bible.

# Acknowledgments

This book was conceived, researched, written, and edited during my first five years at the University at Buffalo, State University of New York in the Department of Jewish Thought and in its predecessor, the Institute of Jewish Thought and Heritage. I must thank my four colleagues, Richard Cohen, Sergey Dolgopolski, Marla Segol, and Noam Pines for creating the intellectually stimulating environment of which this book is a product. It has furthermore been a pleasure to be at the forefront of a new department, introducing students who had little or no connection to Jewish tradition to the riches of Jewish thought. The lively conversations in class and sharp questions to my lectures have helped sharpen the arguments that lay behind this book. Thank you as well to Jim Bono in the Department of History for guiding me as my initial department chair and guide to the university.

I owe a debt of gratitude to Warren Zev Harvey, Hannah Kasher, Danny Lasker, and the anonymous readers at SUNY Press for reading the manuscript carefully, giving me feedback, correcting my mistakes, and helping me better understand the ambiguities in Ibn Kaspi. I would also like to thank my editor, Jackie Newell, who did an incredible job of helping me refine some of the stylistic aspects of this book, thus making it much more accessible to a wider audience. Thank you as well to the questions and comments of participants of the Association for Jewish Studies and the World Congress of Jewish Studies who attended my readings of sections of earlier drafts of this manuscript that began as conference presentations. In addition, I am very grateful for the kind assistance of Libby Garshowitz who helped me with some of the translations and transliterations. Furthermore, my wonderful wife Keren deserves an important mention as she constantly brings joy and excitement into my life, giving me the stimulus to work late hours over the last few years to research and write this book.

Lastly, I would like to dedicate this book to my late grandfather, Patrick Hart Green (Pinchas ben Shlomo). He passed away in 2014 just as I began studying Ibn Kaspi. While my grandfather was not an academic, he was a scholar of life. He was always reading about history, politics, economics, and other topics, and taking adult education classes until a year or two before his death. He proudly identified as a modern Canadian Jew and would have appreciated Ibn Kaspi's two models of history, recognizing the competitiveness of the world from his own experience in business, and the progress of knowledge through his indebtedness to modern science and its advances. Above all, he was a man of ethical character who always maintained a high standard of conduct in his professional and personal life.

# Abbreviations

| | |
|---|---|
| ADK I | Joseph Ibn Kaspi. *'Adnei Kesef*, vol. i. Edited by Isaac Last. London: Narodiczky, 1911. |
| ADK II | Joseph Ibn Kaspi. *'Adnei Kesef*, vol. ii. Edited by Isaac Last. London: Narodiczky, 1912. |
| AS I | Joseph Ibn Kaspi. *'Asara Kelei Kesef*, vol. i. Edited by Isaac Last. Presburg: Alkalay, 1905. |
| AS II | Joseph Ibn Kaspi. *'Asara Kelei Kesef*, vol. ii. Edited by Isaac Last. Presburg: Alkalay, 1905. |
| AM | Joseph Ibn Kaspi. *'Amudei Kesef u-Maskiyot Kesef, Shnei Perushim al-Sefer ha-Moreh le-ha-Rambam*. Edited by Solomon Werbluner. Frankfurt am Main: Baeck: 1848. |
| Politics | Aristotle. *Politics*. Translated by Carnes Lord. Chicago: University of Chicago Press, 1984. |
| BT | Babylonian Talmud |
| EC | Moses Maimonides. *The Eight Chapters of Maimonides on Ethics*. Edited and translated by Joseph I. Gorfinkle. New York: Columbia University Press, 1912. |
| GK | Joseph Ibn Kaspi. *Gevia Kesef*. English Translation in *Joseph Ibn Kaspi's Gevia' Kesef: A Study in Medieval Jewish Philosophic Bible Commentary*. Edited and translated by Basil Herring. New York: Ktav Publishing House, 1982: 125–276. |

| | |
|---|---|
| *Guide* | Moses Maimonides. *The Guide of the Perplexed*. Translated by Shlomo Pines. Chicago: University of Chicago Press, 1963. |
| MK | Joseph Ibn Kaspi. *Maṣref la-Kesef*. Edited by Isaac Last. Cracow: Fisher, 1906. |
| MT | Moses Maimonides. *Mishneh Torah: The Code of Maimonides*. Edited by Yohai Makbili. Israel: Or Vishua Publications, 2009. |
| MT I-E | Moses Maimonides. *Mishneh Torah: The Book of Knowledge*. Translated by Moses Hyamson. Jerusalem: Feldheim Publishers, 1974. |
| MT XIV-E | Moses Maimonides. *Mishneh Torah: The Book of Judges*. Translated by Abraham M. Hershman. New Haven, CT: Yale University Press, 1949. |
| NE | Aristotle. *Nicomachean Ethics*. Translated by Robert C. Bartlett and Susan D. Collins. Chicago: University of Chicago Press, 2012. |
| QK | Joseph Ibn Kaspi. *Qevuṣat Kesef*. English Translation in Barry Mensch, *Studies in Joseph ibn Caspi: Fourteenth-Century Philosopher and Exegete*. Leiden: Brill, 1975: 7–42. |
| SAK | Joseph Ibn Kaspi. *Sharshot Kesef*. Selection published in Isaac Last, "Sharshoth Kesef. The Hebrew Dictionary of Roots, by Joseph Ibn Kaspi," *Jewish Quarterly Review* 19, no. 4 (1907): 651–87. |
| SHK | Joseph Ibn Kaspi. *Shulḥan Kesef*. Edited by Hannah Kasher. Jerusalem: Ben-Zvi Institute, 1996. |
| TAK | Joseph Ibn Kaspi. *Tam ha-Kesef*. Edited by Isaac Last. London: Narodiczky, 1913. |
| TIK | Joseph Ibn Kaspi. *Ṭirat Kesef* or *Sefer ha-Sod*. Edited by Isaac Last. Presburg: Alkalay, 1905. |
| TEK | Joseph Ibn Kaspi. *Terumat Kesef* (on Plato's *Republic*). Edited by Adrian Sackson. In *Joseph Ibn Kaspi: Portrait of* |

|     | *a Hebrew Philosopher in Medieval Provence*. Leiden: Brill, 2017: 263–94. |
| --- | --- |
| YD  | Joseph Ibn Kaspi. *Yore Deʿa* or *Sefer ha-Musar*. English Translation in *Hebrew Ethical Wills*. Edited and translated by Israel Abrams. Philadelphia: Jewish Publication Society, 1926: 127–61. |

# Introduction

Joseph Ibn Kaspi (1280–1345) was one of the most enigmatic Jewish thinkers of the Medieval period.[1] He was a philosopher, biblical commentator, and grammarian, who wrote commentaries on Moses Maimonides' *Guide of the Perplexed*, wrote commentaries on almost the entire Hebrew Bible, constructed a dictionary of Hebrew roots, wrote summaries of Aristotelian logic and even some of his own theological works. He considered himself a philosophic follower of Maimonides and exegetic follower of Abraham Ibn Ezra, though he was willing to criticize the conclusions of both.[2] Ultimately, the two primary works that he looked to for wisdom are the Hebrew Bible and Maimonides' *Guide of the Perplexed* saying that the "*Guide* is the most perfect work written after the Bible that revealed in hints all the secrets of the Bible."[3] On a personal level, we know that Ibn Kaspi was married and had two sons and perhaps a daughter[4] and that his oldest grandson converted to Christianity. Ibn Kaspi was a man with strong opinions, far from politically correct. He was cynical and openly critical of other individuals and groups: he describes the masses as "horses and mules,"[5] derides the appearance and ways of speaking of local Rabbis[6] and blames women for having lower intelligence.[7] Ibn Kaspi was also a frequent traveler, seemingly never staying too long in one place, traveling to Egypt to meet the great-grandson of Maimonides and later traveling around to many cities in Southern France and Northern Spain. It is not fully certain what Ibn Kaspi's true motivation was for moving around so much. Scholars have proposed multiple reasons, which all may be true and that arise from varying statements in his writings, including marriage troubles, escaping Christian persecution, visiting his children, disputes with fellow Jewish scholars, and meeting likeminded philosophical colleagues.[8]

## Writings

Ibn Kaspi's diverse writings are mostly unified through the adjective "silver" (*kesef*) in the title of each book, using different biblical items made of silver to serve in each title. He lists these all collectively in a work describing all of his other writings entitled *Qevuṣat Kesef* (*Collection of Silver*). The list of his works is as following (not in the order present there):[9]

> *'Adnei Kesef* (Sockets of Silver) or *Sefer ha-Mashal*, Commentary on the prophetic books of the Bible
> *'Amudei Kesef* (Posts of Silver), Exoteric commentary on the *Guide of the Perplexed*
> *Gelilei Kesef* (Rods of Silver), Commentary on the Book of Esther
> *Gevia Kesef* (Goblet of Silver), Discussion of esoteric topics in the Bible
> *Ḥagurat Kesef* (Girdle of Silver), Commentary on the books of Ezra, Nehemiah, and Chronicles
> *Ḥaṣoṣrot Kesef* (Trumpets of Silver), Commentary on the Book of Ecclesiastes
> *Kapot Kesef* (Ladles of Silver), Commentaries on the books of Ruth and Lamentations
> *Keforei Kesef* (Bowls of Silver), Critique of earlier Bible commentaries, lost
> *Maskiyot Kesef* (Settings of Silver), Esoteric commentary on the *Guide of the Perplexed*
> *Maṣref la-Kesef* (Refining the Silver), Systematic commentary on the Pentateuch
> *Mazmerot Kesef* (Snuffers of Silver), Commentary on the Book of Psalms, lost
> *Menorat Kesef* (Candlestick of Silver), Explanation of the Account of the Chariot in the Pentateuch, and in the books of Ezekiel, Isaiah, and Zechariah
> *Miṭot Kesef* (Beds of Silver), Intentions of each biblical book from Genesis to Chronicles, lost
> *Mizraq/Mizraqei Kesef*[10] (Basin/Basins of Silver), Explanation of the Account of the Beginning, lost

*Nequdot Kesef* (Studs of Silver), Explanation of blessings and curses in Bible, lost

*Parashat Kesef* (Sum of Silver), Supercommentary on Ibn Ezra's *Commentary on the Pentateuch*

*Qeʿarot Kesef* (Bowls of Silver), Commentary on the Book of Daniel, lost

*Retuqot Kesef* (Chains of Silver), Principles of the Hebrew language

*Sharshot Kesef* (Silver Roots), Dictionary of Hebrew roots

*Shulḥan Kesef* (Table of Silver), Five exegetical and theological essays

*Tam ha-Kesef* (Silver is Finished), Eight theological essays

*Terumat Kesef* (Gift of Silver), Summary of Averroes' *Commentary* on Aristotle's *Nicomachean Ethics* and Plato's *Republic*

*Ṭirat Kesef* (Turrets of Silver) or *Sefer ha-Sod*, Brief commentary on the Pentateuch

*Ṣeror ha-Kesef* (Bag of Silver), Brief treatise on logic

Assigning every work a title with the noun *kesef*, Hebrew for silver, appears at first to merely add a personal signature to each title since the name Kaspi seemingly refers to the place from which his family originated, Argentière, in which *argent* is French for silver.[11] But the connection between the works is stronger than that as the specific items he chooses all thematically hint to his larger project.

One metaphor that Ibn Kaspi employs, through his choice of silver objects in his titles, is to portray himself as the new biblical Joseph who, like his predecessor, was sold into slavery for twenty pieces of silver.[12] Not literally, but metaphorically, in Ibn Kaspi's case. The twenty pieces of silver represent, for Ibn Kaspi, his twenty different writings. Perhaps Ibn Kaspi wants the reader to imagine that just as the brothers received a gift as a result of forcefully removing Joseph from his home and land, Ibn Kaspi's own (possibly forced) departure from his home and land forced him to compose writings that are an intellectual gift to his fellow Jewish brethren. One can extend the analogy to specific titles of works. The silver goblet (*gevia ha-kesef*) that Joseph placed in Benjamin's sack to test his brothers, is the title of the work that engages with the secrets in the Bible that are often missed.[13] The brothers did not notice that Joseph secretly placed the valuable goblet inside the sack and they required Joseph to reveal its presence, so similarly, the philosophic student did not notice the secrets there and require Ibn Kaspi to reveal the valuable secrets hidden inside the Bible that his "brethren" have missed. Ibn Kaspi continues this analogy by naming his summary on logic, the bag of silver (ṣeror ha-kesef), referring to the bag of silver that Joseph secretly gives to his brothers after accusing them of being spies and demanding they return to Egypt with their youngest brother to prove their innocence.[14] Like Joseph who gave his brothers a secret gift for their own benefit leading them to wonder about the source of this reward, Ibn Kaspi's summary on logic is a gift to his own people in order to give them the tool for inquiry. Another example is in Joseph's wise prediction that there will be a famine and, as a solution, he collects all the money in Egypt, so that he can purchase enough food to store and redistribute slowly and equally over the years of the famine. This future period of the famine is a time when the money is spent (va-yitom ha-kesef from Genesis 47:15) and thus Ibn Kaspi refers to his work Tam ha-Kesef as dealing with the vicissitudes of the world and predicting the future. He discusses there the cause of the destruction of the First and Second Temple and the ability to predict the building of a future Third Temple according to his theory about the vicissitudes of history.[15]

Another metaphor employed by Ibn Kaspi in titling his works objects of silver is to portray them all as the lost pieces of silver from the tabernacle and the temple. Ibn Kaspi follows Maimonides here in that one of the goals of the Bible is to liberate the Jewish people from the sacrificial worship in order to achieve true knowledge of God, where the sacrificial laws in the Bible are merely a temporary concession to the Israelite immersion in Egyptian religion.[16] Ibn Kaspi imagines his Maimonidean project not as simply rejecting the physical tabernacle or the temple that was destroyed, but instead to construct a "tabernacle or temple of the mind" following the structure laid out in the Hebrew Bible.[17] He employs the biblical phrases that are used to describe their construction in referring to his project of writing different works. The purpose of these silver objects is to "minister in the holy place"[18] using the language of the priests' duty in the tabernacle and the temple[19] and afterwards says that "I have surely built a house"[20] quoting Solomon upon completing the temple.[21] The external pieces of the tabernacle, the silver sockets[22] and silver posts,[23] are the titles of the commentary on the prophets, *'Adnei Kesef*, and exoteric commentary on the *Guide*, *'Amudei Kesef*, while the internal objects inside the tabernacle, the silver table[24] and the silver menorah,[25] represent the a deeper explanation of the earlier works dealing with the meaning of the Hebrew language, prophecy, and miracles in *Shulḥan Kesef* and the divine chariot in *Menorat Kesef*. These vessels are described by Ibn Kaspi to be "vessels of different kinds,"[26] which according to the rabbinic tradition refers to the vessels of the temple that were taken into exile by the Babylonians and located at Ahasuerus' palace (and thus when the Book of Esther is chanted in synagogue, for those few words in Esther 1:7, the notes of mourning are used unlike the upbeat cantillation of Esther).[27] In employing this image, Ibn Kaspi boldly sees his own writings as symbolically reconstructing the vessels of the temple that were lost in exile!

## Modern Scholarship on Ibn Kaspi's Philosophy of History

The modern scholarship on Ibn Kaspi has mostly rejected the possibility that he is an independent thinker, portraying him instead as a popularizer of the ideas of Maimonides and medieval Aristotelian thought.[28] Nineteenth-century *Wissenschaft* scholars, such as Heinrich Gross, Ernest Renan, and Moritz Steinschneider, gave short historical bibliographies of his life and works, but did not delve deeply into his thought.[29] Early twentieth-century histories of medieval Jewish philosophy, such as Isaac Husik's *A History of Medieval Jewish Philosophy* (1916) and Julius Guttmann's *Philosophies of Judaism* (1933), mention Ibn Kaspi only in passing.[30] More recent histories, such as Colette Sirat's *A History of Jewish Philosophy in the Middle Ages* (1985) and Eliezer Schweid's *The Classic Jewish Philosophers* (2004) have made efforts to expand the canon, though they, in the end, come to the same conclusion as the earlier historians.[31] Hannah Kasher proposes that the reason Ibn Kaspi's thought has not received the attention of other medieval Jewish thinkers is a result of the genre of his writings. He wrote mostly philosophic biblical commentaries and was too philosophic compared to other exegetes and too exegetical compared to other philosophers. She suggests that he was a "philosopher among commentators and a commentator among philosophers." Furthermore, he did not write an independent philosophical work and did not engage in halakhic writing, which differentiated him from both Levi

Gersonides and Hasdai Crescas who did both and thus achieved greater prominence and, as a result, had a larger historical impact.[32]

This book will explore the originality of Ibn Kaspi's thought within medieval Jewish thought in the realm of the philosophy of history.[33] The philosophy of history asks questions such as: are there patterns through the study of the human past such as progress or cycles? Or is the past inherently irregular and beyond models? What roles do the individual or groups have in larger trends in history and what type of individual or group can have an effect? Is history shaped by the most powerful agents? What does it mean to know and write history? For Ibn Kaspi, there is a unique philosophy of history in the Hebrew Bible and his explication of it is a central focus of his philosophical and exegetical thought. He does not engage with these questions in a single work. His comments are scattered in hints throughout his different writings, in some places more explicitly than in others.

In reconstructing this argument across Ibn Kaspi's many writings, I am indebted to the two articles to investigate his approach to the philosophy of history: Shlomo Pines' "On the Probability of the Re-Establishment of a Jewish State According to Ibn Kaspi and Spinoza" (1963) and Isadore Twersky's "Joseph Ibn Kaspi: Portrait of a Medieval Jewish Intellectual" (1979).[34] Both argue that Ibn Kaspi engages with history in reading the biblical text in a way that is almost unprecedented in medieval Jewish thought and exegesis. Pines analyzes Ibn Kaspi's view in *Tam ha-Kesef* that Jews will return to the Land of Israel at some point in the future. While many German scholars read this as a proto-Zionist statement, Pines clearly differentiates Ibn Kaspi from early-Zionist writers. He argues that, according to Ibn Kaspi, the return of the Jews to their ancestral land is not part of a deterministic plan of history, but merely an historical possibility that should not be ruled out. Sooner or later it may happen, just as all reasonable things may happen at some point in the future.[35] Twersky argues that Ibn Kaspi is an historicist who attempts to understand the meaning of many ambiguous statements in the Bible according to their place, time, and context. He does this through taking the Talmudic expression, "the Torah speaks in the language of the sons of man" which was employed by Maimonides to argue that the Bible has a non-anthropomorphic conception of God, but speaks of God in human terms as a concession to human weakness.[36] Ibn Kaspi expands its usage to explain the Bible's concession to errors, superstitions, popular conceptions, local mores, folk beliefs, and customs. Both Pines and

Twersky discovered important facets of Ibn Kaspi's historical thinking, but, I will argue, did not fully explore the depth and complexity of his philosophy of history.

## Maimonides on History

There has been much discussion in the scholarly literature over whether Maimonides is concerned with history.[37] One could easily leap to the assumption that Maimonides has no interest in history from a dismissive comment he makes near the beginning of the *Guide* where he says

> O you who engage in theoretical speculation using the first notions that may occur to you and come to your mind and who consider withal that you understand a book that is the guide of the first and last men while glancing through it as you would glance through a historical work or a piece of poetry.[38]

Salo Baron famously concludes from this that Maimonides was consciously "unhistorical" in the sense of having a theory of how history operates, though unconsciously he referred to historical events throughout his writings.[39] I would argue, instead, that what Maimonides, like Aristotle, means by "history" here, is a collection of accidents where any meaning in it is purely *accidental*, as opposed to literature, which may describe a historical process and teach important lessons, if as Aristotle would say, the author is wise.[40] Like the Rabbis, who had no interest in history except when it could be turned into midrash (i.e., literature), Maimonides was interested in rewriting history in a mythopoetic or literary manner in order to turn it into a pedagogic medium, i.e., in order to turn it into a story with a moral.

Notwithstanding Maimonides' single disparaging comment on historical writing, he engages in a great deal of it, delineating throughout his writings the historical process of educating the Jews into understanding and accepting monotheism and eradicating idolatry through the introduction and development of Jewish law. An example of Maimonides' historical narrative is in the first chapter of his *Laws of Idolatry* where he describes monotheism as the basic human condition and Adam at the first monotheist. This knowledge that Adam obtained was lost among Adam's descendants as they began to worship the stars as intermediaries to God, eventually transforming the intermediary into an end-in-itself and thus worshiped the stars as gods.[41] This was challenged by the next great figure in history, Abraham, who Maimonides says rediscovered monotheism through his own philosophic reflection and was a charismatic teacher who went around teaching and debating others. He clashed with the dominant theology of Ur and thus became a wandering preacher building up tens of thousands of followers. But even Abraham's attempt to educate his progeny and followers was not enough to prevent the next generation from regressing back into idolatry during their period of captivity in Egypt. Moses' introduction and revelation of law represents the next and superior step for Maimonides in the process of educating monotheism and eradicating idolatry, as law has the ability to achieve goals for which knowledge is not sufficient. This is because most people are more interested in the bodily desires than in knowledge, but law can educate by forming habits and good opinions.[42] Moses' law was able to prevent regression to idolatry and stimulate progress toward proper knowledge of God. Moses' law has enforced stability of religious practice over centuries whereas Abraham's educational community was not successfully transmitted between generations. Maimonides goes on to explain in the *Guide* that the purpose of many of the laws of the Torah are to eradicate idolatrous practices.[43] Maimonides' own project in the *Guide* is to take the next step in this historical progress toward a proper knowledge of God by eradicating anthropomorphism: the tendency to think of God of having a corporeal body, which Maimonides thinks is worse than idol worship.[44]

Jewish law after Moses has its own internal logic and history of development, so central to Maimonides' project that he begins his *Mishneh Torah* with an introduction describing the historical development of Jewish law. He argues that Jewish law is built on the recognition of changing historical circumstances and the need to adapt it to new historical challenges.[45] An example is the writing down of the oral tradition in the Mishna by Rabbi Judah because of calamities facing Jews and the resulting dispersal of Jews throughout the world.[46] For Maimonides, the end point of this historical process is in the coming messianic age when the Messiah, as philosopher and political leader, will restore the full practice of Jewish law, regain Jewish sovereignty, and complete the process of educating the entire world in the knowledge of God, thus eradicating idolatry.

Ibn Kaspi differs from Maimonides in examining the workings of history independently from the development and project of Jewish law, and delineates more boldly and openly than Maimonides the power driven competition between nations in history, and the method by which the details of the divine chariot are progressively revealed over time. I do not believe he saw his interpretation, however, as a departure from the *Guide* and *Mishneh Torah*, but as the correct reading of it.[47]

## "The Reasons for the Stories" (*Ṭa'amei ha-Sippurim*)

Both competition for power and progress through history are taught, Ibn Kaspi argues, in the stories of the Hebrew Bible, so he chooses to put greater focus than Maimonides on the narrative part of the Jewish tradition. This may be a reason why Ibn Kaspi explicitly states in *Ṭirat Kesef* that his objective is to discern "the reasons for the stories" (*ṭa'amei ha-sippurim*), an expression constructed to mirror Maimonides' project in the *Guide* of "the reasons for the commandments" (*ṭa'amei ha-miṣvot*).[48] A close look at the structure of the *Guide* reveals that Maimonides spent twenty-four chapters explicating the reasons for the commandments (*Guide* III 25–49) while only one investigating the reasons for the stories (*Guide* III 50). Ibn Kaspi rectifies that imbalance.[49]

To understand these two kinds of teachings in the Bible, it is important to be aware that they are not explicated in any one place, but, according to Ibn Kaspi, divided up throughout the different biblical texts. Thus it is necessary to consider how artfully biblical texts are constructed and interwoven together. The art of the biblical narrative is an important tool to deciphering the underlying meaning. Ibn Kaspi begins *Shulḥan Kesef* by explaining that

> The intention of this work is to explain one question, namely: what is the advantage of our Torah [Pentateuch] and the other books of the Bible with respect to the language (*siddur ha-lashon*) and the writing (*siddur ha-mikhtav*)—that is, the Hebrew language and the way in which the books are written and ordered—over that which is translated from our language [Hebrew] to another language.[50]

Examples that fall under the category of the "language" and "writing" are, for Ibn Kaspi (not all of which are discussed in *Shulḥan Kesef*): the roots of Hebrew words, the contradictions between biblical texts, the structure of biblical chapters and ordering of chapters, the dispersal of ideas through the biblical canon, the existence of mysterious empty spaces, the usage of equivocal terms, the reasons for repetitions of terms, the decision to be selective over what is disclosed, and the reliance on details that are historically contingent to the ancient world. While some of these are explained and employed by Maimonides in the *Guide*, he does not systematically interpret the Bible in light of these considerations. Ibn Kaspi takes on this task, and attempts to explain many of the textual problems apparent in biblical texts, problems that modern biblical critics will use to question the overall authorial intention of the biblical text.

## Gersonides, Ibn Kaspi, and the Ethical-Political Reading of the Bible in Fourteenth-Century Provence

Levi Gersonides (1288–1344) like Joseph Ibn Kaspi (1280–1345) was born in the 1280s and both died in the 1340s. Both lived in Provence, and both considered themselves followers of the philosophic model of religion begun by Moses Maimonides and synthesized with Averroes' naturalism by Samuel Ibn Tibbon (1165–1232).[51] Samuel ibn Tibbon, along with his son, Moses ibn Tibbon, his son-in-law, Jacob Anatoli (1194–1256), and his grandson, Jacob b. Makhir (approx. 1236–1304) continued the project of transforming Judaism into a philosophic religion. This was part of the movement to translate the great works of Aristotelian science and philosophy from Arabic into Hebrew.[52] The challenge with this model of philosophic religion is that it is overly focused on natural science and mostly ignores practical philosophy.[53]

In contrast, both Gersonides and Ibn Kaspi interpret the project of Maimonidean philosophical religion with a new focus on its practical implications. This was carried out under the influence of the Samuel ben Judah of Marseille's Hebrew translation of Averroes' *Commentary on Plato's Republic* and *Commentary on Aristotle's Nicomachean Ethics* in the 1320s. Gersonides and Ibn Kaspi developed the ethical-political implications of these writings in the form of biblical exegesis. The major commonality to the approaches of both Gersonides and Ibn Kaspi is that the Bible prioritizes the bodily necessity for physical survival as both an ethical and political goal, while simultaneously engaging in a process of greater intellectual enlightenment. They differ, however, on whether the emphasis of the Bible should be on individualistic perfection or whether these goals should be viewed as part of a larger process of history.

Gersonides' model adds two new categories of individualistic virtues to Maimonides' model of ethics, virtues of self-preservation and virtues of altruism, which transcend the political nature of moral virtues. The virtues of self-preservation, endeavor (*hishtadlut*), diligence (*ḥariṣut*), and cunning (*hiteḥaḥmut*) in crafting stratagems (*taḥebulot*), arise as a response to "luck," which is an unavoidable feature affecting everything in nature. The virtues of altruism for Gersonides take the form of a non-political and universal altruistic ethics whereby we are obliged to cultivate the virtues of loving-kindness (*ḥesed*), grace (*ḥanina*), and beneficence (*haṭava*) in both knowledge and action independent of the political community and in imitation of God, who, to his mind, created the laws of the universe for no self-interested benefit.[54]

Ibn Kaspi is much more cynical with regard to individual self-preservation, since he sees the human drive for self-preservation as primarily driven by large world empires. Their rise and fall determine who will succeed and who will fail. He highlights the opportunity for Jews to succeed in reviving their own state as a historical possibility, but only in the sense that any future event is possible and therefore, will happen eventually, given an infinite amount of time and thus the infinite number of possibilities as to how historical events will occur. In contrast, the increase of greater enlightenment is a process that takes place throughout the Bible with regard to knowledge of the secret of the divine chariot, which is merely hinted at in Genesis, but is explained in more and more detail by later prophets. Since Ibn Kaspi is harshly critical of the intellectual level of most people and groups, he sees the the progress of intellectual history as restricted to the few great prophets who have come to know these secrets and explained them in greater and greater detail over time.

## Chapter Summary

The thesis of this book is that Ibn Kaspi develops a two-tiered philosophy of history in his interpretation of the Hebrew Bible. He builds on Maimonides' philosophy of history, radicalizing the competitive struggle of nations on the political level and the progressive movement of knowledge of the divine chariot on the intellectual level.[55] The first model represents the endless competition of empires driven by a lust for power and glory; the second model signifies a cumulative process of coming to know over the course of history the nature of the divine chariot and the slow spread of that knowledge to others.

The first chapter analyzes history as driven by power and competition between kingdoms. This model of history is open to unlimited possibilities, as, he argues, the biblical prophets were fully aware. He argues that this teaching is a secret hidden in the Bible. To understand this truth about political history, it is necessary to dissect key verses and chapters. Examples are: "the scepter shall not depart from Judah" (at Genesis 49:8–10), the command to appoint a king (at Deutoronomy 17 and I Samuel 8), the metaphor of the four animals (Daniel 7) and the prophets' predictions on the destruction of the temple and its rebuilding.

The second chapter describes history as a progressive explanation of the details of the divine chariot described in Isaiah 6, Ezekiel 1 and 10, and Zechariah 6. The imagery of God riding on a chariot is considered by rabbinic tradition to be one of the secret teachings of the Hebrew Bible. Ibn Kaspi, building on Maimonides, argues that the divine chariot is a metaphor for the nature and structure of existence, referred to by Aristotle as "metaphysics." For Ibn Kaspi, the Bible describes a historical process in which different prophets came to discover these truths with greater and greater precision, from Abraham to Jacob to Moses, and share more and more details with others, as we move from Isaiah and Ezekiel to Zechariah.

The third chapter argues that the Bible's method of enlightenment comes through its carefully constructed structure and form. He argues that the Bible is the perfect imitation of the philosophy of nature most importantly through its being written in the Hebrew language. He also argues that the form of the Hebrew Bible is a work of art, intended to convey its message to the reader using many different tools.[56] These devices and tools include contradictions, dispersal, empty spaces, repetitions and choosing to give only selective details. Without an awareness of this one will easily conclude that the text is haphazardly pieced together without foresight or plan. Despite this, he argues concurrently that much of the text is not reflective of a higher truth, but is influenced by the historical context of the ancient society and surrounding culture from which the Hebrew Bible originated.

# Chapter 1

# History as Power and Competition

The first model of history that Ibn Kaspi describes in his writings is political history, defined by power and competition between kingdoms, similar to the kind of history written by ancient realist historians like Herodotus and Thucydides. Ibn Kaspi takes it as a given that political history is not guided by a higher code of ethics or standard of justice, but by realpolitik: the advantage of the stronger. This is unfortunate, of course, for any small minority, like the Jews, but Ibn Kaspi does not think the Jews are fated to be continuously oppressed and persecuted throughout history. He even thinks it is possible that they could return someday to rule their ancient land. This is because he sees history as open to myriad possibilities and argues that the biblical prophets were fully aware of this. He claims that this is a secret teaching hidden in the Bible. To understand this truth about political history, he argues, it is necessary to dissect key verses and chapters of the Bible. These include: "the scepter shall not depart from Judah" (Genesis 49:8–10), the command to appoint a king (Deuteronomy 17 and I Samuel 8), the metaphor of the four animals (Daniel 7) and the prophets' predictions on the destruction of the temple and its rebuilding, all of which are examined in this chapter.

## "Man is Political" by "Nature" or "Necessity"

One place to begin in defining Ibn Kaspi's model of political history is by comparing how he and Maimonides interpret Aristotle's famous statement in the *Politics* that "man is by nature a political animal."[1] Maimonides rephrases Aristotle's statement in the *Guide* as "man is political by nature and that it is his nature to live in society. He is not like the other animals for which society is not a necessity."[2] Maimonides explains there that although he says "man is political by nature" he is not saying that political communities simply exist naturally, without human effort, but rather that humans, unlike other animals have a need to form political communities and live in them. He argues that diversity of temperament is unique to man. This makes it necessary for us to live in a community founded by laws. For we need laws to provide order and perfect character, by moderating natural extremes of temperament, pushing us always toward the mean. This is what Maimonides means when he says "that the Law, although it is not natural, enters into what is natural."[3] This law can take place in the form of either political law or divine law, but there is one crucial difference between these laws. Political laws perfect only the body, by abolishing injustice. Divine laws, however, perfect both the body and the mind by teaching correct opinions.[4]

Ibn Kaspi quotes Maimonides' restatement of Aristotle with one subtle but important change of emphasis, stating that "man is political by necessity." This is in his *Commentary on Ecclesiastes*. He applies his version of Aristotle's statement to help interpret the verse "And moreover I saw under the sun, in the place of justice, that wickedness was there; and in the place of righteousness, that wickedness was there":[5] He states that

> Here is another important matter that shows the uselessness of this [political] wisdom, namely that the entire world is sustained by judgment, as our Rabbis said: "by three things is the world sustained: judgment, truth and peace" (*Ethics of the Fathers* 1:18) and they also said: "pray for the peace of the government; for were it not for the fear of its authority, man would swallow his neighbor alive" (Ibid., 3:2). This occurs, without a doubt, when the political ruler is clever and wise. One should pitch one's tent,[6] and fix one's residence in a just and righteous place, in other words, the city in which the clever and wise king rules and most of the people in the political community are righteous and wise because "man is political by necessity." Even more so, when the exalted sage, who delves deeply into his own thoughts, makes choices in

these worldly matters. But we see that what is a place of justice today will be the opposite tomorrow because a new generation or a new king[7] will arise, as it is explained: 'how the faithful city has become an adulterous city! She that was full of justice, righteousness lodged in her, but now murderers." (Isa. 1:21)[8]

It can be seen from this that Maimonides and Ibn Kaspi draw very different lessons from the "necessity" of man's political nature. For Maimonides, man's political nature is necessary like eating or drinking are necessary for his existence. Maimonides takes this as a sign that laws are needed in any human society to establish order and foster moral and intellectual improvement. For Ibn Kaspi, however, the actualization of man's political nature by forming a regime, whether a political or divine law, is dependent on forces beyond human control. Perhaps this is why Ibn Kaspi emphasizes that "man is political by necessity," instead of "man is political by nature," for if politics does not represent a striving toward perfection in human nature, but is instead a force that one cannot fully control; it follows that one should be involved with it only by necessity. A consistent standard of justice cannot be ensured over time, Ibn Kaspi argues, because it is impossible to predict what the nature of the next ruler will be and, therefore, whether or not he will be just or enforce justice. This lesson, he hints here, can and should be taken from events in the Bible. For example, the Pharaoh described in Genesis may have been just, but he proved unable to pass this on to his successor, who had no concern with justice, as is shown in Exodus. Likewise, by quoting Isaiah, in the above passage, Ibn Kaspi shows us that the same is true of justice in Israelite society, again as described in the Bible. There, too, justice depended on the same subjective whims of rulers. Some were concerned with morality and justice, some were not. History, for Ibn Kaspi, is accidental and has no rhyme or reason. Contra to Hegel, history has no progress or direction.

## Why Write an Epitome of Averroes' *Commentary* on Plato's *Republic*?

For Ibn Kaspi, man is political only by necessity since the political community cannot be the foundation for achieving human perfection of character and mind. The vicissitudes of regime change and the inability to ensure a consistent standard of justice makes the political community too unstable for moral and intellectual perfection. Why, then, does Ibn Kaspi write a faithful summary of Averroes' *Commentary on Plato's Republic* entitled *Terumat Kesef* (Gift of Silver)? It may be because Plato advocates, in the *Republic*, having political leaders who are also philosophers. Such a leader is characterized by Averroes as being a combination of "'philosopher,' 'king,' 'Lawgiver'; and so also is 'Imam.'"[9] Does this not contradict Ibn Kaspi's position that one should not rely on an ideal or just political community to come to fruition? Why summarize the *Republic* if its ideal is so rare as to be unrealistic?[10]

Medieval Islamic philosophers were divided between two opposing readings of Plato's *Republic* revolving around the question of the relationship of the philosopher to the political community. Al-Farabi argued in *The Perfect State* that the ideal city described in the *Republic* is a realistic possibility and that philosophers must strive to make it a reality, while Ibn Bajja argued in the *Rule of the Solitary* that the ideal city of *Republic* is not a realistic possibility and philosophers must strive to avoid involvement in the political community, except when necessary.[11] Ibn Kaspi's interpretation of Plato's *Republic* follows that of Ibn Bajja (though he does not cite him) that the philosopher must focus on his own perfection and avoid political rule. Like Ibn Bajja, Ibn Kaspi did not believe that human beings can, by their own power, effect meaningful change in the political community, and thus concluded that political activity is a waste of time. Better to stay home and study.

It is difficult to get a sense of where Ibn Kaspi stands from a quick perusal of *Terumat Kesef*, since it is mostly a summary of Averroes' commentary.[12] In general it is difficult to ascertain the editor's voice in such an epitome since both Averroes and Ibn Kaspi do not often speak in their own voices.[13] One way to decipher Ibn Kaspi's position, in such a close summary of a text, is to notice what Ibn Kaspi leaves out of his summary and consider how he chooses to end it. He ends his discussion of the *Republic* with a summary of how unrealistic a philosopher-king would be, a summary that is taken from Book VI of the *Republic*. He leaves out Plato's famous allegory of the cave of Book VII, his discussion of less than ideal regimes in Book VIII, the case Plato makes for the unhappiness of the tyrant of Book IX and the image of the afterlife he gives in Book X (which are mostly summarized in Averroes' *Commentary*). In moving directly from the critique of the philosopher-king to a case for knowledge as the final purpose for a human being, Ibn Kaspi's summary ends with a poetic defense of a secluded philosophic life.[14]

Ibn Kaspi's interpretation of the *Republic* in *Terumat Kesef* can be fleshed out by examining where and how he quotes Plato's *Republic* or uses political ideas influenced by it, in other writings where he is more forthright. The central lesson Ibn Kaspi draws from the *Republic* is that rule by philosopher-kings is highly unlikely and, absent this, it is necessary for the philosopher to be separate from the non-philosophic citizens in order to avoid trouble. In *Terumat Kesef* he follows Averroes' summary of Plato, showing that political communities do not benefit from the involvement of philosophers for two reasons: first, inhabitants do not care to follow the recommendations of the wise; and second, those who aim for wisdom do not possess all the necessary qualities for leadership, and so will end up doing more harm than good. In a non-virtuous city, therefore, a truly wise philosopher must avoid irritating or even inadvertently harming his fellow citizens, thereby turning them against him. If possible, therefore, he should choose a solitary life.[15] One can see the importance of this position for Ibn Kaspi in his biblical interpretations. In *Tirat Kesef* he states that he has no intention of seeking friendship with others, referring to the masses derogatorily as animals, and using an analogy of an individual with a candle looking to "light the flame," a metaphor for his social relations with others.

> My custom was to minimize friendship with other human beings and I was very careful not to speak about important matters. This was due to my dismay regarding my lack of knowledge of that which is beyond me. I will not be consoled by my superiority over horses and mules. Therefore, my customary way of acting with my contemporaries was analogous to that of an individual who gets up from his bed [in the middle of the night] to do some chore at home and has no candle. He takes a wick and goes to the extinguished stove filled with ash to look for a burning coal or a spark of fire to light his wick. If he finds some, he will light his wick and if not, he will go back to sleep. This is the way I act with regards to other people. If one of them has a spark of fire of what I consider the true religion, I continue speaking with him. If not, I leave his home in peace and close the door.[16]

Ibn Kaspi thus recommends as much separation as possible between the philosopher and the masses and would necessarily suggests that a perfect society must look down upon the ignorant masses, commenting on Proverbs 29:27, "one who endeavors to live in peace with surroundings by hiding views sins to truth."[17]

The only possible role he sees for a philosopher is in the rare occasion when it is possible to rule in a virtuous city in such a way as to spread wisdom to others. Ibn Kaspi praises the biblical Joseph as such a rare case. He interprets the fact that Joseph was named "one who reveals secrets"[18] as significant, since knowledge of secrets and hidden matters are indicative of a prophet. Joseph is also credited by Ibn Kaspi of ruling over the Israelites for eighty years, longer than any other ruler.[19] His greatness is also shown in Joseph's controlled behavior toward his brothers. He was not angry about the loss of his silver goblet,[20] Ibn Kaspi says, because a wise man does not need external goods. Ibn Kaspi also praises the fact that Joseph did not try to kill his brothers for this insult, instead controlling his pain.[21] But the example he chooses of Joseph's rule as an ideal of philosophic rulership also reveals the limits of even such a success, for the next Pharaoh returned to the more common pattern of non-virtuous rule. Furthermore, Ibn Kaspi points to a statement Jacob makes upon being reunited with his son after many years. Jacob says that he was happy to see him, but not happy to discover that he had been in a position of political leadership. According to Ibn Kaspi, Jacob said:

> It is an extremely important matter to me that my son Joseph is alive, but the matter of his high position is not worth mentioning for it is not something that in itself makes me happy about my son, as you may have thought.[22]

Perhaps the reason why we don't have a summary of the third book of *Averroes' Commentary on Plato's Republic* by Ibn Kaspi, is that he did not summarize it, since the third book focuses on the different regimes, while Ibn Kaspi thinks that the difference between them is quite negligible, except in extremely rare cases, like Joseph's. This would fit with Ibn Kaspi's view that the political science of different regimes is not something the philosopher should truly be focused on, politics being a matter to be practiced by philosophers only when constrained by necessity.

## Prophecy as Divination of
## Political History and the Chosenness of Israel

Ibn Kaspi argues that man is a political animal only by necessity and that it is wise for the philosopher to avoid political rule in most cases since most governments and leaders are only concerned with their own venal self-interest. In this, he agrees with Ibn Bajja, but he differs with him over one crucial matter. For, Ibn Kaspi does not suggest that the wise should avoid all interest in the well-being of political communities. Although he is skeptical as to whether the wise can guide political communities toward justice, he argues that prophets have a unique ability to foresee and predict the future especially with respect to the rise and fall of nations and empires, and can make recommendations both to rulers and citizens in light of their predictions.

Ibn Kaspi thus thinks that the role of the prophet is not modeled on that of Plato's philosopher-king. The prophet's role is purely to predict the future. In this regard, he rejects Maimonides' model in the *Guide* of the prophet as philosopher-king and is closer to Averroes, who, in his commentary on Aristotle's *Parva Naturalia* 2.3 (458a33–464b18) restricts prophecy to knowledge of the future.[23] The test of a true prophet, Ibn Kaspi argues in *Shulḥan Kesef*, is to predict the future correctly.[24] His understanding of prophecy is rooted in five key verses in Deuteronomy:

> I will raise them up a prophet from among their brethren, like unto thee; and I will put My words in his mouth, and he shall speak unto them all that I shall command him. And it shall come to pass, that whosoever will not hearken unto My words which he shall speak in My name, I will require it of him. But the prophet, that shall speak a word presumptuously in My name, which I have not commanded him to speak, or that shall speak in the name of other gods, that same prophet shall die. And if thou say in thy heart: "How shall we know the word which the LORD hath not spoken?" Then a prophet speaketh in the name of the LORD, if the thing follows not, nor come to pass, that is the thing which the LORD hath not spoken; the prophet hath spoken it presumptuously, thou shalt not be afraid of him.[25]

He explains the meaning of this verse in the next section of *Shulḥan Kesef*:

> Here [in Deuteronomy 18:18–22] Moses teaches us how to differentiate between a true and false prophet. Namely, that the man who predicts for us a future occurrence in the name of God, saying "so it will be tomorrow or the next day," either for us or for others, for society or for the few, predicts with certainty, of which I mean, it is not conditional, neither on time or place, or without certain limits [and it comes to pass]. If the matter does not occur in the exact way as predicted, he is doubtless a false prophet.[26]

God, he argues, presents the future outcome to prophets through metaphors either in positive decrees, which are described as prophecies of consolation in the Bible,[27] or in negative decrees, which are described as prophecies of doom in the Bible.[28] Prophecies of consolation, he argues, are prophecies of a "necessary future" (*'atida meḥuyevet*), a positive vision of the future that is certain, with no possibility of being reversed. However, prophecies of doom, he argues, provide a "contingent future" (*'atida 'efsharit*), a negative vision of the future which *can* be reversed.[29] Why should one be fixed and the other not, leaving room for human freedom only with respect to the latter?

This is original to Ibn Kaspi, not found in Averroes' discussion of dreams and prophecy. Ibn Kaspi claims it underlies Deuteronomy 18. He makes this claim on the basis of there being two forms of prophesy which he compares to two different kinds of scientific premises. Necessary prophecies are predictions of the future based on unchanging laws, like the laws of physics (unchanging in Aristotle's understanding), and as a result the outcome will happen as predicted without any possibility of an alternate outcome. He compares necessary prophecies to the prediction that the sun will rise tomorrow. No one doubts whether this will happen or not, because it is based on physical laws, which, following Aristotle, are eternal and do not change. Contingent prophecies, however, are dependent on factors that are not fixed so multiple outcomes are possible. He compares contingent prophecies to specific predictions of the weather for a specific day. Predicting the exact amount of rain or snow that will fall on a specific day is a chancy business, as every weatherman knows, because this is dependent on too many environmental factors. Similarly, one cannot assume or predict that the amount of rain or snow will be the same next winter as it was in the previous winter.[30]

One form of prophecy described in the Bible is the prediction of a necessary future outcome, which is positive. Necessary prophecies are not restricted, Ibn Kaspi argues, to a specific time frame, so when a prophet predicts something will necessarily happen, he means only that it will happen at some point in the future, since the potential for it happening is always there. It is necessary, according to Ibn Kaspi because he follows Aristotle in thinking that everything that is potential will at some point happen given an infinite amount of time.[31] In other words, anything that can happen, will happen, at sometime in the future, but no one knows when. Maimonides cites this same Aristotelian principle in *Guide*, II 1 with respect to natural species, but not with respect to historical individuals.[32] Ibn Kaspi differs from Maimonides in the application of this principle to particular events in history. In other words, contingent events are constant and necessary only in the sense that they are potential, but not yet actualized in history. Therefore, prophecies predicting some necessary future can speak only in generalities and cannot be limited to any specific time frame. The examples that Ibn Kaspi quotes in his introduction to this form of prophecy in *Shulhan Kesef*, Exodus 13:17 and Numbers 14:21-23, both affirm God's covenant to the patriarchs that God will take the Israelites out of Egypt and bring them into Canaan in order to build them up into a great nation.[33] In *Gevia Kesef* he explains that the meaning of a "covenant" (*brit*) is as a metaphorical expression of something permanent and necessary whose likelihood of coming to be is as necessary as the sun rising tomorrow. What it is not like is predicting specific weather on a specific day: tomorrow's rain, for example, which is contingent on too many variables.[34]

He goes on to interpret, in *Gevia Kesef*, the covenant with Abraham in Genesis 15 as an example of covenant which is necessary. God predicts that the Israelites will be enslaved in Egypt for four hundred years, "thy seed shall be a stranger in a land that is not theirs, and shall serve them; and they shall afflict them four hundred years."[35] The problem is that this does not appear to fit Ibn Kaspi's criteria of a necessary prophecy, because prophecies predicting bad news, and prophecies predicting that something will happen at a specific time, both fall into his category of contingent prophecy: prophecies that will not necessarily happen. Ibn Kaspi acknowledges this is a problem, but tries to overcome it by arguing, first of all, that God's covenant actually presents a positive outcome, and therefore is good news. Positive outcomes, however, sometimes require suffering and punishment as necessary to achieving them. He gives two very different examples of this: the pain and suffering of pregnancy and child birth being a necessary part of the process of procreation; and the danger of traveling by sea as being necessary for making a profit.[36] He concludes that "servitude and affliction were essential for improving our forefathers in body and soul."[37] Therefore, slavery in Egypt, Ibn Kaspi argues, was necessary to make the Israelites worthy of inheriting the land of Canaan and building the temple. Therefore, according to Ibn Kaspi, God's prophecy of enslavement was actually good news, a metaphor for the natural processes of improvement and education required to achieve physical, moral, and intellectual perfection.[38]

Another central facet of this point is in *Tam ha-Kesef* where he discusses the promise as part of God's covenant with Israel to bring the Jews out of exile and back to the land of Israel. He sees the necessary nature of God's prophetic promise in Deuteronomy 30:4–5:

> If any of thine that are dispersed be in the uttermost parts of heaven, from thence will the LORD thy God gather thee, and from thence will He fetch thee. And the LORD thy God will bring thee into the land which thy fathers possessed, and thou shalt possess it; and He will do thee good, and multiply thee above thy fathers.

Unlike Deuteronomy 18, this statement is undeniably good news, and it does not predict a specific time or place, both of which are characteristics that make it a necessary prophecy, one that promises a necessary future event. In explaining this verse in *Tam ha-Kesef* he says that

> He did not specify a time for this—not one and not two; rather, he said that, from God, it is always true for us. . . . And it is known that He did this once with Nebuchadnezzar and the return of the Second Temple. Why, then, should he not do so again, a second time—or more? He is the First and He is the Last![39]

God's covenant with the Jews is constant, therefore, and predicts an outcome that will necessarily happen at some point in the future because the covenant is a necessary prophecy. In being part of the covenant, the

Jews have the ability to actualize their natural potential because they follow the Torah which is an outcome of Moses' perfect comprehension of the natural world.

Prophecies forecasting doom in the Bible serve a very different purpose, according to Ibn Kaspi, predicting a negative future event which is contingent and changeable because they predict an outcome dependent on specific human events that are limited to a specific time frame. Such a prediction reflects the current trajectory in accordance with human behavior, but such a prophecy can serve as a warning to change their behavior, and thus change the predicted outcome. Often the outcomes of these human choices can even be seen to affect the future of a nation. He provides numerous examples of this through his biblical commentaries.

One example of the unpredictability of the future is God's prediction to Rebecca when Jacob and Esau were in her womb that "two nations are in thy womb, and two peoples shall be separated from thy bowels; and the one people shall be stronger than the other people; and the elder shall serve the younger."[40] Medieval commentators often read this as a prediction of the future of Jews and Christians.[41] Ibn Kaspi finds contingency and not determinism in this statement, in interpretation of Isaac's response to Esau explaining why he cannot give him the same blessing that Jacob stole from him:

> And when I said that he will overcome you and you shall serve him (Gen. 27:40), it is true and will so happen, because it is God's word, but this matter will not necessarily always be so when you will remove his yoke from your neck (Ibid.) . . .and he will not overpower you forever and you will remove the burden from your back for a while. It so happened many times even during the period of the First Temple, let alone when the First Temple was destroyed, as it is written, "remember, O LORD, against the children of Edom the day of Jerusalem; who said: 'rase it, rase it, even to the foundations thereof'" (Psalm. 137:7). And here he did not say to him that he [Jacob] will not serve you because that is what happened [in that Jacob did serve Esau], and God knows all future outcomes.[42]

For Ibn Kaspi, God's prediction to Rebecca, when Jacob and Esau were in her womb, and Isaac's blessing to Esau are not meant as final determinations, but as a prophecy of a contingent future where sometimes

Esau's descendents will rule and sometimes Jacob's descendents will rule. God is teaching that when it comes to the rule of nations, even the Jews are subject to the same laws as other nations. There will be times when Jacob and Esau's descendents will wield greater power.

Prophecies that predict a contingent future are specific with respect to the parties, places, and times involved, which allow multiple contingent prophecies to coexist since different prophecies can have overlapping criteria. Because they do not always specify all the same criteria, they may appear to contradict one another. Ibn Kaspi makes this the central issue in his commentary on the Book of Esther, *Gileli Kesef*.[43] He argues that there are two decrees by King Ahasuerus, one to destroy the Jews and another that allows the Jews to defend themselves. Robert Eisen very astutely suggests that Ibn Kaspi's hints in his discussion of this work that this story is meant to be read metaphorically with King Ahasuerus representing God. Eisen deduces this from statements Ibn Kaspi makes in other writings.[44] This might explain why Ibn Kaspi ends the work with the statement "one of the fundamental doctrines that we learned from this book is God's providence and mercy on us."[45] Otherwise, it is difficult to see how a commentary that analyzes conflicting decrees of a human king and makes little mention of God could teach us about God's providence.[46] The first decree of the king is sent out under the influence of Haman where he orders

> To destroy, to slay, and to cause to perish, all Jews, both young and old, little children and women, in one day, even upon the thirteenth day of the twelfth month, which is the month Adar, and to take the spoil of them for a prey.[47]

The second decree of the king is sent out under the influence of Mordechai where he orders

> That the king had granted the Jews that were in every city to gather themselves together, and to stand for their life, to destroy, and to slay, and to cause to perish, all the forces of the people and province that would assault them, their little ones and women, and to take the spoil of them for a prey, upon one day in all the provinces of King Ahasuerus, namely, upon the thirteenth day of the twelfth month, which is the month Adar.[48]

Reading these as two decrees of God, raises the question of how the latter decree can simply cancel the earlier one. Surely, God cannot be contradicting himself!

Ibn Kaspi's answer is that one must see the two decrees of the king in the Book of Esther as prophecies regarding the contingent future, which therefore can exist simultaneously since they were constructed for different people, at different times, in different places.[49] In other words, neither will necessarily come to fruition, but both are possible outcomes.[50] Indeed, Ibn Kaspi argues, there are crucial differences between the two decrees that limit their interfering with each other. The first difference is that the decrees are written for different actors, for the first decree applies to every country and people, and the second decree applies only to the Jews. The second difference is that neither decree limits the freedom of the actor of the other decree. The first decree is not dependent on the Jews and does not say that the Jews must submit to the yoke and sword or that they should not take revenge or fight back since the command to destroy the Jews applies to nations only. The second decree is written for Jews only, giving them the right to resist and destroy their attackers and does not restrict their attackers from continuing to attack the Jews as commanded in the first decree. Both decrees, therefore, are true at the same time, so much so that Ibn Kaspi goes so far as to say that both would be correct even if the king had sent them both out at the same time.[51] The conclusion to be drawn from this is that God gives freedom both to the Jews and to their enemies. Moreover, Ibn Kaspi argues, prophecies like these forecasting doom often serve as warnings to the Jews so that they can take the necessary steps to protect themselves.

One further issue that concerns both types of prophecy, those that predict a necessary future and those that predict a contingent future, is the question of how do prophets obtain knowledge of the future. Ibn Kaspi does not explain how these prophecies differ explicitly, but gives hints in various places in his writings. His emphasis is on predicting a necessary future in *Menorat Kesef*, and on predicting a contingent future in *Tam ha-Kesef*.[52] One of his most detailed statements about the nature of obtaining knowledge of the contingent future is in *Tam ha-Kesef* where he says:

> God knows contingent future events and how His knowledge alters what may be realized in actu, until, at times, He reveals this secret to his servants, the prophets, without there

26 / Power and Progress

> being any compulsion on His part . . .This is analogous to our Sages, excellent in divination and estimation, who might say of a man whose business and affairs seem jinxed that he will make a poor choice tomorrow or the following day, whether in some matter of matrimony or business or in any mundane matter, whether it be commercial or otherwise.[53]

From these examples, Shlomo Pines, argues that the prophet obtains knowledge of a contingent future based on knowledge obtained through experience in the world. Pines interprets Ibn Kaspi as saying that

> Knowledge of the future, with that of God himself, is like that possessed by experienced people concerning the way in which business transactions or marriages may be expected to turn out—that is, such knowledge is of a probalistic nature. The prescience of the prophets is of the same nature."[54]

Because specific outcomes are rooted in the variability of matter, however, this form of knowledge cannot have demonstrative certainty. Philosophical proofs, therefore, will not help the prophet predict the future, with respect to determining probable outcomes. The prophet can best determine a probable outcome by looking at the specific material factors involved, carefully observing the person, time, and place most likely to affect that event. This is how the prophet can best determine the probable outcome. Scholars of Ibn Kaspi have criticized Pines for reading too much into Ibn Kaspi's comparison between human divination and divine foreknowledge in *Tam ha-Kesef*, but I think Pines' position can be maintained without relying on that comparison alone, and also by restricting it to contingent prophecies where even God's knowledge is less certain by exploring the nature of "experience."[55]

Ibn Kaspi explicitly discusses the nature of "experience" in his interpretation of why Jacob rebukes his sons for taking revenge on Shechem for the rape of Dinah in *Gevia Kesef* chapter 23. Ibn Kaspi begins by approving of the actions of Jacob's sons, for the entire city of Shechem was guilty not only of not opposing this horrendous action, but of remaining silent, and even being amused by it. He adds that the sons' act of wiping out the nations of the land was consistent with the intentions of God's eternal covenant, and is therefore a fulfillment of a necessary prophecy.[56] Notwithstanding, Jacob's response is that

Ye have troubled me, to make me odious unto the inhabitants
of the land, even unto the Canaanites and the Perizzites; and,
I being few in number, they will gather themselves together
against me and smite me; and I shall be destroyed, I and my
house.[57]

Notwithstanding Jacob's rebuke of his sons' behavior, Ibn Kaspi observes that his sons conducted themselves properly according to the standards of eternal God's covenant, but they failed to take contingent matters into consideration. In support of this point, he references Aristotle's argument in the *Nicomachean Ethics* 6.11 (1143b12–14 p. 130) that wisdom from those who have experience is sometimes more important than theoretical knowledge for determining the correct action.[58] Ibn Kaspi states that

> Now even though this is all true, the writer of the Torah
> demonstrated to us the wisdom of old, experienced men, as
> Aristotle said in the *Ethics*, that to listen to the old is no less
> than to listen to demonstrative proof.[59]

The conclusion Jacob drew, in Ibn Kaspi's estimation, is that it would have been wiser to consider the likely result of such an action. Jacob was not as confident as his sons that their military operation was a smart decision for them *at that moment* (even though it was just) since he felt they did not calculate all the contingent variables. Jacob likely feared that while they may have defeated Shechem, his sons did not calculate the potential repercussions of such a victory, including the possiblity of retaliation by another nation in Canaan. Such a retaliation, and the possible consequence of being killed or weakened, would make it more difficult to realize the promise of the covenant of progeny in the land of Canaan. Therefore, Jacob argues, "one should certainly not (endanger oneself) in order to hasten the appointed time that had been told to Abraham."[60]

It seems that the art of prophecy in predicting a contingent future requires the cultivation of practical wisdom which one learns from experience. Aristotle argues that

> One sign of what has been said is the fact that the young
> become skilled in geometry and mathematics, and are wise in
> such things, but a young person does not seem to be prudent.

>The cause is that prudence is also of particulars, which come to be known as a result of experience, but a young person is inexperienced: a long period of time creates experience.[61]

Since practical wisdom is based on complex circumsances that are always changing, learning how to adapt and predict the future requires time and experience. It is not something one is born with.

Ibn Kaspi quotes from the same line in *Nichomachean Ethics* 6.11 to refer to the advisers of King Ahasuerus in the Book of Esther, "those who knew the times"[62] with the comment that "Aristotle says that to listen to the old, who have experience from their long life, is no less valuable than to listen to demonstrative proof."[63] The implication being that the old are the ones with the experience needed to guide the king into making the right decisions. Their advice is based on their predictions on contingent matters coming from their experience. Unlike King Ahasuerus who is quick to anger and rash to act, such advisors can better guide the king because they have practical wisdom. An example of this is seen in the case of Vashti who refuses to bow before the King. His advisors recommend a royal decree expelling Vashti from the King's household and giving her royal estate to another.[64] Their reason for such a drastic action is to pressure wives to submit to their husbands.[65] If we follow Ibn Kaspi's reading of the Book of Esther as a metaphor, in which King Ahasuerus represents God and Vashti represents matter that is rebellious (women serving as a metaphor for matter being a common medieval trope), then these advisors can be taken to understand the unpredictability of matter (represented by Vashti's rebellion) and provide a solution to properly respond to it. This source, not mentioned by Pines, strengthens his reading that King Ahasuerus does not have sufficient knowledge of future contingent particulars and therefore needs to consult with his advisors who are experts in this because they have greater experience. Even God, Ibn Kaspi argues, does not have certain knowledge of future contingent particulars and therefore needs to consult with his "advisors." Perhaps these advisors are a metaphors for the separate intellects which guide the celestial spheres, and through which God knows these contingencies.[66]

One last example elaborates Ibn Kaspi's argument that experience is the basis for knowing future contingencies is Jonah's prediction of the destruction of Nineveh. The story in the Book of Jonah is unique in the Hebrew Bible for God delivers the prophecy to Jonah that Nineveh will be destroyed, but the people repent and are saved from annihilation by fleeing the city. Jonah received this prophecy from God that Nineveh would be destroyed in forty days (Jon. 3:4), but, according to Ibn Kaspi, Jonah did not know if it was necessary or contingent. He only learned the answer to this question by witnessing its destruction while standing outside the city.⁶⁷ Jonah also witnessed the people fleeing the city while it was destroyed, which taught him that the prophecy was necessary with respect to the city, but contingent with respect to the people, allowing them to repent and escape.⁶⁸ Here again, the prophet understands the contingent meaning of a prophecy through his own experience and not through deductive reasoning.⁶⁹

The prophet's process of obtaining knowledge of a necessary future is further described by Ibn Kaspi through the example of Jacob's ladder in *Menorat Kesef* and in *'Amudei Kesef* where he comments on *Guide* I 15, where Maimonides briefly discusses the story of Jacob's ladder as a metaphor.⁷⁰ In the original biblical narrative, Jacob had a dream of a ladder that spanned from the earth to the heavens on which angels of God were ascending and descending.⁷¹ Maimonides interpreted this dream in *Guide* I 15 as a metaphor for the prophet's relationship to the political community. He says that

> For after the ascent and the attaining of certain rungs of the ladder that may be known comes the descent with whatever decree the prophet has been informed of—with a view to governing and teaching the people of the earth. As we have made clear, it is on this account that this is called *descent*.⁷²

The prophet thus leaves the community to "ascend" in order to know the intelligibles and then "descends" to return to the community to share this knowledge with them through teaching and leadership.⁷³ Ibn Kaspi builds on Maimonides' interpretation, but sees it as an example of a prophecy that predicts a necessary future since Jacob's ladder represents the process of coming to know the highest levels of non-contingent reality. He describes in *Menorat Kesef* how

> [Section 1] Chapter 8. One must ask, what is the relationship between comprehension of the theoretical sciences and knowledge of future events in time, whether particular or general, as happened to Jacob, who after comprehending all

of existence, was also told: "the land upon which you lie, to you will I give it, and to your descendents" (Gen. 28:13). It happened similarly to Isaiah when He said to him: "I saw the Lord sitting upon a throne high and lifted up, and His train filled the temple" (Isa. 6:1) and similarly with Ezekiel in the Account of the Chariot and with Zechariah as will be explained further. . . .

. . . Every prophet prophesized through the imaginative faculty, except for Moses whose level of comprehension was superior to anyone before or after him. He comprehended all of existence. [At this point,] he did not comprehend any future events that will happen to him or Israel, like Jacob did in the vision we mentioned, and we find similarly in Isaiah, and similarly to Ezekiel and Zechariah.[74] There is no doubt that knowledge of what is intelligible and necessary is more important than [predicting] future events in time that are potential and possible. However, this occurs to the noble individual from the equivocality of the lower imagination with the discourse of the perfect and this is the first reason.

The second reason is that when the prophet comprehends the separate intellects and the spheres specifically and especially extraordinary knowledge, he will understand the immediate and distant causes and it will lead him to comprehend in general and particular the effects of the separate intellects and the utility of the spheres in that time according to their astronomical observations and changes. In this there are many, and from this he can recognize and see in their essence future matters whether good or bad. Therefore, Jacob saw his success and his descendants' success from the isolation [of his intellect with respect to comprehending] the spheres and the separate intellects. Thus Isaiah predicted the destruction of the people, Ezekiel predicted the destruction of the First Temple, Zechariah predicted the building of the Second Temple, and this essentially arises from intellectual comprehension.[75]

The process moves from comprehension of the sublunar world, to that of the spheres, and finally, to the intelligibles. Once obtaining this theoretical knowledge, the prophet can see astrological predictions of certain future events and use that knowledge to forsee future events, whether good or bad.

There are two apparent problems in this text that seem to undermine the argument that such a prophet sees necessary as opposed to contingent reality. More generally, this seems to contradict the twofold category of prophecy he elaborates in Shulḥan Kesef. The first problem is that the examples he speaks of here are of particular historical events that are both good and bad, of consolation and doom, such as the destruction and rebuilding of the temple, but in Shulḥan Kesef he identified prophecies bearing good news as necessary prophecies and those bearing bad news as contingent prophesies. This may lead the reader to conclude that here, he is collapsing the two categories of prophecy that he laid out in Shulḥan Kesef. It is as if the prophet who understands the secret of the reality underneath the metaphor of the chariot, can look at all the causes and rules in nature and use that knowledge to predict the specific actor, time, and location of an event with certainty, even over matters that Ibn Kaspi earlier identified as contingent. But I think this is a misunderstanding of what Ibn Kaspi means by "particular" (peratiyut) in the prophet's prediction of the destruction and rebuilding of the temple. He is suggesting that the prophets predicted these events in a general sense, but not that they knew the exact actor, time, and location of which the event will occur. In this, he follows Avicenna, who argues that God knows the particulars in a general sense only. God's knowledge is of the universal features and properties of all material particulars, but God does not have knowledge of all the contingent details.[76] The specific times of the temple's destruction and rebuilding are dependent on such contingencies as the rise and fall of larger surrounding empires and the actions of Judean leaders in response to them, but God's promise of the temple and the philosophical idea that it represents is dependent on God's eternal covenant with the Jews in their Torah, which is a mirror reflection of the necessary reality of nature and its structure. These predictions, therefore, are not contingent, but necessary, prophecies.

This may help explain a second apparent difficulty in this text where Ibn Kaspi suggests that Moses' prophecy is unique because it features the rational faculty only and not the imaginative faculty (following Maimonides). Moses, therefore, did not predict future events like other prophets, such as Jacob, Isaiah, and Ezekiel.[77] This seems to be highly problematic since many of Moses' statements in Deuteronomy are predictions of the future, and this is according to Ibn Kaspi's own reading. For example, Moses predicts that after his death the Israelites will fall back into idolatrous worship saying, "for I know thy rebellion, and thy stiff neck; behold, while I am yet alive with you this day, ye have been rebellious against the LORD; and how much more after my death?" (Deut. 31:27). This prediction is actually used by Ibn Kaspi in *Tam ha-Kesef* as the primary example of a prophecy predicting a contingent future, for it is based on Moses' own experience with the Israelites' temptation to return to other gods during his lifetime. Ibn Kaspi suggests that any prophet could predict such a possibility.[78] This reveals a clear contradiction between *Menorat Kesef* and *Tam ha-Kesef*, where in *Menorat Kesef* he presents Moses' prophecy as completely absent of the imaginative faculty and thus not concerned with predicting the future, as opposed to *Tam ha-Kesef* where Moses' prophecy contains examples of predicting the future. The likely explanation is that Ibn Kaspi's objective in *Menorat Kesef* is to defend a model of intellectual progress with regard to teaching the knowledge of the divine chariot, but at the same time he strongly defends the immutability of the Torah against the Christians who present a model of progress that goes beyond the teachings of the Torah. In contrast, Ibn Kaspi's objective in *Tam ha-Kesef* is to highlight the Torah's emphasis on human contingency in order to keep open the possibility of the return of the Jews to their ancestral land, which is a central feature of prophecy, including Moses' prophecy of the Torah. The truth is, Moses' prophecy has both necessary and contingent elements, for Ibn Kaspi, but he is not willing to reveal that everywhere.[79]

To conclude: both forms of prophecy can have an impact on the realm of history of empires competing for power, with some rising and others falling. Their rise or fall is a result of the choices and actions of individuals. The prophet can warn these individuals and help them change their ways and thus influence the future survival or destruction of great powers. On the one hand, Israel is dependent on the contingent vicissitudes of history for its success like other nations. On the other hand, unlike other nations, Israel's existence and future is independent of the vicissitudes of history since its covenant and Torah are a reflection of natural laws that are necessary and not contingent.

## Divine Justice in the Bible and God's Role in History

One implications of prophets' predictions of the rise and fall of nations, cities, and civilizations being not necessary, but contingent, is that God is not directly involved in this level of nature. For this, Ibn Kaspi draws upon Maimonides' argument in *Guide* II 48 and applies it to political history. Maimonides argues that although God is the first cause of everything in nature, nothing in the sublunar world is caused by God directly, but by intermediary causes which form a causal chain that originates in God, who is the first cause and origin of all the rest. This is complicated by one of the pedagogical methods employed by the Hebrew Bible which, according to Maimonides, is to ascribe individual acts directly to God that are in fact caused by intermediary causes.[80] In *Menorat Kesef*, Ibn Kaspi applies this to Moses' project in the Torah which he interprets as guiding its reader from falsely perceiving God as an intermediary cause to comprehending that God is solely the first cause. This is done, he argues through its usage of different names for God. He argues that it is not accidental that Genesis 1:1 refers to God as *Elohim* and not YHVH, since *Elohim* refers to the spheres. Conventional opinion in the ancient world was to attribute creation to the God's intermediaries, the spheres, so Moses began with a conventional opinion and transitioned from *Elohim* in Gen. 1:1–2:3, to YHVH *Elohim* in Gen. 2:4–3:24 to YHVH in Gen. 4:1–6:8.[81]

God being a first cause only and not a proximate cause, means that He does not know all future contingencies that will shape the course of history. This is why Ibn Kaspi refers to God in *Tam ha-Kesef* as the "Lord of intellectual divination" (*'adon ha-shi'ur ha-sikhli*) who knows all the future possibilities, but does not know which of these possibilities will actually happen, or when. In this sense, he is comparing God to an expert investor who knows the stock market and can predict the probable success of certain stocks, but cannot guarantee that all the factors will work out in his favor.[82] Building on our earlier discussion of the Book of Esther as a metaphor, in *Gililei Kesef* this also helps explain why King Ahasuerus is a fitting metaphor for God since King Ahasuerus, like God, created the system but now leaves future events to the whims of the players who operate it and compete within it.

But if God's frequent description in the Hebrew Bible as a proximate cause in nature is to be taken as a metaphor, how can Ibn Kaspi explain God's "decision" to destroy certain civilizations (the flood[83] and Sodom and Gomorrah),[84] or "changing His mind" and saving another, Nineveh in the Book of Jonah? He solves this dilemma by quoting the Talmudic expression that "there is no death without sin, and there is no suffering without iniquity"[85] implying that in both cases their punishment was not a result of God's capriciousness, but a just punishment of sin.[86] The sin and punishment, in Ibn Kaspi's understanding, are not directly caused by God, but are the result of the natural law caused by God. In the case of the flood, God's statements of "seeing" are to be taken metaphorically: "And the LORD saw that the wickedness of man was great in the earth and that every imagination of the thoughts of his heart was only evil continually"[87] applying *Guide* II 48.[88] But what precisely was the evil and sin that the generation of the flood committed? Ibn Kaspi argues that it was following their own physical pleasures instead of following God as their guide to how to live. Consequently, they raised men who misused their physical strength to kidnap and rape women of physical beauty, leading to the violence of that generation.[89] Ibn Kaspi goes so far as to say that their sin spread to animals, plants, and houses, which is why Noah had to bring animals on board the ark along with humans.[90] He does not explain how this violence spread to plants, animals, and houses, but may mean that men who treat women as means to their own physical pleasures are unlikely to show any regard for other creatures and objects. If we rule out God being the direct or proximate cause of the flood, as Ibn Kaspi argues, then we are left with their sinfulness leading to their punishment through natural cause and effect. This makes sense if the flood is taken as a metaphor teaching the following lesson: a society that is premised on the violent fulfillment of their physical desires cannot survive the resulting chaos. Ibn Kaspi's conclusion, therefore, is that it is better to follow God's law as a guide for perfecting oneself and best to live following the natural order.

There is a significant difference between these two stories of God's destruction. The sins of the people living in the time of the flood are explicitly set out in the Hebrew Bible, but the sins of Sodom and Gomorrah are left ambiguous.[91] The only information in Genesis is that "the men of Sodom were wicked and sinners against the LORD exceedingly"[92] and "the cry (*za'akat*) of Sodom and Gomorrah is great, and, verily, their sin is exceeding grievous."[93] Ibn Kaspi's solution is to read the Book of Ezekiel to understand what the sin of Sodom and Gomorrah was, even though this story is in Genesis. He justifies this by arguing that the prophetic writings are written as a commentary on the Pentateuch.[94] Ezekiel says of Sodom and Gomorrah:

> Behold, this was the iniquity (*avon*) of thy sister Sodom: pride, fullness of bread, and careless ease was in her and in her daughters; neither did she strengthen the hand of the poor and needy. And they were haughty, and committed abomination before Me; therefore, I removed them when I saw it.[95]

According to Ibn Kaspi's interpretation, in *'Adnei Kesef*, Ezekiel explains that the fullness of bread and careless ease was not the sin itself, but it was their pride and haughty attitude in having all these riches, while being unwilling to share them or help others. This is why the text goes on to say that they did not help the poor and the needy. Ibn Kaspi argues that Genesis hints at this by using the word "cry," which does not refer to the haughty sinners, but to the poor who were crying for help.[96] The cause of the sinfulness of the people of Sodom and Gomorrah, then, has this similarity to that of the people at the time of the flood: both prioritized their physical desires at the expense of others and against God's law, which advocates a more just way of acting and priorities that transcend the body. God's destruction of Sodom and Gomorrah is thus a metaphor for the natural devolution of any society that prioritizes the fulfillment of the physical pleasures of its members alone.

The only account in the Hebrew Bible of a city that repents and avoids God's decree for destruction is that of Nineveh, as described in the Book of Jonah. God begins by proclaiming their destruction through Jonah saying, "yet forty days, and Nineveh shall be overthrown,"[97] but accepts their repentance and agrees to reverse his decision, stating "and God saw their works, that they turned from their evil way; and God repented of the evil, which He said He would do unto them; and He did it not."[98] The cases of the flood and Sodom and Gomorrah were straightforward since God's destructions were, metaphorically, fulfillments of the laws of nature. But how can Ibn Kaspi account for God suddenly changing his mind in the case of Nineveh if God does not intervene directly, and is only a first cause? The answer given in the biblical text is that the people of Nineveh, including the king, prayed and repented of their sin.[99] Both repentance and prayer are symbolic of overcoming bodily desire, which is what caused the sins that led to the destruction of the people in the other two stories. For repentance requires actions, like fasting, that resist the bodily desires, and prayer, following Maimonides' interpretation, a priority that transcends the needs of the body, for its purpose is to gain knowledge of God and the universe.[100] The conclusion that the king and nobles of Nineveh came to was "who knoweth whether God will not turn and repent, and turn away from His fierce anger that we perish not?"[101] Ibn Kaspi interprets this statement in *Shulḥan Kesef* to mean that they realized that God's decree (at Jonah 3:4) was contingent upon repentance and prayer. They were not sure, however, in what way it was contingent. Could God's decree be averted altogether, or would their city be destroyed in any case, but the people be allowed to escape?[102] They came to discover that the correct interpretation of God's decree was that they could escape the city and be saved. Ibn Kaspi also applies this argument to answer why God presents Himself as a proximate cause when He is actually only the first cause in the destruction of Sodom and Gomorrah. Thus, the statement in the next verse that "God repented" at Jon. 3:10 and changed His mind is considered by Ibn Kaspi to be a prime example of the seventh contradiction in *Maskiyot Kesef*. There he states that when there are two premises, one which presents God as directly involved and cancelling a decree, this is the exoteric view for the masses, while the true view of God is not that He is a proximate cause and does not intervene directly. This is crucial for Ibn Kaspi, because, otherwise, there would be no leaving room left for human freedom.[103] The leaders of Nineveh came to understand this truth and thus saved their people, unlike those at the time of the flood and those in Sodom and Gomorrah who were doomed to destruction.

### "The Scepter Shall Not Depart from Judah" (Gen. 49:8–10)

One of the most important contingent prophecies in the Bible for Ibn Kaspi is Jacob's blessing to his son Judah in Genesis 49:8–10 that predicts that his descendants will merit political rule as kings of Judah and Israel. The meaning of this prophecy is also one of the central points of contention between Jews and Christians.[104] Jacob's blessing is that:

> Judah, thee shall thy brethren praise; thy hand shall be on the neck of thine enemies; thy father's sons shall bow down before thee. Judah is a lion's whelp; from the prey, my son, thou art gone up. He stooped down, he couched as a lion, and as a lioness; who shall rouse him up? The scepter shall not depart from Judah, nor the ruler's staff from between his feet, 'ad ki yavo shilo, ve-lo yekehat 'amim.[105]

For both Jews and Christians, Judah is the ancestor of King David and of King David's son who built the temple, and it is from Judah that the messiah will descend. For Christians, this blessing alludes to the coming of Jesus and the theological and political supersession of Christianity over Judaism as the redemptive force in history,[106] while for Jews it refers to the rule of the Davidic line through kingship which, according to the Talmud, continues through the exilarchs in the Babylonian diaspora.[107] Much medieval polemic between Jews and Christians is rooted in the interpretation of these verses.

Ibn Kaspi's argument is that this blessing is a prophetic prediction of a contingent future of Judean kings from David to Zedekiah. By suggesting that it is contingent and therefore not necessary, he makes Judean kingship dependent, like that of other nations, on power and politics. This blessing, Ibn Kaspi argues, is not a promise of rule by a consistent line of Judean kings for all time. If Jacob's prophecy is contingent, this differentiates it from God's covenant with the Jews, that Ibn Kaspi argues is independent of history and reflects a necessary reality. Ibn Kaspi's teaching here forsees that Jews will not always wield kingly power and that Jacob's prophecy predicted that the success of their rule would be limited in time. However, Ibn Kaspi argues in *Maṣref la-Kesef* that the contingency of Jacob's prophecy is a "great secret" that was hidden for a thousand years.[108] Discovering it requires deciphering the meaning of the metaphors in the biblical passages through an examination of the roots of the Hebrew words. One such example of a metaphor is the description of Judah as a lion, which according to Ibn Kaspi is important since the lion is the king of all the animals, just as Judah's descendants will be kings of the Judean kingdom.[109] Since the relationship between kingdoms is inherently competitive, Ibn Kaspi interprets the line "from the prey, my son, thou art gone up"[110] to mean that Judah went from being a powerless "prey" to being a powerful "lion," reflecting the success of the Judean kingship. The alternation of ups and downs in this passage, he argues, reflects the fluctuation of power that is inherent in power relations between kingdoms.[111]

The contingent and temporary nature of this prophecy is also reflected, Ibn Kaspi argues, in the statement that "the scepter shall not depart from Judah."[112] In *Sharshot Kesef*, he explains the root of scepter, *sh.v.t.*, as referring to a staff or stick, but one which is metaphorically attributed to rulers since it is customary that a ruler has a staff in hand.[113] Therefore, Genesis 49:10 could be read as "the kingship shall not depart from Judah." While this clause taken by itself would seem to propose that the Davidic kingship is eternal, this is not what Ibn Kaspi thinks the clause meant to convey, for he thinks it is limited by the next clause, "*ad ki yavo shilo.*" This can be translated in more than one way, but Ibn Kaspi thinks the correct translation is "as long as they come to Shiloh" (Gen. 49:10). In *Maṣref la-Kesef*, Ibn Kaspi criticizes the Christian interpretation of applying *shilo* to an individual, referring to Christ, and argues that Christian copyists falsely changed the last letter from a *heh* to a *ḥet* and thus read the word as *shaliaḥ*, messenger. Thus, in their reading, God's covenant is with the Jews until Christ (= *shilo* = *shaliaḥ*) comes.[114] Ibn Kaspi criticizes the Christian reading by going back to the root of *shilo*, *sh.l.h*. Because they did not study the text in the original Hebrew, he argues that the Christians misunderstand its meaning since the translation cannot preserve the Hebrew roots and all the different forms that arise from the same root which are connected to one common meaning.[115]

He explains in more detail the meaning of the Hebrew root *sh.l.h* in *Kapot Kesef* in commenting on the verse "her enemies are at ease."[116] He explains that the general meaning of this root refers to a mistake, but its usage in worldly matters has to do with being at rest. He draws a causal link here between making a mistake and being at rest, seeing one as the efficient cause of the other. Applied to political rule, a ruler who makes a crucial mistake will be overcome by a stronger party because of the competitive nature of the world, and put down to rest. By "rest," he means no longer in motion. The verse continues with "for the LORD hath afflicted her for the multitude of her transgressions,"[117] so her rest, or defeat, has an efficient cause, her transgressions. Ibn Kaspi implies that those transgressions were the result of an error in judgment.[118] If this understanding of the meaning of *shiloh* is applied to its use in Genesis 49:10 it would read as follows: "the kingship shall not depart from Judah, until error causes its downfall (though not permanently)."[119] As Ibn Kaspi reads it, Jacob's prophecy was not a uniquely Jewish message in the sense of applying *only* to the Jews, because its prediction of the future is based on understanding the nature of politics, which is true for all nations. Therefore, for Ibn Kaspi, although this verse may predict the end of Jewish sovereignty after the destructions of the First and Second Temples, it leaves open the possibility of a renewed Jewish sovereignty and a Third Temple at some time in the future. He criticizes Christians for interpreting the destruction of the Second Temple as a permanent supersession of Judaism, arguing that they misunderstood the laws of politics, unaware that what happens historically is contingent and is open to the possibility of a renewal of Jewish sovereignty. He explains in *Maṣref la-Kesef* that

The beginning of this [prophecy] is from the time of David and ends in the time of Zedekiah, in other words, it was constant from the time it began and did not cease until the time of Zedekiah. Even though it was weakened and lessened as a result of the division into ten tribes, this is not a problem, because anyway it did not cease, since much of Israel submitted to Judah, a fortiori to Benjamin. Also, in the time of Jehoshaphat and Hezekiah it is explained, for one who is proficient in the Prophets and the Chronicles, that most of the ten tribes came under the protection of Judah. And this does not prevent the return of Zerubbabel and also the Third Temple because [the prophecy] did not intend to limit this motion from its beginning point until its end when the First Temple was destroyed during the time of Zedekiah.[120]

. . . One who posits and reports the beginning of a motion, and determines its end, absence or rest, which is a location of a period [of motion] between the beginning point and the end point, does not exclude the return of this motion at another [later] time.[121]

Applying Aristotelian physics to politics is unique to Ibn Kaspi. In Aristotelian physics, the motion of an object is always caused by the motion of something else, but since such motion is caused by a contingent force, it must at some point come to rest. Maimonides in the *Guide* summarizes Aristotle's understanding of rest and motion in his eight premises, "everything that is moved owing to accident must of necessity come to rest, inasmuch as its motion is not in virtue of its essence. Hence it cannot be moved forever in that accidental motion."[122] Just like one motion can end and then a new motion can begin, applied to politics, one political entity can end and a new political entity can begin and, in the fullness of time, it is possible that the one that ended can begin again and regain power.[123]

Ibn Kaspi is critical of the Babylonian Talmud's interpretation of "the scepter shall not depart from Judah," which argues that Judah's rule is constant and is continued under the exilarch in Babylonia even after Jewish sovereignty ended,[124] a position that Maimonides codifies in the *Mishneh Torah*.[125] Ibn Kaspi, however, argues that taking political power to be a constant motion actually favors the Christian polemic against

Judaism, since they can easily use it to argue that Jesus' rule is a constant motion that is above the competitive laws governing nations and therefore permanent, as is "proven" by the longstanding and powerful Christian empire. He continues to expand in *Maṣref la-Kesef* that

> It is explained that this was the period of motion of the kingdom of Judah from David to Zedekiah, and then this motion ended. If after much or a little time, another motion began, since the first already ended, and between these two motions there was a break and cessation, a period of rest between the two, then it is not correct to say "the scepter shall not depart" applies to the exilarch in Babylonia after the destruction of the First Temple (BT Sanhedrin 5a). Heaven forbid, if we adopt this position, it will give a reason for Christians to argue [against us]. The giver of our Torah [Moses] foresaw all and liberated us from this similarity in using [the subject] *shevet*, as David explained in saying "the scepter of thy kingdom" (Psalm. 45:7). In my opinion, David said this to explain this matter because this is the topic of most of his book and the exilarch is not referred to as *shevet* and also not a government, being a witness to the exile.[126]

Ibn Kaspi's reading frees Judaism from being subsumed under the Christianity, understood as historical progress, and encourages Jews to act independently to restore ruler over their kingdom.

## Kingship (Deut. 17 and I Sam. 8)

Taking the realm of political history to be contingent, because God does not intervene directly, leads Ibn Kaspi to cynicism about the motivations of political leaders. He denounces them as driven by the lower instincts of animals instead of by intellect which, he argues, would want to construct a perfect society to improve the character and knowledge of its citizens. All of this challenges Maimonides' model of kingship as a positive commandment aimed at creating a virtuous society.

The period of Jewish kingship, as described in the Bible was mostly successful in establishing a kingdom and building the First Temple. It lasted, after all, for four hundred years, notwithstanding all the internal problems it faced. The nature of biblical kingship, as debated by the Rabbis, depends on how one interprets Deuteronomy 17:14–20, where the laws of kings are first discussed, and I Samuel 8, where the people ask Samuel for a king. The problem is that these two chapters appear to contradict one another, since one discusses the appointment of a king and the other blames the Jews for asking Samuel for a king. The *Sifra* presents two possible models for reconciling these two chapters, proposed by two different rabbis.[127] Rabbi Nehorai, on the one hand, argues that Deuteronomy does not advocate kingship, as is proven in I Samuel, where, as Rabbi Nehorai argues, the intention of the people is, in effect, idolatrous because they want to replace God with a human king. Rabbi Judah, on the other hand, argues that Deuteronomy does advocate kingship and that Samuel's anger is not because they asked for a king, but because they asked for this at the wrong time and for the wrong reason. Maimonides built upon Rabbi Judah's position, but took it even further. He categorized the appointment of a king in Deuteronomy 17:14 as a positive commandment both in the *Book of Commandments* and in the *Mishneh Torah*.[128] He also devoted the last set of laws in his legal code, the *Mishneh Torah*, to kingship entitling it the *Laws of Kings and their Wars* and ends the entire code with a discussion of the Messiah as the greatest and most perfect king, a kind of "philosopher-king," who returns Jewish sovereignty to the land of Israel making the whole world preoccupied with the knowledge of God.[129] For Maimonides, an ordinary king's primary roles are to lead in war of the state and ensure security and stability. Maimonides goes so far as to condone extra-judicial actions, when necessary, to punish wrongdoers and ensure safety within the kingdom. Maimonides stipulates that the type of individual attracted to political power should be motivated by a desire for honor. Accordingly, he devotes most of the second chapter of the *Laws of Kings* to the ways that the people must awe and revere the king. He balances this, however, with the requirement at the end of this second chapter that the king must cultivate a humble and lowly spirit and show grace and compassion when dealing with his subjects.[130]

Ibn Kaspi's model of kingship challenges Maimonides' paradigm.[131] His position is closer to Rabbi Nehorai in suggesting that the intention of the Bible is not to advocate or require kingship. Instead, he argues, it prefers rule by a judge, a priest, and a prophet. In his commentary on Deuteronomy 17:14, Ibn Kaspi argues that kingship cannot be desirable in the eyes of God, since the laws of the kings are driven by the desires of the masses. Such a reading, he argues, would lower the Bible from being a supernatural text to being one at the whims of the masses:

> "When you have come into the land" (Deut. 17:14). The primary intention of the Torah was that [rulership of the Israelites] would be sufficient with a judge and priest, along with a prophet, as will be mentioned later, like there was in the days of Samuel until the people asked for a king. This was not favorable in the eyes of God because the laws of kingship are laws for the masses. This is clear in every king, even more so in Samuel's advice that "he will take your daughters to be perfumers, and to be cooks" (I Sam. 8:13) and what follows. Indeed, the Torah understood the intent of the masses of Israelites, recognizing that eventually they would yearn for a king in order to imitate the other nations. It was thus commanded to only appoint a king who was chosen by God through a prophet.[132]

Ibn Kaspi repeats this point quite clearly in *'Adnei Kesef* in commenting on I Samuel 8:6 that "it is not appropriate according to the Torah that our people should have a king to judge them."[133] He then compares the command for a king to the command for sacrifices. Presumably, he is building here on Maimonides' argument, in *Guide* III 32, that the command for sacrificial laws was not the true intention of the Torah, but merely a means of guiding people to a higher intellectual end. He thereby accepts Deuteronomy 17:14 as a command (following Rabbi Judah), but undermines it (following Rabbi Nehorai).

Ibn Kaspi resists linking kingship with the rule of a philosopher-king who would aim to cultivate moral and intellectual virtues in its citizens, because he argues that kingship is purely focused on the animalistic drive for survival. He is most explicit about this in *Gevia Kesef* where he lays out an overall taxonomy of the history of the biblical kings:

> Proof is (the history of) the kings of Israel, as is evident from the narrative of their lives, wherein the second (king) destroyed the first, and third destroyed the second, as happened to them all . . . As a rule, whenever there are two people or many wicked nations, it is divine wisdom, as well as complete justice, that one of them will destroy the other

in a manner that is deserved, such as the sword, while subsequently another wicked (agent) comes and destroys the earlier victor. So it is always. . . . Hillel also said, "Because you have drowned others, others have drowned you; those who drowned you shall themselves be drowned" (Mishna Avot 2:7 and BT Sukkah 50a), which is satisfactory and completely just, in that it is universal that a destroyer, whether he be man or some other animal, will be surrounded by his fellow who will plot against his life.[134]

The comparison of kings to animals engaged in the natural struggle for self-preservation is a trope that runs throughout Ibn Kaspi's writings. In Haṣoṣrot Kesef, Ibn Kaspi draws the lesson that humans, like animals, do not naturally incline toward kingship, for they do not require a single leader to rule and guide them. He bases this on the verse "Go to the ant, thou sluggard; consider her ways, and be wise, which having no chief, overseer, or ruler, provideth her bread in the summer, and gatherest her food in the harvest."[135] In effect, Ibn Kaspi is thus saying that kingship is against nature. He also quotes Aristotle from De Animalibus in support of this, who says that mankind resembles bees and ants that are all social animals (holkhot be-ḥaburah), but do not require a king or rule, even though some do choose one.[136] Further, Ibn Kaspi highlights and expands upon Isaiah's wise usage of animal metaphors to describe different kings. In 'Adnei Kesef, he comments on Isaiah's prophecy for Jerusalem's destruction that "they shall roar, and lay hold of the prey, and carry it away safe, and there shall be none to deliver."[137] He expands upon the animal metaphor that the way of animals of prey is to eat some of the corpse and leave the rest in front of them and then return to eat, suggesting that this is what cats do to mice.[138] He also points to another Hebrew root word, q.r.n., that links politics and animal instincts. Its main meaning is strength and exalting. But, it can also refer to the horn on an animal's head used for ramming other animals because it is the strongest and toughest part of an animal's body. By analogy qeren refers to kings because they exemplify that strength and toughness in ruling.[139]

Another consequence of the animalistic nature of kingship and politics that comes out of the above text from Gevia Kesef is that there are no universal standards of justice between nations that protect the weak. Justice is the advantage of the stronger. The way of the world is that the stronger will oppress the weaker. It's a dog-eat-dog world. This is reflected in Ibn Kaspi's recommendations for those in close contact with a king, in his commentary on the Book of Proverbs. Taking, for example, the proverb "when thou sitteth to eat with a ruler, consider well him that is before thee,"[140] Ibn Kaspi warns that rulers may appear to be friendly, but they are not really your friend.[141] He also takes the verse "if thou has done foolishly in lifting up thyself, if thou hast planned devices, lay thy hand upon thy mouth"[142] as warning one that one's life is in danger with a king who is strong willed and easily led to anger since he can easily command your death at a whim. Therefore, act toward kings with humility, or better still, avoid speaking to them at all. If you do speak, do so with awe and fear.[143] Put together, these pieces of advice argue, that one should not make the mistake of thinking that the king is concerned with your best interest or consults a higher moral law that preaches compassion to those weaker or more impoverished than himself. Instead, kings will do whatever they think is to their own advantage, and call that justice.

### Four Animals and Four Kingdoms (Dan. 7)

The competition of animals for survival is the model on which nations relate to one another, according to Ibn Kaspi. Thus it seems fitting that the allegory of four animals in Daniel 7 should apply to the four kingdoms that would rule over the Jews, each overcoming its predecessor. The struggle for power and revenge of one kingdom over another is what leads to the constant vicissitudes of history. In *Tam ha-Kesef*, Ibn Kaspi asks the question "who does not know, and who does not see constantly the revivals (*tekumot*) and collapses (*nefilot*) of constantly alternating (*mithalfot*) nations (*le-am ve-am*)?"[144] We know Ibn Kaspi wrote a commentary on Daniel, *Qe'arot Kesef*, but it is not extant. The theme of the four animals from Daniel 7, however, is a constant trope throughout his writings, so we can extrapolate.[145] Ibn Kaspi goes so far as to argue, in commenting on Isaiah 34:16, that the parable of four animals is one of the secrets of the Pentateuch and of the Prophets that is purposefully hidden, except for a brief hint in Genesis 49:10.[146] This implies that Daniel reveals a secret about the framework of Jewish history that is hidden in all of the earlier biblical writings. This means that the framework of Daniel 7 must be applied to everything before it, and that all previous books of the Bible must be re-read in light of it.

The four animals represent four kingdoms that oppress the Jews. The first is an animal like a lion with eagle's wings. The second is an animal like a bear with three ribs between its teeth. The third is an animal like a leopard with four wings and four heads. The fourth is an animal with large iron teeth and ten horns.[1-7] The fourth animal is different from the first three, for it will "devour the whole earth, and shall tread it down, and break it in pieces."[148] Its ten horns, Ibn Kaspi argues, represent ten kings who will arise from this kingdom.[149] There is much debate in rabbinic and medieval scholarship over which kingdoms this prophecy refers to. The reduction of Jewish history to the subservience to four kingdoms appears throughout *Midrash Rabba*, which identifies the four rivers of Eden (Gen. 2:10), the four kings Abraham fights (Gen. 14:1–16) and the vision of four angels ascending and descending in Jacob's dream (Gen. 28:12) as all hinting at the four kingdoms that Israel would serve.[150] The first three kingdoms are generally agreed upon by medieval Jewish interpreters to be Babylonia, Persia, and Greece, but the identity of the fourth kingdom is the subject of much debate, as is the question of how Christianity and Islam fit into this prophecy.[151] Maimonides argues that the fourth kingdom represents *both* Christianity and Islam, presumably since both religions brought monotheism and knowledge of God to the world—albeit in what he considered perverted form—and prepared the world for the messianic era.[152] Abraham Ibn Ezra argues, instead, that the third kingdom represents both Greece and Rome (of which Christianity is a continuation), while the fourth kingdom must be Islam, because this list is of kingdoms that either exiled the Jews from Israel or occupied the land of Israel, and it was Islamic rulers who were in charge of the land from the seventh century.[153] For Ibn Ezra, the Middle Ages represents the battle between the third and fourth animal. Nahmanides disputes all the above interpretations and argues that the third kingdom is Greece and the fourth is Rome (including Christianity), since the kingdoms on this list are of oppressors of the Jews. They are not simply of large kingdoms that existed contemporaneously. After all, it was the Romans, he argues, and not the Muslims who destroyed the temple and exiled the Jews. He thinks it less important that Muslim rulers later conquered the land of Israel.[154]

Ibn Kaspi's interpretation of the four animals builds on that of his predecessors and adds that it describes the contingent nature of competition between competing kingdoms, especially Christian and Moslem kingdoms. He insists, as always, that because all predictions are contingent, no prophet can foresee more than the first kingdom that will overcome a current one. Predicting two or three conquests beyond that is beyond their scope. He argues, for example, that Jacob's blessing at Genesis 49:10 that predicted the rule of Judean kings under the Babylonians was based upon the laws of how kingdoms compete with one another, but does not predict the next three kingdoms. As evidence of this, he points out that it was the prophets who lived during the time of the Babylonian empire who predicted its downfall (Isaiah, Jeremiah, Ezekiel, Amos, Obadiah, Jonah, Nahum, and Habakkuk),[155] and the prophets who lived in close proximity to the Persian empire who could predict its rise (Isaiah, Ezekiel, Joel, Obadiah, Habakkuk, Zephaniah, Haggai, and Zechariah).[156] He even saw certain of the later prophets—Ezekiel, Joel, Micah, Zephaniah, Zechariah, Malachi, and Daniel—as having successfully predicted events that were to happen to Jews under the Greek and Roman kingdoms, reading these prophetic writings in light of events described in *Sefer Yosipon*.[157] This argument limiting the scope of prophecy is aimed deliberately at Christian biblical hermeneutics that dared to derive the prediction of Jesus' coming from prophets who lived many kingdoms earlier, some going back as far as the earliest narratives of the Hebrew Bible.

Ibn Kaspi agrees with Ibn Ezra that the fourth animal should be identified as Islam, not because he thinks that Islam has overcome Christianity, but because the Muslims were the occupiers of Israel in his time. Ibn Kaspi points to the parallel between the ongoing conflict between Islam and Christianity during this period with the conflict between the third and fourth animals in the prophecy:

> These [revivals and collapses occur] among the Ishmaelites themselves in the passing of their kingdoms, and among the Christians, and between the Christians and the Ishmaelites, as in our days, when the Ishmaelites took Acre from the Christians, having first taken all of the Galilee and Syria, while the Christians took all of the Kingdom of Aragon and the island of Majorca . . . the sons of the third "beast" still wrangle constantly with the sons of the fourth "beast." And how many times has the King of France advanced there without succeeding? Even now, he prepares himself to advance there, and who knows whether he will succeed or not?[158]

It is impossible to know with certainty which "animal" will emerge victorious, as Ibn Kaspi argues, because the fate of kingdoms competing for power is contingent.

Ibn Kaspi argues that the allegory of the four kingdoms as four animals in Daniel 7 should not been taken as an exhaustive list of all kingdoms in history, being merely a prophetic summary of the four kingdoms that will oppress the Jews specifically and is thus written for that purpose. It should not be taken to mean that they are the only oppressors in history or that the Jews are the only oppressed nation. For example, Ibn Kaspi points out, the Bible contains hints that there were other kingdoms that preceded the Babylonians, like the Canaanites, who were also overcome and subsumed by more powerful kingdoms. For Ibn Kaspi, this is the meaning of the mysterious and seemingly out of place phrase "and the Canaanite was then in the land."[159] For Ibn Ezra argues that this verse reveals a hidden secret since it appears to be written at a later time when the Canaanites were no longer living in the land, after the Israelite conquest of Canaan and long after Moses' death. This is one of the places in the Pentateuch that, Ibn Ezra argues, is of non-Mosaic authorship. Unlike Ibn Ezra, Ibn Kaspi is less interested in who wrote this verse, or when, than he is in the nature of its prophetic prediction. He finds in it a contingent prophecy of a future when the Canaanites will be enslaved and no longer rulers of Canaan. Ibn Kaspi writes in *Tirat Kesef* that

> "And the Canaanite was then in the land" (Gen. 12:6) and so it says: "and the Canaanite and the Perizzite dwelt then in the land" (Ibid. 13:7), teaching that they were troubled occasionally because the curse of Noah began to come to pass. Even though the descendants of Canaan were becoming stronger in this land, God will still help Abraham so that his children will inherit [the land].[160]

Ibn Kaspi adds to this in *Maṣref la-Kesef* that

> [Genesis 12:6] is written here for various reasons. First, to indicate that if you are strong, a ruler and in possession of the land God promised to Abraham, this land will be for your children. Abraham himself walked around the land as if it was

his and already divided it up with Lot (Gen. 12:9).... Second, to show us that Canaan and his brothers were always causing trouble because the kings of Assyria were attacking them....[161]

In Ibn Kaspi's reading, this is the result of the moral sin of Ham, which has political repercussions for Ham's descendants, the nation of Canaan. Because Ham laughed, mocked, and failed to cover his drunken father's (Noah's) nakedness, Noah predicted that Ham's descendants would be enslaved at some time in the future.[162] How does one event lead to the other? Ibn Kaspi is not completely explicit, but following the pattern discussed so far: the contingencies of kingdoms are understood to be parallel to those of the human body, but the covenant with God, which is necessary and certain, is understood to be parallel to the mind's knowledge of the unchanging reality of the higher realms. In Ham's focus on the former in the case of Noah's drunkenness, one can surmise that he and his family focus purely on the concerns of the body and therefore will be subject to the whims of competing kingdoms. By referring to the Canaanites in the past tense in both Genesis 12:5 and 13:7, the vantage point of this verse is from when they will no longer live in the land. Ibn Kaspi derives from this that their kingdom would no longer exist in the future and that they would be overcome by a stronger kingdom operating under same principles of competition as the Israelites.[163] This is why he says in *Tam ha-Kesef* that

> we took this land—I mean the Land of Israel and Jerusalem—from the Canaanites, because God so wished. Subsequently, the sons of the first "beast" took it from our hands.[164]

Although Israel has a special covenant with God that is eternal, both the Canaanites and the Israelites still operate under the same laws of politics, laws that predate the parable of the four animals.

## Destruction of the First Temple

Ibn Kaspi attributes the cause of the destruction of the First and Second Temples to the fact that ancient Israelite leadership ignored the prudential political predictions of the prophets. This is central to Ibn

Kaspi's description of the contingent nature of political history, for the destruction of the First and Second Temples happened as consequences of the downfall of the two kingdoms, first, at the hands of the Babylonians (the first animal), and later at the hands of the Romans (the third animal). The attempt to explain the causes of the destructions of the temples and the downfall of the two kingdom goes back to both the Talmud and midrashic literature. Many possible reasons are given, such as idol worship, prohibited sexual relations, bloodshed, love of money, hating one's neighbor, baseless hatred, and judges ruling unjustly.[165] Maimonides provided an alternate political understanding, arguing that the destruction of the temples occurred because the Jews were not sufficiently concerned with politics and war and relied instead solely on predictions based on the stars.[166] As he argues in Letter on Astrology,

> Our kingdom was lost and our temple was destroyed . . . because they found many books dealing with the themes of the stargazers . . . imagining them to be of great science and to be of great utility. They did not busy themselves with the art of war or with the conquest of lands, but imagined that those studies would help them.[167]

Maimonides' project was to teach the Jews to understand that the destruction of the temples was the outcome of a lack of political wisdom. In this regard, Ibn Kaspi builds upon Maimonides' conclusion. He quotes the above letter of Maimonides and, in his *Commentary on Proverbs*, discusses "where there are no stratagems, a people falleth,"[168] both of which support his argument, that the temples were destroyed because the Jews did not perfect themselves in the art of war or the conquest of lands.[169] He adds in *Tirat Kesef* that instead of conquering lands and defending themselves militarily, they merely prayed when the enemy attacked.[170]

Ibn Kaspi builds upon Maimonides here, adding a point that Maimonides does not make explicitly: learning the art of war and conquest is important, but not enough. That art needs to be guided by the practical wisdom of the prophets who can predict the contingent future by knowing many of the particular circumstances, strengths, and weaknesses of the different kingdoms, which makes them valuable advisors. According to Ibn Kaspi, this is why there is a command to listen to the prophet at Deutoronomy 18:15 and his argument that ignoring the prophet's voice is a key cause of the destruction of the two temples. This argument also draws on Ibn Kaspi's cynical portrayal of kings as (most of the time) intellectually weak and driven by the bodily passions and therefore need a prophet who studies empires and history to guide them.

Ibn Kaspi also lists many other causes of the destruction of the First Temple and kingdom, some distant and others proximate, the most distant going back to the actions of David and the most proximate being the actions of Zedekiah. He sees David's sin with Bathsheba and Uriah as the beginning of a long chain of cause and effect that led all the way to Zedekiah who made the final error that led to the downfall of the first kingdom and destruction of the temple.[171] This follows the principle of "visiting the iniquity of the fathers upon the children" (*poqed 'avon 'avot 'al banim*) that is repeated multiple times in the Bible (at Exodus 20:4, 34:7, Numbers 14:18, and Deuteronomy 5:8). Ibn Kaspi argues that this is not a necessary decree that the sin of the father will pass on sin to children, but it is often true that the fathers' sins act as an efficient cause for the sins of their sons, even when these sins only occur multiple generations later. Ibn Kaspi does not see this as deterministic, however, for he argues that there is always a choice as to whether or not to sin.[172] Ibn Kaspi seems to be implying that there may be a natural predisposition to sin, with traits of uncontrolled desire being passed down from one generation to the next, along with insufficient moral education. David's strong, and uncontrolled desires lead him to break two of the Ten Commandments (at Exodus 19:12), by committing adultery with Bathsheba, and killing her husband, Uriah. As punishment, David's son Absalom sleeps with David's wives and chases after his father to kill him.[173] This destabilizes David's family, causing his children and descendants to be at war with one another, for, as Samuel prophecizes, the "sword will never depart from thy house."[174]

David's uncontrolled physical desires are passed down to his descendants, leading to a large variety of sins in succeeding generations. Jeroboam caused an entire generation to worship idols, which led to the destruction of the Israelite kingdom and the exile of the ten tribes.[175] Hezekiah was obsessed with wanting too many possessions and laughed at and mocked the words of prophets, which strengthened God's decree to destroy the temple.[176] His son, Menashe, went further than his father by striving to forget God and killing God's prophets. Menashe is described by Ibn Kaspi as a distant efficient cause (*sibba ha-po'elet ha-reḥoqa*) of the destruction, because it weakened the ability of the prophets to warn of the more serious threat posed by Nebuchadnezzar.[177] The last and most proximate cause of the destruction came when Zedekiah ignored the words of the prophet advising him to submit to the yoke of Nebuchadnezzar and not attempt to fight back at Jer. 27:8–9. Nebuchadnezzar wanted to rule all lands and Jeremiah warned Zedekiah that one cannot overcome such a powerful force.[178] The degeneration of David's royal line was caused by falling away from the intellect in order to satisfy bodily desires. It happened in steps—first, adultery, then murder, then idolatry, then an obsession with possessions, then killing and ignoring of the words of prophets—all of which culminated in the destruction of the First Temple and loss of the kingdom.[179]

### Critique of Christian Eschatology: Reading Isaiah

Many of Ibn Kaspi's statements are written explicitly as a polemic against Christianity. One of his dominant polemical arguments is that Christian interpretations of the Hebrew Bible misunderstand the nature of biblical prophecy. They make the mistake of thinking that it predicts, a necessary as opposed to a contingent, future, and thus mistakenly derive an eschatological messianic teaching from a text that is merely describing political history. Ibn Kaspi's *Commentary on Isaiah* in the collection *'Adnei Kesef* provides an excellent example of this. He is critical there of Christian theologians who attempt to find predictions in the Old Testament text for Jesus' coming. Ibn Kaspi argues that Isaiah is a prophet who prophesized about Judah and Jerusalem from King Uziah to Hezekiah. This was the period when the first animal, the Babylonians, began to come upon them. The Book of Isaiah lends hope for an immediate military victory of Hezekiah over Sennacherib and Zerubbabel over Nebuchadnezzar, Ibn Kaspi argues. It is not, as the Christians would like to think, a prediction of a transcendent redeemer coming at the end of days.[180] Ibn Kaspi argues that his position is a development of the arguments that follows the precedents of both Maimonides and Ibn Ezra.[181]

One difference between Judaism and Christianity, that Ibn Kaspi sees arising from the Book of Isaiah, is over the question of whether history is moving in a redemptive direction that is transcendent and eschatological, or whether history is moved by nothing more than politics and competition between nations, in accordance with the laws of nature. Ibn Kaspi defends the latter reading by building upon Maimonides' model of the Messiah as a political leader who will reestablish Jewish sovereignty in the land of Israel, and his argument that the messianic age will be an era of peace and intellectual enlightenment, all this following the laws of nature.[182] If Maimonides is right about this, then, Ibn Kaspi argues, Isaiah's predictions are not about the messianic era at all. They merely predict an immediate victory over a current enemy.[183] Maimonides and Ibn Kaspi, however, differ on this. For Maimonides, Isaiah 11:6–9 in which the "wolf shall dwell with the lamb" and "the earth shall be full of the knowledge of the LORD, as the waters cover the sea" are texts proving the perfection of the messianic age.[184] Not surprisingly, Ibn Kaspi neglects to comment on these verses, which appear to contradict his conclusion that Isaiah is not predicting the messianic age.[185]

Ibn Kaspi argues that Judaism and Christianity also differ over whether Isaiah is predicting an immediate or distant future. Ibn Kaspi argues that the Christian approach of reading Isaiah as predicting Christ's redemption is incongruous with the rest of the text, since the prophet is not speaking about the end of time, but of the immediate political future of the Israelite or Judean kingdoms in relation to their neighbors. Ibn Kaspi writes that

> The essence of the prophet Isaiah's visions is on Judah and Jerusalem, as he predicted, and the principle of his prophecy concerns this "animal" about Sennacherib and Nebuchadnezzar. . . . Therefore there is no redemption described in this book other than by Hezekiah from Sennacherib and by Zedekiah from the kingdom of Babylonia. . . . On all this I wrote demonstrative arguments and proofs in *Miṭot Kesef* and one of the arguments is that, according to everyone, there is no prediction in this book for the Second Temple, thus how can Isaiah prophesize for the Third Temple? It is necessary that the former temple be destroyed before [one can predict the next one] that will be built. One who attributes other intentions to the author is attributing what the author did not intend, weakening and giving doubts to the belief in the messiah that we are awaiting today, . . .and giving help to Christians to interpret these verses in light of their messiah. . . . If some of our Rabbis interpreted these verses of [the] prophet [Isaiah] as predicting the messiah, this is contradictory and this is not the place for it here.[186]

Isaiah is predicting an event in the immediate future for, once again, Ibn Kaspi argues here that prophets predicting contingent future events can make judgments on the immediate future only based on their own experience of the current geopolitical situation, but they are unable to and predict far off eventualities, such as the Second or Third Temple.

Ibn Kaspi defends his argument by engaging with two metaphors in Isaiah that Christians use as symbol of Christ's coming. The first is the virgin birth referred to in Isaiah 7. Christians interpret Isaiah 7:14 which states that "the Lord Himself shall give you a sign: behold, the '*alma* shall conceive and bear a son, and shall call his name Immanuel" as a prediction that a virgin, named Mary, will miraculously conceive the redeemer of the world. They base this on interpreting '*alma* as meaning virgin. Ibn Kaspi provides two arguments against this claim. First, commenting on Isaiah 7:14, Ibn Kaspi contends that the Christian argument that '*alma* refers to the mother of Jesus ignores the historical context of the text, which suggests that the young woman probably refers to one of the women of the king's court.[187] Second, Ibn Kaspi challenges the Christian translation of '*alma* as virgin (*virgo*) by going back to the root of the word in Hebrew. According to Kaspi, the root '*a.l.m.* refers to hiddenness and '*elem* (m) or '*alma* (f) is an individual young in age. He gives two reasons for the link between hiddenness and youth: (a) that it is appropriate for the young to sit at home and not be seen and (b) their future is hidden since you do not know what lies after childhood for them.[188] Ibn Kaspi adds that if Isaiah meant to say virgin, he would have used the word *betula*, but, instead, he used the word '*alma* which can refer to a young girl whether or not she is a virgin.[189] The second metaphor in Isaiah that Christians think predicts Christ's coming, is that of the suffering servant in Isaiah 52–53. This is interpreted by Christians as a metaphor for Christ's suffering on the cross which they believe paid for the sins of humanity. Ibn Kaspi first response is that "my servant shall prosper" at Isaiah 52:13 is actually a prediction of rebuilding the Second Temple. He argues one can know this by looking at the location of this chapter in relation to the chapter that precedes it (Chapter 51).[190] The suffering that is described in chapter 52 is that of the people of Israel in exile before their return to rebuild the temple. He makes the bold argument that this suffering is not brought upon them by God, but by their own actions.[191] He explains that the meaning of the word "prosper" (*yaskil*) in the expression "my servant shall prosper" is part of the same causative *hifʻil* verbal construct as the Hebrew word for "practical wisdom" (*ha-heskel* or *phronesis*) according to Averroes' translation in his *Commentary on Aristotle's* Nicomachean Ethics.[192] Therefore, by linking *yaskil* to *ha-heskel*, Ibn Kaspi is interpreting Isaiah's prophecy to be that the prosperity of the Israelite nation will be dependent on their cultivation of practical wisdom in this world and not on receiving an eschatological redemption through belief in Christ. Therefore, their suffering in exile can be interpreted as a result of their lack of cultivation of practical wisdom, which may include ignoring the art of war and the advice of prophets.

Ibn Kaspi blames not only Christians, but also other Jewish interpreters, such as can be found in the works of Midrash, such as Yalqut Isaiah 476 and Tanḥuma Toledot 14, who imposed their own eschatology on the text, and used it as evidence for their own messianic vision of a new Third Temple in Jerusalem:[193]

> My reproach is not that Christians interpret these predictions and similar ones to their messiah, but I reproach our own exegetes for applying the same verses to our messiah as in "and there shall come forth a shoot out of the stem of Jesse, and a branch shall grow out of his roots" (Isa. 11:1). For if we "skip over the mountain ranges and hop over" (Song of Songs 2:8) the anointed Hezekiah and Zerubbabel and apply the verse—which was prophesied before the destruction of the First Temple, not to mention the second—to our present condition of exile, we allow the prophecy to refer to the Third Temple and the messiah and thereby give permission to Christians to insert the promise of their messiah right after the end of the time of the Second Temple.[194]

Hence Ibn Kaspi affirms that the attempted justification of such an eschatological reading by Jews actually helps the Christian eschatological argument. Instead of competing with Christians over whose eschatology more correctly reflects Isaiah, Ibn Kaspi argues that Jews should read the prophetic writings, such as the Book of Isaiah, as merely historical and political. Another way of putting this is that the Maimonidean model of the messiah as philosopher-king is the best defense against Christian interlocutors. This would lead to a more accurate understanding of political events in ancient Israelite history, reflecting the competitive and realistic character of world history.

Chapter 2

# History as the Progressive Revelation of the Divine Chariot

The second model of history that Ibn Kaspi describes throughout his writings is one that provides a progressive explanation of the details of the divine chariot described in Isaiah 6, Ezekiel 1 and 10, and Zechariah 6. The image of God riding on a chariot is considered by rabbinic tradition to be one of the secret teachings of the Hebrew Bible.[1] Ibn Kaspi, building on Maimonides, argues that the divine chariot is an allegory for the nature and structure of existence, by which he means metaphysics, to use Aristotle's terminology. For Ibn Kaspi there are three levels of existence: the highest is that of God and the separate intellects, the intermediary level is that of the spheres, and the lowest level is that of the sublunar world of matter. Ibn Kaspi looks upon the Bible as describing a historical process in which different prophets, from Abraham to Jacob to Moses, came to discover these truths with ever greater precision. After this, more and more details of this knowledge were shared with others as we move through the Bible from Isaiah and Ezekiel to Zechariah. Ibn Kaspi thinks Moses had perfect knowledge of the chariot. Later prophets would expand on and describe this knowledge in greater detail without contradicting the teaching revealed by Moses in the Pentateuch. Ibn Kaspi especially appreciated the detailed presentation of this secret by Zechariah so much so that he says that "nowhere else in the Torah nor in the Scriptures is the chariot explained in this lengthy detail,"[2] suggesting that Zechariah's description of the chariot reveals more than the descriptions given by Isaiah and Ezekiel. Here Ibn Kaspi adopts the myth that philosophy and science originated among the ancient Jews and was stolen by other nations. This implies that Aristotle's *Metaphysics* and Maimonides' *Guide* are more detailed accounts of the chariot as articulated first by Moses and later by Zechariah. The fact that metaphysics became an area of study in ancient Greece but was not a central focus of rabbinic Judaism after the destruction of the Second Temple is a direct result of the loss of Jewish sovereignty, Ibn Kaspi argues, and not a reflection of metaphysics being more inherently "Greek" than "Jewish." The project of openly educating others about the secret of the chariot is described by Ibn Kaspi as one of reclaiming lost teachings that had been taken up and taken over by both Christians and Muslims in his own time. Ibn Kaspi praises the proficiency of Christians and Muslims in studying Maimonides' *Guide*.

The Bible itself, according to Ibn Kaspi, employs three different methods of slowly and progressively educating and revealing more knowledge of the chariot to those who are, at the outset, philosophically unprepared for it. The first method is to employ the chariot terminology covertly in the Pentateuch, to prepare the reader for its much fuller explanation in the later prophetic writings. Ibn Kaspi develops a form of "inner-biblical exegesis" through which terminology in later writings builds and comments upon its usage in earlier writings. The second method is a polemic in the Bible against animal sacrifice, beginning as early as Genesis, intended to liberate the Jews from a physical conception of God. In this, he differs from Maimonides who argues in *Guide* III 32 that it is merely a polemic against Egyptian practice, learned as a result of the Israelites' enslavement in Egypt. The third method is the employment of different names of God in the Bible, such as YHVH, YHVH *Elohim*, and *Elohim*, each metaphorically representing a different level of nature, according to Ibn Kaspi.

## The Divine Chariot as the Structure of Existence

In *Menorat Kesef*, Ibn Kaspi continues the Maimonidean tradition of identifying "the account of the chariot" (*ma'ase merkava*) with the philosophical metaphysics of Aristotle.[3] The divine chariot is described differently by three different prophets who employ this image at Isaiah 6, Ezekiel 1 and 10, and Zechariah 6. The common features that Ibn Kaspi

## History as the Progressive Revelation of the Divine Chariot / 57

derives from them are of an individual riding a wheeled chariot pulled by horses. He interprets it as follows:

> The totality of existence is a complete chariot because the world of the separate intellects are the riders that stand on the surface of the carriage, the world of the spheres are the horses, and the world of the elements are the wheels. . . .[4]

Ibn Kaspi takes these three different elements in of the image to reveal three different levels of reality. He states that the division of metaphysical reality into three levels is agreed upon by all the interpreters of Aristotle, including Averroes, Alexander, and Al-Farabi.[5]

The lowest level of metaphysical reality is the world of the elements. It represents the sublunar realm which is composed of matter drawn from the four elements of land, water, air, and fire. The middle level is the realm of the nine spheres of the celestial bodies. Eight of these nine spheres are likened to tracks followed by a star or a set of stars revolving in a circular motion around the earth. The ninth and highest sphere, however, is composed of a special matter that is unified and spherical but has no physical qualities. The nine spheres from the lowest to the highest are: the moon, the sun, Mercury, Venus, Mars, Jupiter, Saturn, fixed stars, and the starless sphere.[6] The highest level of metaphysical reality is the world of the separate intellects, nine intellects that control the nine spheres, plus an Active Intellect that controls the sublunar world, and ultimately God who is the intellect above them all. Following Al-Farabi's synthesis of Aristotle and Neo-Platonism, God's intellect overflows or emanates "images" of Himself, as a separate intellect, which by contemplating itself emanates the sphere below it. Similarily, as each of the other intellects contemplates itself, it creates a new separate intellect and a new sphere below it. The circular motion of each sphere is caused by its desire to emulate its corresponding intellect which has a circular motion because that is considered perfect motion.

Ibn Kaspi's identification of the divine chariot as a metaphor for Aristotelian metaphysics is not unique nor innovative. What is unique to Ibn Kaspi's rendition of the divine chariot is first his presentation of it as part of a larger historical process that enables and illuminates the teaching of the divine chariot and second, his argument that this image is not simply a hidden doctrine revealed in a few select texts, but rather, that it is the ultimate purpose of the Bible from beginning to end, and is consistent throughout.

## Secrecy and Progress in Post-Maimonidean Thought

Maimonides states that one of the purposes of the *Guide* is to revive the lost secret tradition of the divine chariot. Maimonides applies, what Moshe Halbertal calls, the "paradox of secrecy."[7] Before discussing the divine chariot in *Guide* Book III, Maimonides lays out the two sides of this paradox: if a secret is too out in the open, it is no longer a secret since it is accessible to anyone; but if a secret is too hidden and restricted to only a limited few, it is also no longer a secret, since it no longer exists once they die.[8] Secrecy is always "secrecy from"—it is always a relationship. Paradoxically, for it to be a secret there must be the possibility of finding out the secret. Therefore, there are times when a secret has been brought back to life after being so hidden that it has disappeared altogether, and there are also times when a secret is too out in the open and must become more hidden. The intention of the Rabbis in Mishna Hagiga 2:1 was for the secret to be passed down orally from teacher to student, but Maimonides writes that in his time the secret has become lost due to the instability of exile, which has prevented it from being transferred orally from teacher to student. So, he devised a means of putting it into writing in a unique esoteric way that maintains a proper balance of hiddeness and openness.[9] Since the secret is put in writing, which is accessible to anyone, its true meaning requires knowing the correct method to decipher it.[10]

Samuel Ibn Tibbon, the translator of Maimonides' *Guide of the Perplexed* into Hebrew, downplayed Maimonides' argument that his understanding of the divine chariot is a radical break from previous generations and instead suggested that earlier generations did in fact teach and transmit the secrets. He argues that the philosophers or sages of every generation repackaged these secret truths in new metaphors to communicate them effectively to the next generation. He derives this from the Midrash (following Maimonides in *Guide*, Intro., p. 11):

> To what were the words of the Torah to be compared before the advent of Solomon? To a well the waters of which are at a great depth and cool, yet no man could drink of them.

> What did one clever man do? He joined cord with cord and rope with rope and drew them up and drank. Thus did Solomon [join] allegory with allegory and word with word until he understood the words of the Torah.¹

Ibn Tibbon interprets this Midrash to be referring to the secrets of the Bible since both the water in the well and the secrets of the Bible, like that of the divine chariot, are deep and unseen by most and require a special art to obtain them from the hidden depths. Just as obtaining the water requires constructing a series of interlinking cords, obtaining the secret requires constructing a series of allegories. The implication is that every generation needs to construct new cords and allegories to speak to the unique character and individuals of the next generation.¹² The model of history that arises from this is linear and consistent, because, although the truth is constantly hidden, it is always presented in new allegories designed to convey the truth to those who are able to decipher them. Accordingly, the secrets of the Bible have been conveyed in new allegories by Solomon in Ecclesiastes, Proverbs, and the Song of Songs, by Isaiah and Ezekiel through the chariot metaphors, by the Rabbis in Mishna Hagiga, and finally, by Maimonides using Aristotle's philosophy. There is no implication in Ibn Tibbon's model that later generations have revealed more detail. They have simply obtained and conveyed these secrets by different means.¹³

Ibn Tibbon argues that the specific challenge of his generation is that Christians are studying the secrets of the divine chariot in greater numbers than Jews, and have taken ownership of its teachings. He argues in *Ma'amar Yikavu ha-Mayyim* (*Treatise of the Gathering of the Waters*) that

> "It is time to act for the sake of God" (Psalm. 119:126). I saw that the truths that were concealed since [the time of] our prophets and the Sages of our Torah have become well known among the nations of the world, and in most places they interpret Scripture in accordance with the truths concealed in the Torah and in the words of the prophets and those speaking by means of the holy spirit. Our nations is ignorant of them completely, and by virtue of this ignorance they [the gentiles] mock us and abuse us saying that we only possess the shells of the words of the prophets . . .I, the youngster

> who follow him [Maimonides], also saw that [the number of] those understanding his hints has greatly declined, all the more so those who understand the hints in Scripture. I saw also that the true sciences have become much better known among the nations under whose sovereignty and in whose lands I live—much more than the familiarity with them in the lands of Ishmael.[14]

Ibn Tibbon follows the rabbinic precedent that certain matters are meant to be orally transmitted and not put into writing, but argues that this law can be broken and these matters can be written down in order to preserve them from being lost.[15] He quotes the verse "it is time to act for the sake of God, for they have infringed Thy Law"[16] to justify breaking rabbinic precedent.[17] Ibn Tibbon is building here on Maimonides, who quotes this same verse to justify his writing of the *Guide*.[18] In addition to the loss of the oral tradition of these secrets in exile, Ibn Tibbon adds two more justifications. The first is that the Christians know the secrets, speak about them openly, and mock the Jews for their ignorance in these areas. Jews thus need to speak about them openly as well in order to show that the secrets were originally Jewish, not Christian, and that Jews have not lost their tradition here. The second is that Moses hid these secrets during the composition of the Torah because the people of his time did not recognize the existence of God or that of the separate intellects. The implication here is that these secrets do not have to be hidden at all times, but were hidden by Moses only because of philosophic ignorance in ancient times. In other words, the tension between philosophic secrets and popular ignorance can be minimized or overcome in a more enlightened age. Ibn Tibbon, of course, is implying that his own time is such a time.[19]

Ibn Kaspi differentiates his approach from that of Ibn Tibbon in that he explicitly writes that his commentaries are *not* intended to copy the words or ideas of others.[20] He suggests that if one is interested in understanding the ideas of his predecessors, one should read their books and not his own. Instead, he asserts that he is writing to innovate and present new interpretations. He may feel this is justified because he views the Bible as revealing only limited details on many matters simply for the sake of brevity, thus requiring the reader to unpack the arguments for themselves. Ibn Kaspi argues in *Maṣref la-Kesef* that

> If God would have written all He knew, the books [of the Torah] could not contain it[21] . . . and if he intended and wanted to teach all He knows and or a part, He would still be sitting on the mountain teaching it. From this we can see the method of every author and teacher.[22]

Ibn Kaspi holds Moses up as the perfect philosopher who understood God's knowledge and the secret of the divine chariot perfectly, but could not reveal everything in the Pentateuch. To explicate all the arguments of all the laws of nature described in the divine chariot would be too long for one book and too deep for most people. As a result, all the prophets after Moses studied the Pentateuch, the part of the Torah that Moses revealed, and based themselves on it, but, Ibn Kaspi argues, none reached Moses' depth of wisdom. Later prophets built on earlier prophets and came to understand more and more of the secret knowledge that Moses hinted at in the Pentateuch, and they described it in new metaphors, none of which contradict the Pentateuch.[23] After Moses, Ibn Kaspi argues, the quest for truth has been inherently progressive, which leaves room for Ibn Kaspi to innovate and differentiate his position from that of his predecessors.[24]

Progress toward understanding the secret of the divine chariot was also accomplished by Aristotle and his philosophic interpreters, who discuss these matters openly in their books. This makes hiding the divine chariot less necessary, not to say less possible. He writes in *Menorat Kesef* that

> The fourth aspect [explaining why I am justified in explaining the secrets of the Torah in writing] is that I am just copying the words of the philosophers like Aristotle and his followers who wrote about these matters in their books, in other words, the explanation of the worlds that are known to us as the Account of the Chariot. Their books are available to all and, by the way of truth, are hidden from our people because of our sins.[25]

Aristotle's open discussion of the secrets conveyed to the Jews by the chariot is reason enough that the secret no longer needs to be hidden, Ibn Kaspi argues, especially since the study of the chariot is not being spread by Jews, but by Christians and Muslims. In *Sefer ha-Musar* he praises Christians for honoring, studying, and translating the *Guide* and Muslims for establishing colleges for this purpose.[26]

## The Jewish Origins of Philosophy and Science

Ibn Kaspi's model of history as progressing toward greater knowledge of the divine chariot is based on an adaptation of the Jewish myth that the origins of philosophy and science were Jewish.[27] In Ibn Kaspi's narrative, progress toward knowledge of the divine chariot is part of a long historical process that began with Abraham and was pieced together in stages over time by the biblical prophets. This secret was held by the Jews until they lost their kingdom, which he blames on "our sins."[28] For example, in *Menorat Kesef* he says

> Maimonides wrote in the *Book of Knowledge* . . .that the highest separate intellect cannot know the first cause in the manner that it is the cause of all [that exists]. Since no intellect is separate from the ten officers [separate intellects], one cannot say any of them is truly one . . . One will not understand this from what I wrote, until you understand completely the proofs in the works of natural and divine science that were stolen from us because of our sins.[29]

The main sin that led to destruction (as discussed in the last chapter) was ignoring the words of the prophets and their practical wisdom based on experience, showing how kings should best act. In connecting "our sins" to "being stolen from us," he draws a direct line between political loss and intellectual loss.

Furthermore, he argues that the reason "metaphysics" is known as "Greek" philosophy and not "Jewish" philosophy, and that the tripartite division of nature would come be known through the term "metaphysics" and not through the image of the "divine chariot," is an outcome of the Greeks reading the works of the Torah and studying with the Jewish wise men during the time of the Second Temple, and then writing books of philosophical interpretation based on what they had learned from the Jews and the Torah. When the Romans conquered the Greeks and destroyed the Second Temple, they stole this wisdom from the Jews, in effect plagiarizing it, and claiming it as their own, which they saw as a right of conquest.[30] Ibn Kaspi expands upon this in *Tirat Kesef* saying:

> This book [Exodus] will include in it all of what is in Aristotle's *Physics* and also what is included in Aristotle's *Metaphysics* . . . Here it is very possible that Aristotle and those with him saw and studied our Torah because it was found among all the nations. I have no doubt also that all the prophets and the wise men who came after them, like Solomon and his colleagues, wrote many books to explain these matters found in the Torah with general premises and went into explanations of the different types. These books were copied into Greek, which is the third animal described in Daniel, and they exiled us, as is well known, a fortiori, they who came after them [the Romans] who forced upon us many tragedies and evils of all the nations, which is why they obtained the credit for the sciences.[31]

As a result of this theft and open dissemination of the secrets of the chariot by the Greeks and Romans, Ibn Kaspi's purpose in openly discussing of the divine chariot is to encourage Jews to regain their stolen possession and reclaim it for Judaism.[32]

## Biblical Characters as Historical Actors

Ibn Kaspi's model of history progressing toward ever greater knowledge of the divine chariot covers a long period of time and multiple biblical characters, who play important roles as key actors in this large historical process. But what exactly is the nature of a literary character in the Bible? This raises the important question of what does it mean for the narratives of the Bible to be understood as philosophic? Does a character in a biblical story testify to the existence of a unique historical individual with that name and character, or is that individual to be taken as a metaphor for some metaphysical principle? This issue arose in a heated debate during the Maimonidean controversies when Abba Mari ben Moses of Montpellier wrote to Solomon Ibn Aderet of Barcelona in 1303 to request a censure on a group of philosophic allegorists in Languedoc.[33] Abba Mari reports that this preacher declared that Abraham and Sarah were a metaphor for form and matter, the four matriarchs served as a metaphor for the four elements, and Jacob's twelve sons represented the twelve constellations of the Zodiac.[34]

In his *Commentary on Proverbs*, Ibn Kaspi explicitly criticizes the scholars of his generation for carrying out such preaching and biblical interpretation.[35] He writes that

> I have seen the little foxes of our generation who begin to study the sciences and they strive to climb the mountain which God hath desired for His abode (Psalm. 68:17). [But, in doing so] they open their mouths to degrade the sages of Israel, they teach to the masses the repudiation of the [biblical] miracles, and they turn the stories of the Torah into metaphors, like Abraham and Sarah into matter and form, and others like this. . . . It is not enough for them that they sin, but they cause the masses to sin. And they are the reason that the masses hate the sciences because one who does not know such matters upon hearing their words will not think they are lacking wisdom, but will think they have achieved perfection in it.[36]

As a response to this, he asserts in *Gevia Kesef* that the proper reading of the Bible must affirm the historical existence of biblical characters discussed like Adam, Noah, Abraham, Isaac, Jacob, the twelve tribes, and Job, but concedes that it is possible that some events occurring to these individuals, such as the binding of Isaac, may have occurred in a dream.[37]

The position of the teachers of philosophy in the Jewish community of his time, whom Ibn Kaspi is criticizing, is that the biblical narrative is a poetic construction arising out of the imaginative faculty of the prophet to teach lessons about Aristotelian science. According to this stance, there is no need for the stories of the Bible to conform to any historical reality. In fact, they could be completely made up and, as such, would probably be more successful in teaching these lessons than a story that is based on an actual historic event. Ibn Kaspi must also contend with some Rabbinic precedent for this position, for the Rabbis wrote that Job "had not existed and was not created, but was a parable," a position that Maimonides also affirmed in the *Guide*.[38]

The danger inherent in this position, according to Ibn Kaspi, is that it is difficult to set the proper limits in applying this principle, both (a) in terms of the boundary between and within narrative texts and (b) in terms of the boundary between narrative and law. First, if we take it that Job "had not existed and was not created, but was a parable," how can we avoid applying this to all biblical characters and narratives? Why apply it selectively to the Book of Job, but not to all biblical books?[39] This is all the more compelling because the Rabbis said "Moses wrote his book and the Book of Job."[40] If one of the books of Moses is an allegory, does it not raise the possibility that all of them are?[41] In Ibn Kaspi's *Commentary on Job*, he argues that one should assume that all biblical narratives reflect an empirical reality and an historic event, unless there is a clear indication in the text that the narrative is describing a dream or vision ("in that its [occurrence] while [one is] awake is impossible").[42] He argues that although both the Pentateuch and the Book of Job teach practical and theoretical lessons, the entire Pentateuch should not be read as a parable like the Book of Job, even though parts of the Pentateuch also have parables and metaphors, like that of Jacob's ladder.[43]

Second, Ibn Kaspi—very subtly—raises the problem that if the entire narrative of the Torah can be interpreted as an allegory, this undermines the practical authority of the Torah's commandments. He asserts that "if the truth is that Esau and Jacob never existed, then neither did Moses and Aaron, and if Rebecca [likewise did not exist], then neither did Miriam exist."[44] The implication here is that allegorizing some characters could easily lead to allegorizing the individuals and generations from which the law itself arises. But if Moses and the revelation of the Torah on Mount Sinai is purely an allegory, then who laid down the laws and why should we obey them? Ibn Kaspi makes the compelling point that taking the narratives of the Bible to be allegories can easily undermine the entire legal framework of the Bible and all of Jewish tradition.

Part of Ibn Kaspi's argument against the transformation of the Bible into an allegory and his defense of the historical existence of biblical characters and narratives is that characters who are real are better models for imitation. To appreciate the progress in coming to understand the divine chariot in ever greater detail as later prophets expanded upon what is revealed in the Penateuch, Ibn Kaspi argues, it is necessary to understand the unique character of each individual. Ibn Kaspi may be following Aristotle here, in arguing that ethics—the cultivation of both moral and intellectual virtues—is fully persuasive only if based on actual characters that existed as opposed to literary constructs. For Aristotle, ethics does not begin with knowledge, but with repetition, with habits formed in the family from early childhood and are then reinforced by law. Aristotle argues that "by habituating citizens, lawgivers make them good" and "it makes no small difference, then, whether one is habituated in this or that way straight from childhood but a very great difference—or rather the whole difference."[45] Ibn Kaspi adds to this that the cultivation of virtues and ethical actions requires belief that the patriarchs, the matriarchs, and the prophets actually lived and acted as described in the Bible. Such belief is necessary, Ibn Kaspi argues, if the Bible is meant to improve mankind and be part of the larger historical process of human development.

## The Biblical Discoverers of the Divine Chariot

Ibn Kaspi explains in *Menorat Kesef* how the Bible reveals a historical process in which prophets who come before Moses discovered different aspects of the nature of the divine chariot, culminating with Moses, who achieved perfect knowledge of it. Some of the prophets who came after Moses also sought to uncover and reveal the secret of the divine chariot, hidden within the Torah.[46] Each expanded upon and described the chariot in greater details without contradicting the teaching revealed by Moses in the Pentateuch.[47] According to Ibn Kaspi, the knowledge of the divine chariot began with Abraham who was the first to discover God's unity as a separate intellect that exists above the spheres. The people in Abraham's time, he says, understood the second, and intermediary level of the spheres, but because they lacked knowledge of the highest realm—that of God and the separate intellects—made the mistake of thinking that the spheres were God. Abraham was the first to ask: how do the spheres cause themselves to move?[48] This led him to discover the true nature of God. Ibn Kaspi very cleverly reinterprets the Talmudic statement that "Our father Abraham kept the whole Torah"[49] to mean that Abraham discovered the first five commandments of the *Mishneh Torah*, by arguing that the "whole" does not mean the 613 commandments, but refers to what Ibn Kaspi considers the *true* Torah, which is knowledge of God, as exemplified in the first five commandments of *Mishneh Torah*.[50] These commandments are: (1) to know there is a God, (2) do not think that there is another God, (3) acknowledge His unity, (4) love Him, and (5) fear Him.[51] If we accept this argument,

Abraham's model of existence recognized God as a separate intellect, but lacked knowledge of the other separate intellects.[52]

Jacob building on Abraham's discovery, revealed three separate levels of existence through the metaphor of Jacob's ladder to heaven upon which angels were ascending and descending.[53] Ibn Kaspi argues that Maimonides had already recognized that Jacob's ladder teaches the existence of these three levels. Ibn Kaspi's addition to this is to see it as a development in a historical process that started with Abraham.[54] Neither Maimonides nor Ibn Kaspi explicitly link each element of Jacob's ladder with each of the three realms, but presumably God and the separate intellects are at the top of the ladder, the sublunar world at the bottom of the ladder, and the spheres are represented by the angels ascending and descending the ladder. Jacob, however, like Abraham had no knowledge, Ibn Kaspi argues, of the highest level of the separate intellects, other than God, and did not posit a specific number such as ten or twenty.[55] This is why the story of Jacob's ladder at Genesis 28:12 describes God alone in the highest level and does not go into specific detail about the number of separate intellects.

Next in this development of knowledge, Moses built upon Jacob's conclusions describing the perfect, but hidden, model of the divine chariot by adding ten intellects that are separate from and below God.[56] Ibn Kaspi considers Moses' detailed instructions, in the portion of *Teruma* (Exod. 25:1–27:19), for building the tabernacle and its internal furnishings to be a metaphor for the divine chariot. Ibn Kaspi argues that God's intention when telling Moses "and let them make Me a sanctuary, that I may dwell among them"[57] is to build it in imitation of the "heavenly temple":[58]

> No one who possesses a soul can have any doubt . . .that these artificial matters are exalted and wonderful imitations of natural things in order to make an impression on the soul of Moses and on the High Priest . . .and on any man who sees . . It is as if God said to Moses "make a complete world, including three worlds, as I myself made." All of this is for the purpose of copying, imitating and emulating, for to know this is the goal of every man.[59]

God's complicated and detailed technical instructions for building the tabernacle, Ibn Kaspi argues, express Moses' perfect apprehension of the divine chariot and presentation of it in metaphorical form. The practice of rituals in the tabernacle, so constructed, he argues, would educate the priest and the people in the nature of the divine chariot.[60]

According to Ibn Kaspi, the tabernacle represents the three realms as revealed through the metaphor of the divine chariot in the following ways. The tabernacle has both an inner tent and an external courtyard. The external court is an imitation of the sublunar world where all is matter, so there are four copper rings on the altar which represent the four elements.[61] Inside the tent, which represents the intermediary level of the spheres, are the ark and its cover which represent Moses and his soul, and the two cherubim which represent the Active Intellect and the rational faculty.[62] The utensils and the menorah represent God and the separate intellects.[63] The seven candles on the menorah correspond to the seven separate intellects that are the causes of seven of the nine spheres, those that correspond directly to the planets. The candles are lit to signify the planets' influence on the sublunar world.[64] The table and the showbread are intended to remind Moses and the High Priest that even though the rational faculty is conjoined to the active intellect, they cannot ignore bodily needs.[65] According to Ibn Kaspi's interpretation of the tabernacle, as a model for understanding the structure of existence, the sublunar realm which is accessible to all is outside the tent in plain view, while the higher levels are hidden within.

Ibn Kaspi next examines the prophecies of Isaiah, Ezekiel, and Zechariah, the three prophets after Moses who described the divine chariot. Ibn Kaspi states emphatically in *Menorat Kesef* that it is a common mistake of the masses to think that the divine chariot is found only in Ezekiel. In fact, he says, it is found in multiple places in the Hebrew Bible. Ibn Kaspi describes these three post-Mosaic prophets as being both conservative and revolutionary. He states that of "all the prophets [after Moses], their prophecies are only imitations of the prophecy of Moses, like a monkey makes imitations of man."[66] The implication is that although a monkey can mimic a man, it is not able to fully understand and reflect human complexities. This suggests that, in Ibn Kaspi's view, no later prophet could reach the depth of Moses' understanding. In another section, he seems to contradict this, however, when he praises Zechariah's vision stating "nowhere else in the Torah nor in the Scriptures is the [divine] chariot explained in this lengthy detail."[67] So it appears that at least one of the later prophets described and revealed certain aspects of the divine chariot in greater detail than Moses was willing to divulge. Nevertheless, Ibn Kaspi insists that none surpassed Moses' knowledge of it.

Isaiah sees the divine chariot as operating on three distinct levels and adds details that are not explicitly stated in Moses' description. Isaiah reports:

> In the year that king Uzziah died I saw the Lord sitting upon a throne high and lifted up, and His train filled the temple. Above Him stood the seraphim; each one had six wings: with twain he covered his face and with twain he covered his feet, and with twain he did fly. And one called unto another, and said: Holy, holy, holy, is the LORD of hosts; the whole earth is full of His glory.[68]

God is likened in this metaphor to a king, the seraphim to the separate intellects, and the earth to the sublunar world. God is sitting on a throne because He is the first cause, Ibn Kaspi argues. This puts God above the other separate intellects that cause the motion of the spheres. The evidence for this, according to Ibn Kaspi, is Isaiah's use of the verb "sitting,"[69] which is explained by Maimonides in *Guide* I 11 as showing that he is "the stable One who undergoes no manner of change, neither a change in His essence as He has no modes besides His essence with respect to which He might change—nor a change to His relation to what is other than Himself. . . ."[70] The "temple," Ibn Kaspi argues, reflects this same realm of the separate intellects which are represented here by the seraphim.[71] Ibn Kaspi explains that Isaiah describes the seraphim as being "above Him," because Isaiah is following common convention derived from human kingdoms that the king sits and everyone else stands around him, either beside him or in front of him.[72]

Ibn Kaspi does not himself explain the metaphor of the seraphims' wings, but points the reader to *Guide* I 43 saying "I cannot add more to his [Maimonides'] explanation because I have sworn [not to]."[73] Maimonides argues there that both the seraphim and the separate intellects have no bodies and the wings of the seraphim cover their bodies in order to show that the cause of their motion is concealed.[74] Isaiah says that the seraphim "called unto another" which Ibn Kaspi interprets as meaning that the separate intellect contemplate the highest level of existence, but cannot comprehend the levels that are below them (the spheres and the sublunar world).[75] They call "holy" three times since three hints at the division of the separate intellects into three: God, eight of the nine separate intellects, and the ninth separate intellect, the Active Intellect.[76] The last element of Isaiah's prophecy is that the "whole earth is full of His glory" which Ibn Kaspi argues shows that the sublunar world originates from the higher worlds that oversee and, in God's case, know them, which makes God the efficient, formal, and final cause of the sublunar world.[77]

Ezekiel's vision of the divine chariot also presents it as representing the three realms, but while Isaiah's prophecy focuses mostly on details about the separate intellects, Ezekiel's prophecy adds many more details about the intermediary level of the spheres and their impact on the sublunar world, a point only hinted at in the Pentateuch, according to Ibn Kaspi. In other words, Isaiah's prophecy treats of metaphysics, while Ezekiel's treats of celestial physics. Ibn Kaspi's decision to present Ezekiel's vision after Isaiah's appears to repudiate Maimonides' position, that Ezekiel's vision of the chariot was flawed and more problematic than Isaiah's. Maimonides makes this case by quoting the Bayblonian Talmud's statement that "all that was seen by Ezekiel was [likewise] seen by Isaiah. Isaiah is like unto a city man who saw the king; whereas Ezekiel is like unto a villager who saw the king."[78] This suggests that Ezekiel was less familiar with the divine chariot, and therefore described it in much greater detail, like an individual who grew up in the country and moved to the big city, while Isaiah's description is much simpler since he was more familiar with the divine chariot, like an individual who grew up in the big city and is not as excited by the tall buildings and action.[79] Maimonides considers two possibilities for why Isaiah would provide less detail than Ezekiel: either Isaiah had reached a higher intellectual level than Ezekiel, or they were both at the same intellectual level, but Isaiah's audience is of a higher intellectual level than Ezekiel's audience and thus needed less instruction.[80]

Maimonides hints at III 6 that Ezekiel's prophecy is imperfect, but it is only by connecting this chapter to earlier chapters in the *Guide* that one can piece together a detailed account of the two mistakes he sees in Ezekiel's description of the divine chariot.[81] Ezekiel's first mistake is attributing sound to the motion of the spheres. Maimonides uses Aristotle to criticize Ezekiel for this, in *Guide* II 8, without ever mentioning Ezekiel by name. Indeed, Maimonides conspicuously fails to cite Ezekiel 1:24 so much as a single time in the *Guide*: "And when they went, I heard the noise of their wings like the noise of great waters, like the voice of the Almighty, a noise of tumult like the noise of a host; when they stood, they let down their wings."[82] Ezekiel's second error, according to Maimonides, is that he gives an incorrect number and order for the spheres. This is because Ezekiel describes four animals, which Maimonides takes to represent the spheres. Ezekiel's mistake is in having only four animals (spheres), whereas according to Aristotle there are nine spheres. Maimonides hints at this mistake in *Guide* II 9, but again without mentioning Ezekiel by name.[83] Warren Zev Harvey argues that Ezekiel's errors are a paradigm for what happens when you rush to study celestial physics before studying terrestrial physics. This is why he thinks Maimonides ranks Ezekiel so low in the hierarchy of prophets at *Guide* II 45[84] and why Ezekiel is not mentioned in the summary of the chariot in the *Mishneh Torah* in *Laws of the Foundations of the Torah* Chapters 1–2.[85]

In *Maskiyot Kesef*, Ibn Kaspi interprets Ezekiel's mistake of attributing sound to the motion of the spheres as an outcome of his prophecy not being constant, containing moments of cessation and weakness like "lightning flashes," where the prophecy is lowered in status to a dream and comes under the influence of the imagination.[86] In mentioning Ezekiel in his commentary on *Guide* II 8, Ibn Kaspi makes explicit what Maimonides only hints implicitly. Ezekiel's mistake is not one of making a faulty argument, but is a mistake that is characteristic of every prophet other than Moses, because their prophecies are dependent on the imagination and, therefore, cannot avoid incorporating physical elements in it. Ibn Kaspi defends Ezekiel in a different way in *Menorat Kesef* where he proposes that Ezekiel did not actually reach the conclusion that the spheres make noise, but merely presents it that way with a deliberate imaginative falsity (a "noble lie") in order to present it more effectively to the masses. Ibn Kaspi makes a similar argument, there with respect to Ezekiel's four animals. He claims that this is not a scientific error on Ezekiel's part implying that there are four spheres as opposed to the Aristotelian calculation of nine spheres, but an imaginative method of conveying the nature of the spheres.[87]

Ezekiel's prophecy of the divine chariot adds to Isaiah's by describing the animals and the wheels of the chariot, which are taken to represent the spheres and the sublunar world. Ibn Kaspi identifies the faces of the four animals, those of a man, a lion, an ox, and and an eagle,[88] as metaphors for eight out of nine spheres: those spheres that contain stars. The face of man, Ibn Kaspi argues, represents the sphere of the fixed stars that causes the motion of the seven spheres below it. It is represented by man since man rules over all the animals, just as this sphere controls all the other stars. The face of a lion represents the five spheres of Mercury, Venus, Mars, Jupiter, and Saturn; the face of an ox represents the sphere containing the sun; and the face of an eagle represents the sphere of the moon.[89] The four wings of each,[90] Ibn Kaspi argues, represent the four causes of their motion: the spherical shape of the sphere, its soul, its intellect, and the separate intellect which is its beloved.[91] Ibn Kaspi defends this interpretation by pointing out to the reader that he is connecting Maimonides' dispersed discussions at *Guide* I 49 and II 10.[92] Maimonides takes the fact that the wings are all joined to one another[93] to symbolize the single unified motion of each sphere, which does not change direction, or twist or turn.[94] The feet of the animals are taken to represent heavenly matter and the comparison of the soul to the sole of a calf's foot is relevant, Ibn Kaspi argues, since the root of the Hebrew word for calf, *'egel*, is similar to the word for circle, *'igul*. Therefore, since a calf's foot is spherical, Ibn Kaspi takes it to be a metaphor for the spherical nature of heavenly matter.

The wheels of the divine chariot, are taken to represent the sublunar world. Its motion is caused by the motion of the spheres, just as the motion of the wheels of a chariot is caused by the motion of the horses.[95] The relationship of the intellects and the spheres to the sublunar world is expanded upon in a second prophetic vision at Ezekiel 8:1–11:1:

> And behold six men came from the way of the upper gate, which lieth toward the north, every man with his weapon of destruction in his hand; and one man in the midst of them clothed in linen, with a writer's ink on side.[96]

The seven men mentioned are metaphors and are taken by Ibn Kaspi to be metaphors for the seven separate intellects that cause the motion of the seven planets of seven of the nine sublunar spheres below them: the sun, moon, Mercury, Venus, Mars, Jupiter, and Saturn. Ibn Kaspi sees everything that happens in the sublunar world as a result of the position of the seven planets. Ibn Kaspi next converts a second metaphor, at Ezekiel 9:2, into yet another metaphor: that of a celestial court with God as the king, and the separate intellects as his servants and ministers.[97] He argues that the actions of the separate intellects are "sometimes for good and sometimes for evil,"[98] which is why different intellects are described by him at different times as good angels, bad angels, the angel of death or Satan, since the motion they cause to the spheres has repercussions on events and people in this world, whether for good for ill. Ibn Kaspi thinks this helps explain why Ezekiel describes the divine chariot in two seemingly repetitive visions that differ only in that they approach it from different perspectives: The first vision starts from the more exalted upper realm before it stoops to describe the lower sublunar realm, while the second vision starts with the sublunar realm before it rises to the upper realm.[99]

Of all the post-Mosaic prophets, Zechariah is considered by Ibn Kaspi to give the most lengthy and detailed vision of the divine chariot. Indeed, Ibn Kaspi argues that four of Zechariah's seven visions are of the chariot.[100] The first gives more details of the celestial spheres:

> I saw in the night, and behold a man riding upon a red horse, and he stood among the myrtle-trees that were in the bottom; and behind him there were horses, red, sorrel, and white.[101]

Ibn Kaspi takes the man riding on the horse to represent the Active Intellect that is responsible for the sublunar world, which is represented by the red horse. The horse is red because fire is the element that is closest to the Active Intellect and fire is red. Zechariah, Ibn Kaspi argues, represents the element of fire as a horse, not only because fire is the lightest of the elements, according to Aristotle, and therefore closest to the heavens, but also because its lightness makes its movement the quickest.[102] The four elements naturally move up and down and fire is the lightest of the elements, according to Aristotelian science.[103] The myrtle trees, Ibn Kaspi argues, are symbols of the human intellect's capacity to move from potential to actual. Ibn Kaspi builds this on Maimonides' argument that one of the definitions of *ruah* is the divine intellect overflowing into a prophet, making actual what previously had been only potential.[104] This is relevant, Ibn Kaspi argues, because the rabbis understood the myrtle as unique for its nice smell, its *re'ah tov*,[105] and *re'ah* and *ruah* share the same root, *reish, vav, het*. Lastly, the three riderless horses in Zechariah's vision, Ibn Kaspi claims, represent a division of the sublunar spheres into three: red representing the five spheres of Mercury, Venus, Mars, Jupiter, and Saturn; sorrel representing the sphere of the sun; and white representing the sphere of the moon.[106]

Zechariah's fifth prophetic vision of the divine chariot contains a seven-piped gold candelabra:

> I have seen, and behold a candlestick all of gold, with a bowl upon the top of it, and its seven lamps thereon; there are seven pipes, yea, seven, to the lamps, which are upon the top thereof and two olive-trees by it, one upon the right side of the bowl, and the other upon the left side thereof.[107]

Taken together, the seven candelabras and the two olive trees represent nine of the separate intellects, the bowl on top refers to God as the separate intellect above them all. The metaphor of the candelabra suggests two divisions: the seven lamps with pipes refer to the intellects that cause the motion of the seven spheres with stars: sun, moon, Mercury, Venus, Mars, Jupiter, and Saturn. The two olive trees refer to the two topmost spheres of the fixed stars and the outer sphere which has no stars. How does one explain why Moses' calculation of the number of separate intellects was ten, while Zechariah's calculation was nine separate intellects?[108] Ibn Kaspi solves this dilemma very simply by stating these divisions are all imaginative constructs based on Maimonides' sixteenth premise at the beginning of *Guide* II that the intellect cannot grasp multiplicity in substances that are not physical bodies.[109]

Zechariah's sixth prophetic vision refers to a flying bun that is a metaphor for the motion of the elements in the sublunar world, based upon the premise that the sublunar world, the world of matter, is the source of evil and sin. Ibn Kaspi compares the movement of the elements in the sublunar world to the movement of the spheres and intellects. Movement in the sublunar world is in an upwards and downwards direction, and requires exertion, which is tiring, unlike the movement of the spheres and the intellects that move without exertion or tiring.[110] The upward and downward motion of the sublunar world is taught by Zechariah in chapter 5 through the image of two women lifting a measure between heaven and earth, the two women according to Ibn Kaspi signifying the two directions of movement.[111] The flying bun leads to a curse "that goeth forth over the face of the whole land."[112] This indicates, in Ibn Kaspi's reading, that the physical nature of humanity is what leads most individuals to evil and sinful actions. This is an odd reading, since the Book of Zechariah focuses on two specific sinful actions, neither of which satisfy physical desires: stealing and swearing falsely with God's name.[113] Ibn Kaspi cites Maimonides' explanation of this point that "all man's acts of disobedience and sins are consequent upon his matter and not upon his form."[114] In other words, these sins are unavoidable in the sublunar world due to the physical composition of its creatures.[115]

Zechariah's seventh prophetic vision is of four chariots each with different colored horses, emerging between two mountains of brass:

> And again I lifted up mine eyes, and saw, and, behold, there came four chariots out from between the two mountains; and the mountains were mountains of brass. In the first chariot were red horses; and in the second chariot black horses; and in the third chariot white horses; and in the fourth chariot grizzled bay horses.[116]

Here, the red horses, Ibn Kaspi argues, represent the fixed stars, the black horses represent the five stars (Mercury, Venus, Mars, Jupiter, and Saturn), the white horses represent the sun, and the grizzled bay horses represent the moon.[117]

## The Divine Chariot and Miracles

Prophetic knowledge of the divine chariot, Ibn Kaspi argues, gives prophets the ability to understand and manipulate the laws of nature and to fashion miracles at will.[118] This arises in the context of his discussion of how Maimonides thinks philosophers differ from prophets. Maimonides raises this question in *Guide* II 37 where he contrasts the philosopher, the statesman, and the prophet. The philosopher, he says, is concerned with obtaining knowledge, but not in communicating it to others, having perfected his rational faculty, but not his imaginative faculty. The statesman is concerned with ruling others and does so through the imaginative faculty, but lacks the perfection of the rational faculty, either because he lacks the natural disposition or is not sufficiently trained. The prophet is unique in having perfected both his rational and imaginative faculties, and thus can communicate rational truths through education and legislation.[119]

Ibn Kaspi, like Maimonides, highlights the common ground of the prophet and the philosopher. But, unlike Maimonides, Ibn Kaspi argues that prophets are superior to philosophers. In commenting on Maimonides' *Guide* II 32 in *Maskiyot Kesef,* Ibn Kaspi interprets Maimonides' three opinions of prophecy as an example of the seventh contradiction where the true meaning is dangerous to the non-philosophic reader and thus purposely concealed.[120] The first opinion is the Pagan view that all prophecy is caused entirely by the divine will, the second opinion is the philosopher's view that prophecy is entirely the result of human perfection, and the third opinion comes from the Torah which agrees with the philosophers, that prophecy is the result of human perfection, but adds that God can withhold prophecy.[121] In Ibn Kaspi's reading, the third opinion, that of the Torah, is, in truth, but covertly, the same as the second opinion, that of the philosophers, but Maimonides hides this from the masses. He maintains that

> The third opinion that he postulates is "the opinion of our Law and the foundation (*yesod*) of our [religious] doctrine." . . .But [if it is] so that it is "the opinion of our Law and the foundation (*yesod*) of our doctrine," why is it not included in the Laws of the Foundations of the Torah [in the *Mishneh Torah*] in enumerating the foundations? And so it says in Chapter 7 of the Laws of the Foundations of the Torah: "it is one of the foundations of our religious doctrine that God inspires men with the prophetic gift, but the spirit of prophecy only rests upon the wise man who is distinguished by great wisdom and strong moral character, whose passions never overcome him in anything whatsoever." It did not say that this particular foundational principle is separate from the opinion of the philosophers. And further, where does one find in the Torah and the prophetic writings this condition [that God withholds prophecy] and only some biblical verses can be interpreted in this way and it is possible to interpret them otherwise, as he himself does in undermining all [that he said here]. Thus, it seems to me that all this language, was written by Maimonides using the seventh contradiction.[122]

To solve this problem, Ibn Kaspi goes to the *Mishneh Torah* and shows that Maimonides' legal code does not distinguish between the opinion of the philosophers and that of the Torah, nor is there any mention there of God withholding prophecy. Since the divine will endows the perfect individual with prophecy, saying that the divine will withholds prophecy implies that nature does not always guarantee that the worthy succeed (as Maimonides argues in *Guide* II 48). Saying that the divine will withholds prophecy also hides the truth, which is that God is only a distant cause of all.[123]

Ibn Kaspi repeats once again that the prophet is superior to the philosopher. This is consistent throughout his writings. In *Shulḥan Kesef*, for example, he states that "the level of the prophet is superior to that of the philosopher, and the ways of prophecy do not follow the roots of philosophy."[124] In *'Amudei Kesef* he argues that "the view of the prophet is always true, so that even if philosophers are divided between two interpretations, prophecy settles the debate . . .since prophecy is superior to philosophy"[125] and in *Maskiyot Kesef* that the "prophetic soul is superior to the philosophic soul."[126] Ibn Kaspi argues that the superiority of the prophet lies not in combining knowledge with leadership, but in his speed and ease of acquisition of knowledge and his ability to control nature at will.

Ibn Kaspi adopts Avicenna's concept of "intuitive prophecy" (*ḥads*) to explain the miraculous nature of the prophet's understanding of nature.[127] For he is able, Ibn Kaspi argues, to arrive at conclusions instantaneously and can do so with no external aid or prior learning, qualities which today would be called "gifts" or "genius."[128] Ibn Kaspi takes exception to Maimonides with respect to this, in his commentary in *'Amudei Kesef* on *Guide* I 34. This is the chapter where Maimonides deals with the reasons why most people cannot study divine science. The third of these reasons is the length of time it takes to gain such knowledge. Most people, Maimonides says, desire to obtain knowledge of the heavenly spheres, but few can or will abandon their occupation in order to devote themselves to the extremely detailed preparation required: "it is certainly necessary for whoever wishes to achieve human perfection to train himself at first in the art of logic, then in the mathematical sciences according to the proper order, then in the natural sciences, and after that in the divine science."[129] Maimonides operates under the assumption that all the prophets completed such a curriculum of study. Ibn Kaspi, however, argues that true prophets are an exception to this rule, since they have an unique intuitive ability to obtain the knowledge of the divine chariot without spending all the time learning the prerequisites, having the ability to arrive at the conclusions of the divine sciences without studying all the intermediary steps, such as logic, mathematics, and the natural sciences.[130] Ibn Kaspi discusses his second criteria of intuitive prophecy: the speed and ease of the prophet's acquisition of knowledge in contrast to the rigorous education of the philosopher, in *Shulḥan Kesef*. There he suggests that the prophetic soul is higher than philosophic soul because the prophet comes by his knowledge easily, while the philosopher comprehends these matters with difficulty.[131] Ibn Kaspi quotes Averroes' *Epitome of Aristotle's Parva Naturalia* as evidence for the existence of intuitive prophecy:

> . . . unless a person assumes that we have here a species of man that can comprehend the theoretical sciences without training. Now this species, if it indeed existed, would be called "man" only equivocally, but actually it would be closer to angels than to man.[132]

Averroes' next sentence, however, casts doubt on this claim: "it will be seen that this is impossible from that which I shall say."[133] Ibn Kaspi, tellingly, chooses not to quote this. He finds better support in Avicenna, who, in *The Healing*, gives a similar view to Ibn Kaspi's, of the prophet as a quasi-god:

> And whoever, in addition to this, wins the prophetic qualities, becomes almost a human god. Worship of him, after the worship of God, becomes almost allowed. He is indeed the world's earthly king and God's deputy in it.[134]

Ibn Kaspi builds on Avicenna in order to present his image of the prophet having knowledge of the divine chariot which gained without difficulty, patience or skepticism; but with ease, speed, and certainty.

Prophets have such a deep comprehension of nature's laws, Ibn Kaspi argues that they can use their will to cause miracles. Ibn Kaspi goes so far as to say that the prophet imitates the Active Intellect in endowing matter with new forms, just as the active intellect imparts intelligible forms to the physical universe.[135] Kalonymous ben Kalonymous criticizes this in his letter to Ibn Kaspi:

> You ascribe to one who possesses the most perfect knowledge possible in reality the ability to change the course of those events that can be changed in nature. Although you do not say so explicitly, this is your opinion, that when one has an encompassing knowledge of all the propositions necessary to effect any activity in nature, he will also have knowledge of the causal connection of those propositions, one to the other, so that he may establish his work in place of nature.[136]

For Ibn Kaspi however, it is active involvement in the world that differentiates the prophet from the philosopher. The philosopher may also understand nature, Ibn Kaspi concedes, but he can do so only with difficulty, and lacks the ability to use his knowledge to cause miracles. In his *Commentary on Proverbs*, Ibn Kaspi states that "the perfection of the human intellect . . . attained by Moses, our master . . . the perfection of the prophetic soul . . . for Moses did [wonders] with the four [elements] according to his will, deeds that are impossible for every wise man to do."[137] Ibn Kaspi does not think miracles are against nature. Instead, he sees them as rare natural phenomena. Here, he follows Maimonides who distinguishes between miracles impossible by nature and miracles possible by nature in the *Letter on Resurrection*.[138] Maimonides argues that miracles that are impossible by nature happen only for a very short period of time before everything reverts back to the normal pattern of nature. This demonstrates that they are not natural. Examples include a staff turning into a snake, splitting the Red Sea so the Israelites could escape Egypt, splitting the Jordan River so they could enter Israel, and the land opening up to swallow Korah.[139] Miracles that are possible by nature can also be predicted by a prophet, Maimonides argues; they have a low probability of occurring, but can continue over a considerable length of time. Examples include many of the plagues in Egypt.

Moses is Ibn Kaspi's paradigm of the prophet. Ibn Kaspi argues that Moses had perfect knowledge of the divine chariot (encompassing all of nature, a.k.a. the four elements, the spheres, and the intellects), which gave him the knowledge of how these different parts of the natural order interact and operate. This, in turn, gave him knowledge of how to manipulate them at will, as Ibn Kaspi argues in *Tirat Kesef*:

> There is no doubt that Moses our master, peace be on him, reached the ultimate perfection of intellectual apprehension possible for the human mind to attain in accordance with its nature. His actions will prove that, which is why Solomon described the miraculous actions of Moses, saying: "Who has ascended heaven and come down? Who hath gathered the wind in his handful? Who hath bound the waters in his garment?" (Prov. 30:4). And in general he described the higher types of miraculous actions which included miracles that are impossible by nature. One cannot claim that Moses ascended [only physically] to the top of the mountain because it is written "I have talked with you from heaven" (Exod. 20:18) which was preceded by "and Moses went up unto God" (Exod. 19:3). . . . There is no doubt that he worked [miracles] with

the wind, and in general with the element of air, and also with the element of water, most of them impossible to us, until these [miraculous] actions were, metaphorically, like collecting wind in handfuls or binding water in a garment. It is as if the air was soot of the furnace or flour, and the water was myrrh or silver. In general, his actions were done according to his will.[140]

Ibn Kaspi argues that the Bible presents Moses' control over nature metaphorically as if the four elements were physical objects or substances that Moses could hold in his hands and combine at will, much like a chemistry formula.

A prime example, for Ibn Kaspi, that demonstrates Moses' complete knowledge and miraculous manipulation of nature is his causing the ten plagues against Egypt. What makes them miraculous is not that plagues are impossible by nature, but that Moses was able to summon them. Ibn Kaspi describes the ten plagues not as ten separate natural occurrences, but as one causal chain that was begun by Moses. The plagues he set in motion moved from affecting the lowest to the highest of the four elements, first from water, next earth, then air and finally, fire. Moses initiated this process when he took his rod and put it in the Nile, turning its water into blood, causing the first plague.[141] Ibn Kaspi takes this as a metaphor for Moses using heat to change the chemistry of the water into blood, since water is cold and wet, and blood is also wet, but hot.[142] This led to the death of all the fish in the Nile, and forced the frogs to multiply on land, causing the second plague.[143] The transformation of the water of the Nile into blood also caused a lack of rain, drying up the land so that the earth became dry like sand on a beach. The drought, in turn, was optimal for lice and fleas, which constituted the third plague.[144] The drought also caused the fifth plague, a disease that afflicted the Egyptian livestock, including the horses, cattle, sheep, and camels, while encouraging the increase of wild animals, the fourth plague, such as snakes, scorpions, spiders, wasps and flies. Ibn Kaspi notes that the Bible purposefully refers to the fourth plague ambiguously as a "mixture" or "swarm" ('*arov*) in order to hide the unlimited number of species grouped within this category.[145] This disease also, eventually spread to the air affecting three different levels of air, causing the next three plagues: boils on the lowest level, hail on the intermediary level, and locusts on the highest level. Boils were caused by the spread of disease through the air from the livestock to other animals and humans. Its spread into the air also caused thunderstorms to rain down destructive hail and fires that, in turn, caused the deaths of good birds and the survival of destructive birds, hence the plague of locusts.[146] The last two plagues were caused by the effect of air on the element of fire. The darkness of the ninth plague was caused by murkiness that was caused by heat and dryness existing in the element of fire and the absence of the dry and cold of the element of water. This, in turn, caused the last plague, the death of the firstborn of Egypt, which Ibn Kaspi argues refers to the death of the weak, because they were overcome by intense heat.

Ibn Kaspi distinguishes the miraculous abilities of Moses from those of other prophets who he places on a lower level, even if they carried out miracles that seem more wonderous than those of Moses. In *Shulhan Kesef*, Ibn Kaspi writes that

> It is a mistake and a transgression of the true religion to believe that Joshua, Elijah, Elisha or others carried out actions more miraculous and sublime from Moses our master. If Joshua made the sun stand still by the will of God and Elijah and Elisha revived the dead, I say that so did Moses our master, even if he did not write it in his book. No doubt Moses did not write in his book all the actions he carried out.[147]

So, although other prophets coming after Moses were able to study the divine chariot and use that knowledge to perform miracles, none, Ibn Kaspi argues, were comparable to Moses' miracles because no other prophet attained Moses' superior level of knowledge. Ibn Kaspi goes so far as to argue here that Moses could have created any miracle performed by later prophets, and probably did, but did not always bother to write it down.

## The Project of Teaching the Chariot: Inner-Biblical Exegesis from Genesis to Zechariah

Ibn Kaspi argues that the details of the divine chariot were discovered and revealed by biblical characters through a long historical process described in the narratives of the Hebrew Bible from Genesis to Zechariah. He champions Moses as the pinnacle of perfect knowledge, even though this can only be maintained by arguing that Moses did not reveal all that he knew in the Bible, at least not explicitly. According to Ibn Kaspi, Moses and later biblical authors constructed multiple texts in order to create a dialogue between them by interconnecting them through certain common images and forms of language that prepare and guide the reader to understand hidden secrets. Modern scholars of the Hebrew Bible refer to this literary method as that of "inner-biblical exegesis," in which later passages will often compel readers to revisit earlier ones, subjecting them to inquiry, revision, and deeper examination.[148] Ibn Kaspi argues that Moses did this, deliberately constructing Genesis as an introductory guide to understanding the divine chariot in order to lead his readers, to build up their skills, little by little as they scrutinize his use of language, in order to gain greater knowledge.[149] Later prophets, he argues, continued to build on Moses' method, and developed his lessons further, using more complex imagery.

The clearest example of inner-biblical exegesis can be seen in the relationship between the terms used to describe creation in Genesis 1 and the fuller development and explanation of creation by later prophets. Ibn Kaspi states near the beginning of *Maṣref la-Kesef* that "most of the terms of this supernal account [of the beginning] were explained further by the prophets, and moreover this is true about the entire Torah, so much so that if you understand the explanations of the prophets, you will not need the commentary of Ibn Ezra and others."[150] One example of this is the division of nature into three realms in the image of the divine chariot, as presented by later prophets. Ibn Kaspi argues that Moses covertly hints at this in the first few chapters of Genesis by using three different names for God: *Elohim* between Genesis 1:1–2:3, YHVH *Elohim* between Genesis 2:4–3:24, and YHVH between 4:1–26.[151] Ibn Kaspi argues that this is not accidental. In *Menorat Kesef*, he claims that the account of creation has three different sections with three different names of God, corresponding to three different opinions on the nature of God, in order to slowly bring a reader from the simple to a more complex understanding of God. According to his interpretation *Elohim* represents the spheres, YHVH *Elohim* represents the separate intellects, and YHVH represents God as the highest separate intellect.[152] Ibn Kaspi posits that Moses should have begun Genesis with "in the beginning YHVH (the highest intellect) created the heaven and the earth," but instead wrote "In the beginning *Elohim* (the spheres) created the heaven and the earth" as a concession to the common view in Moses' time that the world came into being through the spheres. While Moses is presenting a false premise at the very beginning of the Bible, he is doing so with the intention of gradually shifting the reader away from this error toward the truth.[153] Ibn Kaspi argues that more detailed descriptions of the creation by later prophets provide a commentary and further explanation of it.

The different parts of nature other than God, Ibn Kaspi argues, are also presented in Genesis 1 in terms that are explained only by later prophets. For example, Genesis begins with the ambiguous statement that "In the beginning God created the *shamayyim* and the *'areṣ*" (Gen. 1:1), but Genesis does not say what the *shamayyim* is. The Christians translated this word into Latin as *caelum*, heaven, but Ibn Kaspi disputes this, adamant, as always, that biblical words are always connected to their root and grammar, making it necessary to read the Bible in Hebrew in order to avoid losing its complexity of meaning. Unlike the Christians, Ibn Kaspi interprets *shamayyim* to refer to heavenly matter that is spherical, moves in a circular motion, and exists in multiple locations when viewed from different angles.[154] He bases this on *shamayyim* being the plural of *sham*, "there," which refers to a location, and therefore hints at a plurality of locations. He argues that this teaches an essential characteristic of heavenly matter; it is not restricted to one physical location, in contrast to the sublunar world of the four elements that moves in a linear direction, upward and downward. Ibn Kaspi argues that the prophets continued to explain the nature of heavenly matter by referring to God's action of "planting (*linṭo'a*) the heavens" at Isaiah 51:16.[155] The verb *naṭa'* can refer to planting a plant or pitching a tent (such as Genesis 31:25). Both these worldly meanings, if projected onto heavenly matter, appear to mean that God set up the structure of the heavens.[156]

Another ambiguous element of the account of creation in Genesis 1 is God's construction of a *raqi'a* in the midst of the waters that divided the waters that were below it from those above it.[157] Ibn Kaspi agrees with Maimonides that the *raqi'a* refers to the celestial spheres that divide the sublunar world from the separate intellects, but does not think Maimonides is needed to establish this, since Maimonides was merely expanding on Isaiah.[158] On the second day of the creation, the waters are divided into two: the water below the *raqi'a* is indeed water, Ibn Kaspi argues, but the water above the *raqi'a* is a different substance that is described as water only metaphorically.[159] To justify this, Ibn Kaspi points to examples of how the later prophets expanded upon God's construction of the *raqi'a* as the celestial spheres. One example is in Jeremiah 10:13 where Jeremiah describes the second day of creation as follows: "at the sound of His giving a multitude of waters in the heavens, when He causes the vapors to ascend from the ends of the earth; when He makes lightning with the rain, and bringeth forth the wind out of His treasuries."[160] According to Ibn Kaspi, Jeremiah is expanding on Genesis 1:6 saying that God purposefully made the spheres of a different substance than that of the sublunar world or the world of the intellects, which is shown by His separating the "water" above from the "water" below.[161] Isaiah describes this same action of God in Genesis 1:6 saying that "[I] have covered thee in the shadow of My hand, that I may plant the heavens."[162] Ibn Kaspi is quite terse in his explanation of Isaiah's statement, but he suggests that "plant the heavens" refers to the celestial spheres only and argues that the nature of the verb "to plant" must be explored. Therefore, not every form of planting must directly touch the ground, for "planting" can also be like pitching a tent where the tent is rooted in the ground only through the intermediary of the tent pegs. He seems to be suggesting here that the sublunar world is "planted" in the universe through the "pegs" of the celestial sphere and that is why the creation of the spheres is a necessary prerequisite to the more detailed description of the details of the sublunar world.[163]

Ibn Kaspi describes a similar relationship between Genesis 1 and the later prophets in deciphering *tohu va-vohu*, the darkness and void, described at the beginning of creation.[164] The relationship between Genesis 1:1 that describes God's creation and Genesis 1:2 that describe this vacuous state of darkness and void is ambiguous. If 1:1 describes God's creation, why is there still a vacuous and unformed state in 1:2? Ibn Kaspi's answer is that we need to read Genesis 1:2 in light of Isaiah 45:18–19.[165] Isaiah describes creation as follows: "for thus saith the LORD that created the heavens, He is God; that formed the earth and made it, He established it, He created it not a waste (*tohu*), He formed it to be inhabited: I am the LORD, and there is none else."[166] According to Ibn Kaspi's reading of Isaiah, Genesis 1:1 states that the purpose of God's act of creation is so that the universe is "to be inhabited."[167] Thus, in light of Isaiah, one should not read Genesis 1:1 as chronologically preceding Genesis 1:2, but Genesis 1:1 refers to the goal and Genesis 1:2 refers to the nature of the material before the process of creation began.[168]

History as the Progressive Revelation of the Divine Chariot / 85

## The Sacrifices and the War on Idolatry

Idolatry is one of the central obstacles to Ibn Kaspi's argument that intellectual progress toward knowledge of the divine chariot is an historical process. Ibn Kaspi follows Maimonides, here, who makes eradication of idolatry the main principle of the Torah. Maimonides writes that

> The intent of the whole Law and the pole around which it resolves is to put an end to *idolatry*, to efface its traces, and to bring about a state of affairs in which it would not be imagined that any star harms or helps in anything pertaining to the circumstances of human individuals. . . .[169]

Idolatry is not simply a mistaken action of worshiping a physical idol as if it were God, under the incorrect belief that any such physical object governs the heavens. It is also a well-intentioned error of the understanding in believing that some intermediary between ourselves and God must be worshipped as a means to worship God.[170] The danger of such a simple, and perhaps naïve mistake is that over time it leads the worshipper to forget that the intermediary is no more than a means to worship a non-corporeal God, and instead leads them to worship the corporeal intermediary as if it were God.[171]

The difference between Maimonides and Ibn Kaspi is over the historical context of idolatry, with respect to animal sacrifice. The problem with animal sacrifice is that it is a form of worship premised on the assumption that God is a physical being who needs to be assuaged with gifts. Maimonides famously states that biblical animal sacrifices were not in essence a Jewish ritual, but were originally a form of Egyptian idolatrous religious worship, picked up while the Jews were enslaved in Egypt, and instituted in the Bible's as a ruse intended to slowly wean the Israelites from this form of idolatry.[172] The war on idolatry is thus a correction of the mistakes of Egyptian religion. Nahmanides famously criticizes Maimonides' account of the origins of animal sacrifices in Judaism arguing instead that sacrifices preceded idolatry in the Hebrew Bible, as is evident from the accounts of sacrifices made by Abel and Noah.[173] Nahmanides even finds an example in Maimonides' own *Mishneh Torah*, from *Laws of the Temple* 2:2, of Adam offering a sacrifice to God![174] Ibn Kaspi, agreeing implicitly with Nahmanides' criticism, radicalizes

Maimonides' philosophic battle against idolatry and treats it as a battle that goes all the way back to the beginning of Genesis.

The battle to eradicate idolatry moves being from completely concealed in the first line of the Hebrew Bible to being addressed openly in the later writings of the prophets. As we discussed in the last section, Ibn Kaspi argues that Moses should have begun Genesis with "In the beginning YHVH (the highest intellect) created the heaven and the earth," but instead wrote "In the beginning *Elohim* (the spheres) created the heaven and the earth" in accordance with the common view of people in Egypt in Moses' time that the world came into being through the spheres. Although this means that Moses presents a false premise at the very beginning of the Bible, he is to be understood as doing so with the intention of gradually shifting the reader away from this error toward the truth.[175]

Discouraging animal sacrifice and idolatry is hinted at, according to Ibn Kaspi, as early as the story of Cain and Abel, which has slightly more detail than the first few lines of Genesis. Cain and Abel both made sacrifices to God, but Ibn Kaspi suggests that the verb indicating God's response is telling. It says, very neutrally, that "the LORD paid heed (*va-yish'a*) to Abel and to his offering" but "unto Cain and to his offering He had paid no heed."[176] This is in contrast to more positive statements such as "that he may be accepted (*li-reṣono*) before the LORD"[177] or that "the LORD smelled the sweet savor."[178] In both the case of Cain and that of Abel, God's response indicates that sacrifices are not his true desire, Ibn Kaspi argues. This is why he thinks Adam and his chosen son Seth are not described as making sacrifices.[179]

The next significant character described as making a sacrifice to God is Noah who "built an altar unto the LORD; and took of every clean beast, and of every clean fowl, and offered burnt-offerings on the altar,"[180] but Ibn Kaspi argues that a careful reading shows that the intention of this passage is to lessen sacrificial ritual by presenting this sacrifice without naming what specifically was sacrificed. The same omission is made when the children of Gad, Reuben and Gibeon, make a sacrifice to God in Joshua 22:10.[181] This pattern is repeated in the very general description of the sacrifices Jacob makes, especially when the biblical text reports that "Jacob offered a sacrifice in the mountain,"[182] without giving any information about the purpose or form of the sacrifice. Ibn Kaspi interprets this absence of information to mean that the sacrifice is for food and therefore not a sacrifice to God at all, since the verse continues "and called his brethren to eat bread; and they did eat bread."[183] In another case, the Bible reports: "And Israel took his journey with all that he had, and came to Beer-Sheba, and offered sacrifices unto the God of his father Isaac."[184] The mention of God in this case is intended, according to Ibn Kaspi, to show that this sacrifice is for God and not to demons, though this is another case where the details of the sacrifice are left out, which for Ibn Kaspi is part of this larger biblical battle against idolatry and sacrifices.[185]

Abraham, Ibn Kaspi argues, advanced this battle in two areas: first, by showing the superiority of prayer to sacrifice and second, by coming down hard against child sacrifice. Ibn Kaspi cites as evidence that Abraham "called upon the name of the LORD" and "and Abram called there on the name of the LORD" as references to prayer, specifically to the *amida* (which consists of eighteen benedictions).[186] The lesson Ibn Kaspi draws from such statements is that prayer is more appropriate than building temples and performing sacrifices.[187] Interestingly, Ibn Kaspi diverges from Maimonides in his *Laws of Prayer* by arguing that structured prayer was created in response to the destruction of First Temple. Before that, he claims that prayer was spontaneous.[188] For Maimonides, structured prayer, like the structured sacrificial ritual, was constructed to respond to a specific historical problem, thus hinting at the possibility that in the future ordered sacrifices and even prayer may no longer be necessary.[189] Ibn Kaspi, however, describes sacrifices as a constant problem and prayer as a constant good. Ibn Kaspi defends the philosophers against the accusation that they do not pray to God, by arguing that even for philosophers, the order of prayer has a purpose: it teaches that God is the first cause and that God is one.[190]

Abraham's skirmish with sacrifices is, of course, embodied in the narrative of the binding of Isaac, where God asks Abraham to sacrifice his son Isaac.[191] Ibn Kaspi argues that this story is actually a subtle critique of child sacrifice albeit in covert language.[192] He states:

> The purpose [of the command] was to uproot, undermine, and weaken the established belief that was in the heart of the people that those who are punctiliously careful take of their children to make sacrifices to their gods.[193]

A superficial reading of this chapter in Genesis would appear to recommend child sacrifice, but if one assembles all the subtle clues, according to Ibn Kaspi, one can see that it was written to undermine it.[194] The first of these clues, Ibn Kaspi argues, is the opening line, "God did test (*nisa*) Abraham." *Nisa* is related to trial and error by experience, which Ibn Kaspi argues is the the primary basis for a contingent prophecy.[195] His implication is that the command given to Abraham to sacrifice his son was contingent (not necessary) and thus Abraham had the freedom to refuse.[196] The second clue is the three days that elapsed between God's command and Abraham's attempt to carry it out.[197] According to Ibn Kaspi, this is to show that the action of sacrificing his son was not carried out in confusion and haste, but after consideration as to how God could command him to commit such a horrible deed.[198] By portraying Abraham as questioning this command, Ibn Kaspi, presumably, wants to promote skepticism over whether God condones this practice. Abraham's doubts and reluctance to carry out this commandment are also shown by the fact that Abraham did not kindle any fire below the wood once Isaac was placed on the altar.[199] The third clue is that the command to "offer him there for a burnt-offering" lacks the key detail of naming the recipient of this offering "to the Lord," which Ibn Kaspi takes as a sign that God did not actually recommend it.[200] The fourth and final clue is that the story is so constructed that God stops Abraham from carrying out this command, and the command stopping him is stronger than the command to commit it.[201] This comes out in a few other details as well: the initial command came from *Elohim*, while the latter command came from YHVH;[202] the first command mentioned Abraham's name only once, while the latter command mentioned his name twice, which is taken to show greater force;[203] and, finally, there is the praise Abraham receives for not sacrificing Isaac, "because thou hast hearkened to My voice," which implies that the latter command comes from God's true voice.[204] Unfortunately, this story was not successful in persuading the ancient Israelites to completely abandon child sacrifice,[205] which is why Moses had to address this point directly, stating "thou shalt not do so unto the LORD thy God; for every abomination to the LORD, which He hateth, have they done unto their gods; for even their sons and their daughters do they burn in the fire to their gods."[206]

The technical details of the sacrificial order are laid out in Leviticus, but Ibn Kaspi brushes this aside, writing in *Maṣref la-Kesef* that there is no need for him to further comment on these sections, since "God has no desire for sacrifices and burnt-offerings."[207] Ibn Kaspi here takes Maimonides' argument in the *Guide* that sacrifices are not the true form of divine worship, but pushes this further, since Maimonides dedicated two of the fourteen books of his *Mishneh Torah* to codifying all the details of sacrificial worship. Ibn Kaspi develops this point in '*Amudei Kesef*, where he draws connections between certain chapters of the *Guide*, and ritual sacrifices that Maimonides does not make explicitly. Maimonides, for example, dedicates a chapter to interpreting Aristotle's concept of "equity,"[208] which is a form of legal reasoning meant to adapt laws that were constructed in response to certain individuals and certain times to apply justly to different individuals in different times.[209] Maimonides does not mention sacrifices in III 34, but Ibn Kaspi connects that chapter to the discussion of the sacrifices in III 32, saying that God knew when He gave Torah that there would come a time and place to command an end to all sacrifices, for they were only necessary during a limited time.[210]

## The Divine Chariot and the Tripartite Structure of the *Guide*

The division of the divine chariot into three levels of reality, the intellects, the spheres, and the sublunar world, explains Maimonides' many threefold divisions within the *Guide*, according to Ibn Kaspi. While Maimonides does not link these patterns of three explicitly, Ibn Kaspi thinks there is a distinct continuity between the first group, the second group, and the third group in each division, and argues that we need to follow Maimonides' advice of putting together the pieces of the puzzle that he disperses throughout this book.[211] He thinks the purpose of Maimonides' recurring tripart divisions is to reclaim and reinstitute the tradition of contemplating the divine chariot which, in Ibn Kaspi's narrative, was stolen by gentile nations. Ibn Kaspi strives to show that writing in patterns of three in order to mimic the division of the divine chariot into three is not a hermeneutical invention of Maimonides, but follows the precedent of the Bible itself, which he argues employs this method, most visibly in the parsha of Genesis which can be broken into divisions of three.[212]

Ibn Kaspi expands upon this by highlighting Maimonides' tripartite divisions in his commentaries on the *Guide*. Ibn Kaspi's first observation of this is in *Maskiyot Kesef* where he notes that Maimonides divides the biblical term "man" (*adam*) into three possible meanings at *Guide* I 14.[213] The first meaning refers to Adam, the character, described in the Garden of Eden, who, according to Maimonides, represents the perfection of theoretical intellect.[214] Ibn Kaspi suggests that this also refers to Moses who, he argues, acquired the understanding of God as the highest separate intellect. This is also, Ibn Kaspi argues, what Ezekiel meant when using the word "man" in describing one of his visions: "and upon the likeness of the throne was a likeness as the appearance of a man upon it above."[215] The second meaning of "man," as delineated in *Guide* I 14, refers to the human species. Ibn Kaspi interprets Maimonides' use of it there to mean that Adam's perfect theoretical knowledge was hidden from mankind after the fall of Adam, because he ate the fruit of the tree of the knowledge of good and evil. He hints to the fact that this is because most people are divided between their desire for theoretical knowledge and desires coming from their imagination and their bodily needs, which are all obstacles to gaining perfect knowledge of God.[216] Maimonides' third meaning of "man" refers to the masses, who, Ibn Kaspi argues, are weak in intellect. Prominent among this group are rulers, who are primarily concerned with victory and rule.[217] This division into three meanings of "man" represents the three possible audiences of the *Guide*, who have reached three possible levels of understanding: the first understand the level of the separate intellects, the second that of the spheres, but the third are limited to the level of the sublunar world.

Ibn Kaspi also highlights Maimonides' division of "figure" (*temuna*) into three possible meanings, representing three different levels of formal knowledge of an object. The first is apprehension of the physical form of an object through the senses, the second is apprehension of the physical form in the imagination after the sense data is no longer present, and the third is apprehension of its true form by the intellect.[218] In his commentary on *Guide* I 4 in '*Amudei Kesef*, Ibn Kaspi raises the question of why Maimonides divided this into three, when it could easily be divided into two: the senses and the intellect. Ibn Kaspi's answer is that the threefold division is not necessary for this, but it is there to serve a different purpose.[219]

Ibn Kaspi continues in '*Amudei Kesef* to argue that Book II of the *Guide* is structured in a tripartite manner in order to imitate both these three levels of understanding and the three levels of reality represented by the divine chariot. Accordingly, *Guide* II 1–12 investigates God's existence as an incorporeal and unitary being, the heavenly spheres, and the angels (aka the intellects). Similarly, *Guide* II 13–31 analyzes the question of how the universe originated, whether it is eternal or whether it was created at a specific point in time. This is an issue related to the level of the celestial spheres, whereas *Guide* II 32–48 deals with the meaning of prophecy, an issue for the sublunar world.[220]

Next, Ibn Kaspi looks at one of the clearest and most debated threefold divisions in the *Guide*, the relationship between the three opinions concerning creation and the three opinions concerning prophecy.[221] Maimonides intentionally directs his reader to compare these two sets of opinions in stating that

> The opinions of people concerning prophecy are like their opinions concerning the eternity of the world or its creation in time. I mean by this that just as the people to whose mind the existence of the deity is firmly established, have, as we set forth, three opinions concerning the eternity of the world or its creation in time, so are there are also three opinions concerning prophecy.[222]

The way to match these two sets of three opinions has been debated by contemporary scholars.[223] The three opinions on creation are those of (1) the Torah, (2) Plato, and (3) Aristotle. The three opinions on prophecy are those of (1) Pagans, (2) the Philosophers, and (3) the Torah. The problem with interpreting this is deciding which position on creation matches which position on prophecy. Three contemporary scholars have provided three different solutions to this problem: Lawrence Kaplan (building up on Mordechai Jaffe in the sixteenth century) proposes the division of 1:3, 2:1, 3:2; Herbert Davidson (building on Isaac Abarbanel) proposes the division of 1:1, 2:3, 3:2; and Warren Zev Harvey proposes the division of 1:1, 2:2, 3:3.[224]

In commenting on this section, Ibn Kaspi challenges the relationship between the second and third opinions (those of Plato and Aristotle) in the case of creation, and the second and third opinions (those of the philosophers and the Torah) in the case of prophecy. He suggests that these are both examples of the seventh contradiction. In the case of creation, in *Guide* II 25 Maimonides presents Plato's position, creation from pre-existent matter, as closer to that of the Torah than Aristotle's position, the eternality of the universe, while in II 13 he presents Plato's position position as equivalent to Aristotle's position.[225] Ibn Kaspi argues in 'Amudei Kesef that II 13 is Maimonides' true view, defending Aristotle's position of the eternality of the universe, and II 25, defending

Plato's position of creation from pre-existent matter, is a false view for the masses. He argues this on the basis that creation is not presented as one of the five foundations of the Torah at the beginning of the *Mishneh Torah*.[226] In the case of prophecy, Ibn Kaspi writes in *Maskiyot Kesef* that the third opinion of the Torah, prophecy as human perfection with God withholding prophecy, is covertly the same as the second opinion of the philosophers, of prophecy as human perfection, and is only artificially presented as a separate and false view for the masses.[227] But if Ibn Kaspi views the second and third positions as secretly equivalent, how does he understand Maimonides' reasoning for dividing these sections on creation and prophecy into three?

Ibn Kaspi's solution to this is not stated explicitly, but, piecing it together in order to connect this division into three with Maimonides' other divisions into three laid out above, these three levels appear to correspond to the three levels of intellectual understanding of reality. In doing this, Ibn Kaspi defends this structure of the *Guide*, 1:1, 2:3, 3:2, in a way that is later defended by Abarbanel and Davidson (though it leads them to different conclusions as to Maimonides' true view).[228] The first opinion on creation, God's creation of the world *ex nihilo*, and the first opinion on prophecy, that God chooses the prophet with no human preparation necessary, both present a voluntaristic God. This is the opinion of the masses who have knowledge of the sublunar world but lack knowledge of the spheres and the intellects. The second opinion on creation is that of Plato's position of creation from pre-existent matter, and the third opinion on prophecy is the Torah's position of prophecy as human perfection with God withholding prophecy. What they have in common is that they both understand nature as operating self-sufficiently, except for God's occasional intervention into the natural order. While Ibn Kaspi is clear that this position is hinting at the Aristotelian view, the quasi-voluntarism of God in this position may be a midway point for those who have some but not complete philosophic knowledge. He may be suggesting that this is the level of those who have knowledge of the celestial spheres, but no knowledge of the intellects: they understand natural science and its relationship to the spheres, but do not fully comprehend the role of God and the intellects in the level above the spheres, which is why this portrait of God shows Him intervening in nature. The third opinion on creation, that of Aristotle, and the second opinion on prophecy, that of the Philosophers, see the universe as eternal and prophecy as a purely naturalistic phenomenon.

# History as the Progressive Revelation of the Divine Chariot / 93

For Ibn Kaspi, this is the true view for it alone demonstrates knowledge of all three spheres: the sublunar world, the celestial spheres, and the separate intellects.

The following chart summarizes Ibn Kaspi's analysis of Maimonides' division of the *Guide* into sections of three to imitate the three levels of reality:

| Chapter | Sublunar World | Celestial Spheres | Separate Intellects |
|---|---|---|---|
| I 3 Figure | Apprehend by senses | Apprehend in imagination | Apprehend by intellect |
| I 14 Adam | Adam = masses | Adam = species | Adam = Adam I = Moses |
| II Intro | II 33–48: Prophecy | II 13–32: Creation vs. Eternality | II 1–12: God's existence, not body, one, heavenly spheres and angels |
| III 13 Creation | (1) Torah View | (2) Plato's View | (3) Aristotle's View |
| II 32 Prophecy | (1) Pagan View | (3) Torah's View | (2) Philosopher's View |
| II 45 Levels of Prophecy | Levels 1–2 | Levels 3–7 (5 levels) Dream | Levels 8–11 (4 levels) Vision |

## Ethical Implications of the Knowledge of the Divine Chariot

Ibn Kaspi claims that knowledge of the divine chariot, which entails the knowledge of all three levels of reality, leads to an ethics of love and compassion for the lower parts of nature. It seems just as likely that knowing all that exists could lead, instead, to withdrawal from the world and immersion in solitary contemplation. Ibn Kaspi, however, argues that in recognizing the commonality one has with all parts of nature, the lowest as well as the highest, should lead sages who have attained this knowledge to strive to benefit the weaker parts of the natural world, since they, themselves, partake in it. This includes cultivation of the moral virtues of compassion, modesty, humility, lowliness, generosity, and magnanimity, all of which recognize the commonality of human beings not only with their fellow human beings, but also with animals, plants, and even material objects. Ibn Kaspi argues that the love inculcated by the laws of the Torah and the character traits the Torah aims to cultivate are rooted in what is a uniquely human love and compassion for all the other beings within the natural world.[229] In other words, this love ranges across all four levels of the Aristotelian hierarchy of nature from the human, to the animal, to the vegetative, to the material. Ibn Kaspi explains in *Maṣref la-Kesef* how the Torah achieves this goal. He says that

> The Torah inculcates in us a sense of our humility (*'anava*) and lowliness (*shiflut*), that we should ever be cognizant of the fact that we are of the same stuff as the ass and the mule, the cabbage and the pomegranate and even the lifeless stone.[230]

This is a startling conclusion to derive from a Maimonidean approach to the Bible that understands humanity as unique and therefore separate from than the rest of nature, because of our intellect, both theoretical and practical. But Ibn Kaspi argues that it would be a mistake to think that this makes human beings completely distinct from the lower order of nature.[231] While recognizing the uniqueness of humanity, his argument is that it would take the intellectual superiority of humans too far if it leads us to forget that even those of us who are sages share much in common with other human beings (even those who have little concern for perfecting their intellect) as well as with animals, plants, and even lifeless material objects, such as stones.

Ibn Kaspi argues that some laws in the Torah teach what we have in common with other human beings, some teach what humans have in common with animals, still others laws teach what we have in common with plants, and finally, there are laws that teach what we have in common with lifeless material objects.[232]

He gives many examples. With respect to humans, he points to the allowance the Torah gives to marry a woman captured in war, followed by the command that "thou shalt not deal with her as a slave." For, Ibn Kaspi argues, the Torah teaches mercy on all people, notwithstanding what nation they come from.[233] Similarly, the command to "love thy neighbor as thyself" and others like it teach loving behavior toward members of one's own nation.[234] The purpose of the laws that prohibit looking upon the nakedness (*'erva*) of one's close relatives in Leviticus 18, he argues, is to create peace between individuals and avoid conflict. He admits that the purpose of these commandments is not stated explicitly, but argues that it is only hinted at. He points to the only place where this comes out explicitly, in is Leviticus 18, where it is explained that a man should not marry a woman and her sister, because that it will create rivalry between them (*liṣror*).[235] This comes immediately after the command that prohibits marrying both a woman and her daughter. Obviously, in both cases, such a relationship would foment jealousy.[236] Ibn Kaspi cites Aristotle, saying in support of this, that jealousy is strongest among relatives.[237] Because of the purpose Ibn Kaspi discerns behind so many of these biblical laws, he is able to argue that many of the laws of the Torah aim at creating peace.

As for laws in the Torah that teach us to act mercifuly toward animals since humans have much in common with animals, Ibn Kaspi gives two examples. The first known as *shiluaḥ ha-ken*, the command to send away the mother bird, in order to avoid cruelty, if you find a nest with her young and eggs inside, when foraging for food, in order to distance oneself from the trait of cruelty.[238] Showing compassion to animals, he argues, is also an important component of the dietary (kosher) laws: the prohibition against cooking a kid in its mother's milk, for example. Ibn Kaspi argues that humans were commanded to be vegetarians before the flood, but because of the human desire for meat, God relented and allowed Noah and those who came after him to kill animals, but only for food, and with the stipulation they be killed mercifully.[239] Ibn Kaspi argues in *Ṭirat Kesef* that the reason for the command to be merciful toward animals (*ṣa'ar ba'alei ḥayyim*) is because "we humans are very much like them and we and they are children of the same father."[240]

With respect to laws in the Torah that show the commonality of humans with plants, Ibn Kaspi points to a command given in the laws of war, in Deuteronomy 20, that forbids destroying trees upon entering a city to conquer it, because "man is like the tree of the field."[241] With respect to kindness toward material objects, Ibn Kaspi asserts that the purpose of leaving fields fallow during the sabbatical year, as set out in the Torah, is to show compassion to the earth, which needs rest, just like humans.[242]

## Moral Virtues

Ibn Kaspi provides a model of ethics that emphasizes the commonality of humanity with *all* of nature. His list of moral virtues governs far more than actions within one's own political community, far more even than interactions with all of humanity. It encompasses everything in the sublunar world, including actions affecting animals, plants, and even material objects. This may be, in part, in response to the Averrostic reading of Maimonides, which Ibn Kaspi thinks overemphasizes development of the intellect as the main goal for human perfection. Ibn Kaspi corrects this imbalance by reminding us that humans share much in common with animals, plants, and material objects. But what exactly is the purpose of virtues that govern our interaction with lower forms of nature? For Maimonides, showing mercy toward animals, plants, and material objects is only for inculcating compassion toward other human beings. For Ibn Kaspi, however, the practice of these moral virtues is actually meant to benefit animals, plants, and material objects, as well.

It is interesting to note the parallels between the debate between Maimonides and Ibn Kaspi on the question of whether love of all of nature is inherently valuable in itself, or valuable only as an instrumental action, to the modern debate in Kantian ethics over whether Kant's categorical imperative should be applied to animals as well as humans. Kant thinks there *is* a need to treat animals and humans lacking rationality with sensitivity and compassion, not for their sake, however, but as a means of ensuring that we will treat other rational human beings in an equally compassionate manner.[243] Martha Nussbaum criticizes Kant's position, here, for its limited sensitivity. She fears that Kant's radical split will necessarily lead to the unjust treatment of non-rational creatures: that it will prevent extending the universal will to restricting the unjust treatment of these creatures.[244] To treat animals with sensitivity and compassion requires recognition of the commonality that humans and animals share. Nussbaum's critique of Kant is very much like Ibn Kaspi's extension of the moral virtues of love and compassion to all of nature, just as Maimonides' position, like Kant's, is that the cultivation of these virtues toward the rest of nature is purely for human benefit.

In this matter, there is a key difference between Maimonides and Ibn Kaspi over how they understand the purpose of humility (*'anava*), lowliness (*shiflut*), and the mercy (*ḥemla*). Like Aristotle, Maimonides understands virtuous human action to be a result of the perfection of certain character traits, which are rooted in the appetitive part of the soul that deals with emotions and temperaments. Ideal character— what Maimonides calls the "right way" (*derekh ha-yeshara*) or the mean (*midda ha-beinonit*)—lie at the mean, or midpoint between two opposite extremes. Courage, for example, as Aristotle explains, lies at the midpoint between two opposite vices: cowardice and foolhardiness. Maimonides breaks away from Aristotle, however, with respect to certain moral extremes, especially those inspired by religion. For example, he approves of the pious man (*hasid*) who is exceedingly scrupulous with himself and moves toward one extreme. With regard to these certain character traits, Maimonides thinks it is wrong to keep to the mean and that one should, instead, embrace the approved extreme. Take honor, for example. Maimonides argues that we embrace the extreme of humility, and avoid all need and concern for the pursuit of ego and self-worth.[245] In this, Maimonides argues, we should follow the example of Moses who is described in the Torah as being "very meek, above all the men that were upon the face of the earth."[246] Maimonides argues that the moral virtues are set down by divine law for the sake of order in the political community He says that its purpose is the "acquisition by every human individual of moral qualities that are useful for life in society so that the affairs of the city may be ordered."[247] In contrast, Ibn Kaspi argues that the purpose of the divine law, which cultivates humility and lowliness, is not to promote political order, but to teach us that we are not so exalted because we are intelligent beings such that we do not have the right to treat other parts of nature as tools for human ends. For, we too, are physical beings who have much in common with animals, plants, and material objects. Therefore, we must treat them with compassion because they, like us, are part of the sublunar world.[248]

Ibn Kaspi's dispute with Maimonides, here, is primarily over the reasoning behind many of the commandments. Maimonides, for example, explains why the Torah permits the soldier to have sexual relations with the woman captured in war by using the Talmudic rationale that "the Torah only provided for man's evil passions."[249] He explains that the relationship of the soldier with the captive woman is a concession to the uncontrollable passion of soldiers. Instead of pretending that soldiers will act morally, the Torah provides a framework for channeling their immoral action toward a more positive outcome. Maimonides does not derive a positive and universal lesson from this law, but sees it as an example of crisis management: in other words, weakening negative damage.[250] Ibn Kaspi, however, draws a lesson in humility from this story, as we saw in the previous section of this chapter, focusing on "thou shalt not deal with her as a slave" if the sexual relationship does not work out satisfactorily. He argues that this teaches a universal lesson about how the stronger should not abuse their strength, but should show compassion to the weak, even of an enemy nation.[251] In other words, Maimonides sees this law as channeling the immoral tendencies in less harmful ways, rather than attempting to restrain them altogether, while Ibn Kaspi sees this law as premised on the belief that we should recognize our common humanity.

Ibn Kaspi's explanation of the reasoning behind the many different laws regarding slaughtering and eating animals in the Hebrew Bible is thus, because humans and animals have much in common, we should slaughter animals mercifully, and do this for the sake of the animals, as well as to cultivate compassion. Maimonides' explanation of the rational behind these laws is concerned with cultivating moderation, in this case, as the mean between lust and insensibility to pleasure.[252] One can see from this that the ultimate intention of these commandments, according to Maimonides is not for the sake of the animals, but for the sake of the moral character of the humans slaughtering them. Maimonides explains that the dietary laws encourage moderation by placing limits on which animals can be eaten, which restrains gluttony[253] and protect against disease. He provides multiple examples of this. He argues that the reason for the prohibition against eating pork is because pork is harmful for humans, since pigs feed on all manner of dirty things.[254] The prohibition against eating blood and dead carcasses is because they are difficult to digest and are harmful nourishment.[255]

Maimonides comes closer to Ibn Kaspi's position, however, in his discussion of certain merciful practices toward animals that are, seemingly, for the sake of the animal and not just for our moral perfection.[256] Maimonides gives three examples of this: choosing a method of slaughtering animals in the kindest possible manner, prohibiting the slaughter of an animal and its young on the same day, and sending the mother bird away when taking her young and eggs for food.[257] Maimonides concludes that

> In these cases animals feel very great pain, there being no difference regarding the pain between man and other animals. For the love and tenderness of a mother for her child is not consequent upon reason, but upon the activity of the imaginative faculty, which is found in animals just as it is found in man.[258]

Following this statement, Maimonides thinks, like Ibn Kaspi, that some of the laws toward animals command mercy for the sake of the well-being of the animal. But I think Maimonides' ultimate point can only be discerned by putting together Maimonides' disparate discussions of mercy toward animals. Authority for doing this is contained in Maimonides' own instructions in his Introduction to the *Guide*, where he says that he is scattering his discussions throughout the work.²⁵⁹ First, as discussed earlier, all these commandments are grouped under the section in the *Guide* dealing with moral perfection with respect to man's lusts and desires.²⁶⁰ Second, Maimonides says that part of the secret behind the divine laws is that they represent God's attributes, as can be discerned from God's actions in the world. The role of the prophet, as lawgiver, he argues, is to foster God's attributes through the laws. In *Guide* I 54, he discerns God's attribute of mercy in His gift to all living beings of the faculties necessary for survival.²⁶¹ The purpose of the Torah, therefore, in describing God's attributes is for the prophet to imitate them by giving laws that inculcate these virtues.²⁶² Third, while *Guide* I 54 may seem to imply that God's mercy extends to nonhumans, this is contradicted by Maimonides' statement in *Guide* III 17, so it seems that God's providence extends only to humans and not to other living beings, implying that God's mercy does not extend to animals after all, at least not according to Maimonides.²⁶³ Anticipating the objection to this statement, that God is described as being merciful to animals, Maimonides explains that mercy, "is set down with a view to perfecting us so that we should not acquire moral habits of cruelty and should not inflict pain gratuitously without any utility but that we should intend to be kind and merciful even with a chance animal."²⁶⁴ The purpose, therefore, of being merciful and compassionate toward birds and other animals, for Maimonides, is that humans may become habituated into transferring that compassion to other human beings. Ibn Kaspi differs from Maimonides here, only in that he thinks that Ibn Kaspi's model has the additional purpose of teaching us to recognize the commonality between animals and human beings.²⁶⁵

Ibn Kaspi and Maimonides differ in a similar way over the purpose of the laws dealing with the treatment of plants. One example is the command against destroying fruit-bearing trees upon conquering an enemy city.²⁶⁶ This injunction in Deuteronomy suggests that trees that give food and are thus useful for people be saved, but trees that do not give food may be cut down, if useful for other purposes. Ibn Kaspi argues that the reason for this command is that "man is like the tree of the field"[267] and is made of the same matter as "the cabbage and the pomegranate."[268] Maimonides however, analyzes this commandment very differently, in *Laws of Kings and their Wars* 6.8–10 where he argues that the merciful treatment of the tree is not the issue, but whether and in what way the tree is useful for humans, in this case, of course, it is useful as a source of food. This is why a fruit-bearing tree may be cut down for many reasons: if it causes damage to other trees, if it does not bear fruit, or if it produces too little fruit. In all these cases, it is simply a matter of utility. In fact, Maimonides argues that the command "not to destroy," here is not even inherently about trees, but that trees simply serve as an example for an entire category of objects. Maimonides pushes this further and argues that it is also forbidden to destroy the property of people you have conquered. He gives many examples here, forbidding such as destroying household goods, tearing clothes, demolishing a building, stopping up a spring, and destroying goods.[269]

Ibn Kaspi and Maimonides also differ over the reasoning behind the laws of the sabbatical year. For Ibn Kaspi, their purpose is to teach compassion toward matter, for the land needs to rest, just like humans.[270] Maimonides, instead, explains that the laws of the sabbatical year teach the moral virtue of generosity, pushing us toward the extreme of prodigality, so that we move far away from the extreme of stinginess in order to establish the mean of generosity firmly within us.[271] He expands upon the political significance of the sabbatical laws in the *Guide*, where he argues that their purpose is to encourage pity and help for all, to make earth more fertile and stronger by leaving it fallow and to increase benevolence toward slaves and the poor.[272]

The nature of humility and lowliness understood as virtues, rooted in recognizing one's common material nature with animals, plants, and matter, is hinted to by Ibn Kaspi, as can be seen in exegesis of Numbers 12 in *Maṣref la-Kesef*. His interpretation arises from ambiguity over the identity of the Cushite woman Moses marries in the account in Numbers 12:1. He questions whether she is the same woman as Moses' wife, Tzipporah, and also asks why this marriage is followed by the statement in Numbers 12:3 that Moses "was very meek, above all the men that were upon the face of the earth." Assuming that these verses are not placed together haphazardly, what could the relationship be between Moses marrying the Cushite woman and his extreme humility? In Ibn Kaspi's interpretation, this Cushite woman is *not* the same as his wife,

Tzipporah, indicating that he made a second, bigamous marriage.²⁷³ Ibn Kaspi goes on a polemic over this, criticizing certain Christian sects for their ascetic tendencies. He differentiates Moses' behavior from that advocated in such ascetic movements, for ignoring the physical nature of man. Ibn Kaspi thus draws a link between the perfection (presumably moral and intellectual) of several prominent biblical characters who took multiple spouses:

> However, we should not be amazed if he [Moses] married two wives. Look at all the early ones that did this, even if they were very perfect. Abraham was the first to marry two wives, Jacob married four wives, David married eighteen wives, and Solomon, the master of the wise, married a thousand wives and the actions of the fathers produced children.²⁷⁴

Ibn Kaspi is not advocating bigamy or polygamy since most people who embrace it do so out of lust, but he does think that it is permitted for those who had achieved moral and intellectual perfection in early biblical times. For those few individuals who have achieved that level of perfection, multiple marriages can be taken, he argues, as a sign of physical vitality. Perhaps Ibn Kaspi's point is that Moses' humility and lowliness results from Moses not separating his intellect from his material self. He was humble because he understood who he was, indeed, and that he was united with the lower parts of nature.²⁷⁵

## Moral Mistakes

Ibn Kaspi is notable for his willingness to criticize the actions of biblical characters. He sees their reprehensible actions as resulting from gratifying their bodily desires, and therefore agrees with Maimonides' statement that "all man's acts of disobedience and sins are consequent upon his matter and not upon his form, whereas all his virtues are consequent upon his form."²⁷⁶ But, at the same time, as I show above, Ibn Kaspi praises the virtues that recognize the commonality and compassion of humans with all the lower parts of nature. This gives rise to the question, why does he blame the former as sinful, and praise the latter? His answer seems to turn on whether they gratified their bodily desires out of hubris and self-interest or with humility and mercy, since humility inspires compassion for similar weaknesses in others. His rationale for this seems to be that humility comes as a result of recognizing that you are a weak physical being who shares much in common, in this respect, with other people, animals, plants, and matter. He draws from this a duty to act mercifully toward everything else in nature. Hubris, on the other hand, he condemns, as it leads to arrogant, self-interested behavior, because you think yourself superior to other people, animals, plants, and matter and therefore treat them like tools that you have the right to use in any way you please.

The first example of Ibn Kaspi's critique of biblical characters based on their succumbing to physical desires is his explanation for the sin and punishment of Ham and his descendants (the entire nation of Canaan) in *Tirat Kesef*. He explains that Noah made wine after the flood so that he could fulfill the lusts of his body, and he got so drunk that he sprawled in his tent naked. This is the reason that the Nazir is forbidden from drinking wine since wine is associated with the body and its pleasures.[277] Noah's son Ham's behavior is apparently more reprehensible than Noah's because he looks upon his father's nakedness and "told his two brethren without." His brothers, however, covered their father with a garment, without looking at him.[278] Noah's response was that he "knew what his youngest son had done unto him" and cursed Ham's descendants with being slaves to the descendants of Ham's brothers.[279] The story is ambiguous about what exactly was Ham's sin. Ibn Kaspi rejects the view that he committed a physical act with his hands, such as castration or sodomy.[280] Instead, Ibn Kaspi contends that Ham's sin was that he laughed at and mocked his father and failed to help his brothers cover him up. Lack of helping, Ibn Kaspi writes, is like actively removing the garment. Noah's reference to Ham as his "youngest son" indicates his villainous intent in not properly honoring his father.[281] What arises from Ibn Kaspi's comments on this story is that Ham's mockery of his father shows his pride and sense of superiority. Because he thinks that he is better than his father, he feels no compassion for his father's weakness, and therefore no obligation to show respect toward him.

Ibn Kaspi also criticizes biblical patriarchs and matriarchs for being overly promiscuous and sexually permissive. In the case of Lot's daughters who got their father drunk in order to trick him into committing incest with them, and justified this with the claim that "there is not a man in the earth to come in unto us after the manner of all the earth."[282] Ibn Kaspi does not buy this claim. He speculates that, in truth, no one wanted to have sex with them because they may have been ugly and their father did not care about this.[283] Ibn Kaspi seems equally shocked that Jacob kissed Rachel upon meeting her.[284] He writes in *Maṣref la-Kesef* that "I apologize for this occurrence, but say yet that it is not the custom of this land to kiss on the lips or cheek. God forbid on the lips! And if, God forbid, Jacob did this, what can we do?"[285] Ibn Kaspi also has a problem with Jacob loving Leah (though less than Rachel) and hating her at the same time.[286] Ibn Kaspi speculates is that Jacob loved Leah only after he slept with her, implying that this love was purely physical, but that he hated her on a non-physical level.[287]

## Judaism vs. Christianity on the Popular Dissemination of the Divine Chariot

Ibn Kaspi's teaching that there has been historical progress in understanding the image of the divine chariot and its ethical implications is not without a polemical angle. He argues that the philosophical founders of both Judaism and Christianity knew the secrets of the divine chariot, but that the Torah is superior because it tries to guide its unphilosophic adherents to the secrets of the chariot, whereas the New Testament reserved those secrets for the few and left the masses with false teachings. Ibn Kaspi is making the case for a common philosophy between Judaism and Christianity, while criticizing the Christian Bible (and likely Christian ritual) for deficient methodology.[288]

In *Gevia Kesef*, Ibn Kaspi argues forcibly that the Christian doctrine of the Trinity is actually in agreement with Judaism. For God can be referred to as either a singular entity or a plural one, depending on whether God is referred to as being the first cause, or whether He is referred to in His more general role of encompassing the world of the separates intellects. Ibn Kaspi cites Al-Farabi's division of God into the Primary Intellect, secondary intellects, and the Active Intellect, in support of God's plural aspect.[289] He contends that the Trinity became a conventional way of expressing God's plurality in many traditions, including Judaism and Christianity. He writes

> One can understand the verbal similarity between us and the Christians in that with regard to the trinity they speak of "Father," "Son," and "Spirit," asserting that they are both

> three and one, which is similar [to what we say]. . . . Yet we are really far-removed from the Christians in opinions despite an external similarity in phrases and in speech, even though some individuals among them are similar to us (in opinions).[290]

Ibn Kaspi thus defends the Christian description of God as Father, Son and Holy Spirit as consistent with the Jewish view that the father represents the highest of the separate intellects, the son represents the lower separate intellects, and the holy spirit represents the Active Intellect.[291] This, he argues, is what Isaiah was referring to in repeating the word "holy" three times, when he says, "holy, holy, holy, is the LORD of hosts."[292]

Christianity's error is not in dividing God into three parts, Ibn Kaspi argues, but in presenting God as a corporeal being, even though the founders of Christianity knew full well that God is not corporeal. Ibn Kaspi expounds on this point in 'Amudei Kesef in his explanation of Guide I 35, where Maimonides lays out an exception to the general prohibition against teaching divine science (a.k.a., the divine chariot) to the masses: the necessity to teach God's incorporeality to all. Although Maimonides is discussing Judaism in this chapter of the Guide, Ibn Kaspi finds in it a point of comparison with other religions:

> Here, included in this chapter, Moses' Torah is superior to religions founded by others, and similarly to those scholars who claim to follow the Torah. And even though the Torah has innumerable statements that teach God's corporeality, and also His physicality and responsiveness in some place, nevertheless, in rare cases it makes clear that this is not true with relation to God, may He be exalted. As it says, "for ye saw no manner of form on the day that the LORD spoke unto you in Horeb out of the midst of the fire" (Deut. 4:15). And it is appropriate according to the weakness [in intellect] of the masses that there will be [only] few statements such as these [which accord with] the true opinion, while the [number of statements that accord with] the former [indicating God's corporeality, physicality and responsiveness] are more prevalent. This is like an individual who holds a rope by the two ends. The rest of the religions do not even preserve [both] because

all of their statements are to settle in the hearts of the masses [the belief in] the corporeality of God. The founders of the [rest of the] religions know it is false, but employ this [method of describing God purely in corporeal terms] out of fear that once they will say the truth to the masses, they will leave the religion completely and deny the existence of God. But the giver of our Torah chose to follow the convention [of revealing the truth], however infrequently and in covert language. This is one of the reasons that the world to come is not [explicitly] discussed in the Torah, its truth only discernible through interpretation, except in parables and riddles, like the Garden of Eden. . . . And Avicenna wrote: there is no need to bother the masses by teaching them about the details of the knowledge of God, may He be exalted, except that he exists and he is one with nothing similar. It will confound their religion to teach them that He does not change and that He is not outside the world nor inside it and all that is similar to this. They have no faculty to perceive this matter and instead it will deceive them, or create conflict and prevent them from performing the [proper] political actions.[293]

Judaism and Christianity, according to Ibn Kaspi, are in agreement on the theoretical truths about the nature of God and the divine chariot, but are divided on the political question of whether it is better for the masses to have some knowledge of God's incorporeality or whether they should be left with the false belief that God is corporeal. Ibn Kaspi argues that Judaism believes in teaching the non-corporeality of God to the masses, while Christianity does not belief in teaching the non-corporeality of God to the masses. His comparison of Judaism to holding a rope at both ends to obtain the water at the bottom of the well may refer to *Song of Songs Rabba* 1:1:8 where the allegory used to discover the secrets about God's true nature is compared to a set of interlinking cords and ropes. For Ibn Kaspi, the Torah provides the ropes, but Christianity does not.

Ibn Kaspi goes on to explain the difference between Judaism and Christianity through this debate over their two very different approaches to teaching metaphysical truths to the masses through religious texts. Ibn Kaspi quotes, disapprovingly, from Avicenna, who argues that the masses do not need to know anything more about God, than his existence and unity, which suggests that he thinks that teaching about God's incorporeality could lead people away from the necessary practices of the community.[294] This is in stark contrast to Maimonides who insists that teaching God's incorporeality as a central doctrine is necessary even in popular religious texts, which is why it he makes it one of the thirteen principles of faith.[295] As Ibn Kaspi sees it, Christianity follows the model of Avicenna and other Islamic philosophers such as Al-Farabi and Averroes, whereas Judaism follows the much superior model of Maimonides.[296] For Ibn Kaspi disagrees with Avicenna about the ethical and political implications of hiding this truth from the masses. He argues that the founders of Christianity followed Avicenna's advice, presumably because they thought that knowing God's true nature would confuse the masses. Therefore, they chose instead to mislead them with a myth in order to ensure their practice of the proper moral virtues. In other words, Ibn Kaspi disparages Christianity for thinking, like Avicenna, that intellectual virtues are only for the few who are wise, whereas moral virtues, based on a lie, are the best that can be hoped for from the ignorant masses. Ibn Kaspi counters that some knowledge, at least, of God's incorporeality is necessary for the cultivation of moral virtue. It is only by providing this teaching, if only in hints, that the serious believer can discern how these moral virtues are grounded in universal truths. Lacking this, Ibn Kaspi hints, is the source of Christianity's deficiency in the ethical realm.

The uniqueness of the Torah for Ibn Kaspi over Christianity and other divine laws is not that Judaism and Christianity, for example, disagree about theoretical and moral truths, or that one is less knowledgeable, philosophically. For Ibn Kaspi, the superiority of Judaism lies only in the fact that Torah is constructed in such a way as to guide its ordinary, unphilosophic, adherents to deeper truths. To this end, he argues, the Torah contains many literary features and hints that are "roadmaps" or "signs" intended to slowly and progressively enlighten its readership.

Chapter 3

# The Pedagogical Structure of the Hebrew Bible

Ibn Kaspi mounts a multi-pronged defense of the structure and form of the Hebrew Bible. He argues that the Hebrew Bible is the perfect imitation of "nature" because it is written in Hebrew. He thinks each root word in Hebrew is a conventional imitation of some part of the natural world. Therefore, in order to understand the true meaning of the Bible, it is necessary to go back to the common conceptual ideas underlying each root. According to Ibn Kaspi, what the Rabbis meant when they said that "the Torah is from Heaven" (*torah min ha-shamayyim*) is that the underlying language of the Hebrew Bible reflects God's rational construction of nature. He argues, therefore, that translating the Hebrew Bible into another language, as the Christians did when they translated it into Latin, necessarily loses much of its deeper meaning. They see only the superficial meaning of the words, but do not understand what lies behind them, in their roots. Moreover, he argues that the form of the Hebrew Bible is a work of art, intended to convey its message to the reader in subtle ways, using many different hermeneutical devices including contradictions, dispersal, empty spaces, repetitions, and suppression of all but selective details. If this is not understood, it would be easy to make the mistake of thinking that the Hebrew Bible is haphazardly pieced together without foresight or plan, as indeed, modern biblical critics have concluded. At the same time, however, he argues that much of the text is *not* reflective of a higher truth, but merely a reflection of the historical context of ancient Jewish society and the surrounding culture from which the Hebrew Bible emerged. Building on the precedent set by earlier medieval Jewish thinkers including Maimonides, Ibn Kaspi argues that the true teaching of the Bible is of a non-anthropomorphic conception of God. The problem with this argument is that the Torah speaks undeniably of God as if He resembles an all-powerful human being. Ibn Kaspi gets around this difficulty by arguing that the Bible speaks in this way by employing the rabbinic phrase, "the Torah speaks in the language of the sons of men." Ibn Kaspi expands the application of this rabbinic phrase to explain the Bible's resort to and utilization of concession to errors, superstitions, popular conceptions, local mores, folk beliefs, and customs.

## "The Torah is from Heaven" and the Hebrew Language

The principle that God is the source and origin of the Pentateuch is a central dogma of rabbinic theology. This is articulated in the tenth chapter of tractate Sanhedrin in the Babylonian Talmud which states that "he who says the Torah is not from heaven (*ein torah min ha-shamayyim*) has no portion in the world to come."[1] This position was codified by Maimonides as one of the thirteen principles of faith in his *Commentary on the Mishna*. Indeed, Maimonides expands on this dogma, saying that "the whole of this Torah which is in our hand today is the Torah that was brought down to Moses, our teacher; that all of it is from God."[2] This is challenged, however, by divergent voices that agree as to the divine origin of the Pentateuch, but concede that certain parts of it were added by later writers, after Moses' death.[3] In the Babylonian Talmud, tractate Baba Batra 15a, there is a debate over how to reconcile the claim that Moses was the author of the Deuteronomy, with the fact that the last chapter of Deuteronomy describes Moses' death and burial. One opinion is that Joshua wrote this chapter, or at least its last eight verses, after Moses' death.[4] Abraham Ibn Ezra expanded upon this much later, in the Medieval period, with his "secret of the twelve" (*sod ha-shnem asar*), which points to parts of the Pentateuch that do not seem to have been, or could not have been, authored by Moses. These include: "and the Canaanite was then in the land," "these are the words which Moses spoke unto all Israel beyond the Jordan," and "and Moses wrote this law."[5] The problem with this approach is how to determine which passages were written by Moses, and which were not? In other words, how can we determine what is holy in the Bible, and what is profane, without compromising belief, by historicizing everything?

In a few spots in his writings, Ibn Kaspi deals with this problem by criticizing those who attempt to attribute the authorship of the Pentateuch solely to Moses, arguing instead that it is clear that God is the author. In *Menorat Kesef*, he writes that even though the Rabbis made the statement that "Moses wrote his own book [Deuteronomy],"[6] God wrote everything, which is why God says "I will write upon the tables the words that were on the first tables, which thou didst break" and "and I will write on the tables the words that were on the first tables which thou didst break, and thou shalt put them in the ark."[7] Ibn Kaspi does not want to diminish the authority of God as the cause of all, because once it is doubted that God is the author of the Pentateuch, it could also be doubted that God is the cause of creation, as is claimed in Genesis 1.[8] Ibn Kaspi is determined to transmit what he maintains is the knowledge that God is the first cause of everything, whether it be the construction of nature in Genesis 1 or the ideas at the core of the Pentateuch, which he believes was written in imitation of nature. If God is the author of everything, however, but only in the sense that He is the first cause of the universe, this leaves open the question of who were the proximate authors of the Bible. There may have been many authors, but God was really the true author, since He is the first cause of the universe.

For the most part, however, Ibn Kaspi's solution to the problem of reconciling the rabbinic position, that the Torah is of divine origin with the position that parts of it were *not* written by Moses under God's direction, is that the holiness of the Pentateuch lies not in its authorship, but in the language in which it is written. This is because of Hebrew's unique system of three letter root words (*shorashim*). Of course, this is also true of later books of the Bible, which were also written in Hebrew. The reason why the Hebrew language is so central for maintaining the divine origin of the Pentateuch for Ibn Kaspi is, he argues, because Hebrew is the only language with a structure that imitates nature.[9] Ibn Kaspi has to contend, here, with Aristotle's argument that humans are not born with language: that all languages are merely conventional, constructed by individuals in order to communicate with others. Aristotle argues in *On Interpretation* that language is an arbitrary, man-made system of symbols created by individuals to express their thoughts. Different people use different symbols, which is why different languages arise.[10] If so, it follows that their linguistic structure is not constructed to reflect the laws of nature, or to guide people toward achieving human perfection. Ibn Kaspi accepts Aristotle's argument that language is, for the most part, arbitrary and conventional, but he makes one exception. That, of course, is Hebrew, whose words, he argues, were invented by philosophers to express the nature of reality.[11] For example, he writes in *Qevuṣat Kesef* about

> . . . the perfection of the Hebrew language . . . The founders of the Hebrew language had such a complete knowledge of the sciences that they knew the nature of existence in its entirety. Therefore, they knew that the external word is an imitation of what exists outside the soul. And they knew that that which exists outside the soul comes to exist in its being and its essence from the four well-known causes, that is, the material, the formal, the efficient, and the final, and that various properties and accidents cleave to it. Consequently, when they gave names to each existent, they observed those things which are found in the nature of that particular existent and they chose that quality of a thing, that element, which would relate it to the totality of existence, that is, to the three worlds [of existence].[12]

Ibn Kaspi believes it is possible to understand all the secrets of natural science (*ma'ase bereshit*) and divine science (*ma'ase merkava*) purely through a study of Hebrew. Each root word in Hebrew is a reflection of nature, Ibn Kaspi argues, because it expresses a phenomenon or principle in the natural world and because all the different forms of each root reflect one central meaning in some way. Ibn Kaspi wrote a dictionary of Hebrew root words, entitled *Sharshot Kesef*, to prove this theory. In order to accomplish this, he had to contend against two other dictionaries of Hebrew roots, one by David Kimḥi and another by Ibn Jannah. In *Retuqot Kesef*, he argued that neither Kimḥi nor Jannah correctly understood the general meaning underlying all the usages of each root:

> Consequently, because of how the abovementioned scholars [Ibn Rushd and al-Ghazali] understood it, what Ibn Janaḥ and Ibn Kimḥi defined in their dictionary—and in most cases, they divided the understanding of the root into a number of subjects, and for each definition they provided, they wrote

"and another matter . . . ," without introducing the root with its general meaning—deviated from the true meaning according to Ibn Rushd's understanding.[13]

Thus, Ibn Kaspi argues, each usage of a Hebrew root is different, but all are connected by a general principle. This means that Hebrew does not have complete homonyms: two words from the same root that have completely unrelated meanings. Nor does it have complete synonyms, where two words from different roots have exactly the same meaning.[14]

Let me give some examples of how Ibn Kaspi goes about finding a common general principle to each Hebrew root word, while at the same time allowing for a diverse set of applications and derivations. My first example is the root *aleph, bet, lamed*, which he argues, refers to loss and nonexistence, as opposed to acquisition and existence. One form of this root is mourning ('*evel*) the death and loss of another person. Another form of this root is mourning attributed metaphorically to inanimate objects, as in "the land mourneth and languisheth."[15] Here, the land is mourning its destruction or absence.[16] This is also the root of the conjunction "but" ('*aval*), which Ibn Kaspi explains fits this pattern because it also carries the sense of death or loss, since a clause that comes after "but" negates what was said before the conjunction.[17]

Ibn Kaspi interprets another root, '*ayin, reish, mem*, as a gathering together of many parts. Its two main uses in the Bible refer to individuals who are either cunning or naked. The connection between these two characteristics is suggested, Ibn Kaspi argues, by the fact that Genesis 2 ends with "and they were both naked ('*arumim*), the man and his wife,"[18] followed by Genesis 3 with "now the serpent was more cunning ('*arum*) than any beast of the field."[19] Although the connection between these two characteristics may seem tenuous at best, Ibn Kaspi finds a common thread. He argues that a cunning individual is referred to as '*arum* because he gathers in his heart many stratagems and keeps to himself until necessary, while a naked individual is referred to as '*arum* because he is cold and collects his limbs together to keep warm and hide his nakedness.[20] In other words, both uses share the act of gathering, but one applies to the mind, and the other to the body. Another example is the root, *quf, reish, nun*, which Ibn Kaspi interprets as strength and exalting. It can refer to the horn on an animal's head that is used for attacking or defending against other animals. Because of its strength and toughness, it is called a *qeren* because it is tougher than other parts of the animal's body. By analogy, *qeren* can also refer to strong and tough individuals, like kings, as in Daniel 8.[21] It can also be used metaphorically, Ibn Kaspi argues, to describe Moses' strength and exaltation over others in the knowledge he gained on Mount Sinai:

> And it came to pass, when Moses came down from Mount Sinai with the two tables of the testimony in Moses' hand, when he came down from the mount, that Moses knew not that the skin of his face *qaran* while He talked with him.[22]

Ibn Kaspi rejects the literal interpretation that Moses' face sent forth beams of light, arguing instead that we should read this metaphorically in light of Ecclesiastes 8:1: "a man's wisdom maketh his face to shine, and the boldness of his face is changed." So, *qaran*, he argues, refers here to Moses' superior knowledge over others that he obtained on Mount Sinai and Moses' face glowing with newfound wisdom.[23]

Ibn Kaspi launches a polemic, defending the divine origin of the Hebrew Bible. He disparages its translation into Latin by showing the inadequacy of Latin to convey the full meaning of the Hebrew. In *Shulḥan Kesef* and *Maṣref la-Kesef* he argues that the complete meaning of the biblical text is lost when it is translated into another language.[24] This, of course, is a problem with any translation from one language to another. But Ibn Kaspi pushes this further when it comes to translating from Hebrew. For, he argues, the roots of the Hebrew words were constructed by expert philosophers who reflected upon the natural world unlike the founders of Latin who, he argues, were not philosophers and as a result did not construct their language with essential reasons, thus the Latin words, he argues, are just a conglomerate of letters randomly assembled.[25] Ibn Kaspi chooses the first line of Genesis, as an example of a problematic translation into Latin. The Christians translated *bereshit bara Elohim* to *in principio creavit Deus* (In the beginning God created). Ibn Kaspi explains that *bereshit* is an equivocal term, indicating priority in time to the ignorant masses, but priority in cause for the philosophic few. The Latin, *in principio*, however, conveys only the popular understanding and obscures the philosophic one. The next word, *bara* he argues, is different from similar Hebrew verbs such as *'asa* and *yaṣar*. Whereas *'asa* refers to the production of matter and *yaṣar* refers to the production of form, *bara* combines the production of both matter and form. The Latin translation of *bara*, however, is *creavit*, which he argues does not convey both meanings of *bara*, in fact, he implies that *creavit* is closer in meaning to *'asa* (production of matter).[26] Lastly, Ibn Kaspi thinks that translating *Elohim* as *Deus* is problematic since *Deus* refers to God's personal name, YHVH (God as the first cause), but Moses did not intend to reveal this meaning of God until Genesis 2:4. This is important, Ibn Kaspi argues, because *Elohim* refers to the spheres, which was the common conception of God at the time the Bible was written. The Latin translation frustrates Moses' entire purpose, Ibn Kaspi argues, which was to guide the reader away from the simple conception of God as *Elohim*, to the true concept of God as YHVH, the first cause. Therefore, Ibn Kaspi chastises Christian translators, writing that, "Christians who copied *Deus* diverged from God's intention in this book."[27]

It is important to note that, for Ibn Kaspi, the Bible is merely a repository and written form of a living and fluid language, which flourished before the Jews were exiled and were forced to adopt the languages of other nations, leading them to forget Hebrew. Ibn Kaspi builds on Maimonides' acknowledgement, that "we know today that we have no complete understanding of the science of our language," as Ibn Kaspi embarked on his attempt to reconstruct it, because he thought it was the key to uncovering the secrets of the science of nature.[28] Ibn Kaspi refers to this statement of Maimonides throughout his writings saying, for example: that "the sage Maimonides said what is no doubt the truth, that these [earlier] generations knew the language of Hebrew much better than we do,"[29] "if we had in our hands all the works written by our forefathers, we would see this root used a lot,"[30] and "we do not have our language, as Maimonides said, just a little of it, only what is written in these books, because the rest was lost in our exile."[31] Ibn Kaspi criticizes other Jewish commentators for trying to explain some problem in a biblical verse, using their local language (*lo'azi*), instead of going back to the Hebrew. He sees this as the opposite of the Bible's intention.[32] Because of the importance he assigns to the Hebrew language, he is confident that in the messianic days, all nations will speak Hebrew. This is how he explains the verse "in that day there shall be five cities in the land of Egypt that speak the language of Canaan, and swear to the LORD of hosts."[33] He derives from this the lesson that, in the future, when the Egyptians return to the God of Israel and study his Torah, they will only need to study Hebrew.[34]

## Structure of the Text

Ibn Kaspi views the Hebrew Bible as a work of art that conveys its message to the reader in many different ways, not all of them obvious. A great deal can be learned, for example, by looking for the purpose behind its structure, especially if, as Ibn Kaspi argues, it is divided, deliberately, to convey a specific purpose. Ibn Kaspi writes that "the beginning of understanding a book is to understand its division [into different parts]."[35] Here he comes to a very different conclusion from that of modern biblical critics who argue that the Pentateuch has no logical order, is structurally disordered, and its parts are glued together haphazardly. If Ibn Kaspi could be transported through time to have read the writings of Julius Wellhausen, his response would likely have been similar to Martin Buber's: "even this theory so dear to the eighteenth and nineteenth centuries, has been badly shaken. It appears that a book like the Book of Genesis could not have been put together like a cheap newspaper, with the help of scissors and paste."[36] Anticipating the objection that he makes the false assumption that the Bible is structured like a work of Aristotelian philosophy, Ibn Kaspi writes that "the philosophers wanted to imitate our holy Torah, but did not [truly] imitate it, doing so in the way that a monkey imitates the actions of man."[37] In other words, the structure of the Torah is far more philosophic than that of a work of philosophy.

Ibn Kaspi argues that, "the beginning of understanding a book is to understand its division [into different parts]."[38] The first division, of course, is the division of the Pentateuch into five books, of which Ibn Kaspi considers Genesis and Exodus to be more important than the other three books.[39] Presumably, although he does not state his reasoning where he says this in *Maṣref la-Kesef*, it is probably because Genesis and Exodus contains the creation, Abraham's discovery of God's unity, and the story of Moses, who Ibn Kaspi argues reached the highest levels of human perfection by learning the secret of the divine chariot and conveying this knowledge metaphorically through the form of the tabernacle. The remaining three books of Moses are of less interest to Ibn Kaspi, because they lay down laws, many of which are not necessary by nature. This is true, he argues, of the sacrificial order set out in Leviticus, for example, and in Moses' repetition of the law in Deuteronomy, which is a completion of what was stated earlier with the addition of some new ideas.[40] In fact, Ibn Kaspi argues that it is necessary to look for order and structure *only* in the narrative parts of the Pentateuch, but not in the legal sections, where he thinks the order is of little or no significance. But on what basis can he justify slighting entire books of the Bible? His answer is based on the distinction between nature and convention. As he sees it, the narrative sections are written to reflect a necessary reality, while many of the laws are not necessary by nature, like the sacrificial order. For example, in commenting on the order of the Ten Commandments, he writes that there is no necessary reason for their order, instead recommending the reader to study every commandment on its own.[41] Similarly, in beginning to comment on the section that deals with civil laws (Exodus 21:1–24:18), he writes that one should not spend time attempting to discern the order of these laws and why they were placed in a specific order, since it was not constructed to reflect what is necessary in nature.[42]

A second structural feature of the Pentateuch is its division into weekly Torah readings, known as *parshiot*. Ibn Kaspi considers that this division is not haphazard, but done with wisdom despite the fact that he attributes it variously to Moses acting for God or to the men of the Great Assembly.[43] He explains the division of Genesis into twelve *parshiot*, each corresponding to the main patriarch it focuses on. *Parsha* 1 is Adam to Noah, *parsha* 2 is Noah to Abraham, *parsha* 3–5 is Abraham, *parsha* 6 is Isaac, *parsha* 7–8 is Jacob and *parsha* 9–12 is Joseph.[44] Ibn Kaspi further divides the first *parsha*, that of Genesis (1:1–6:8), into three, which he subdivides again into three, based on the three different names of God, which he argues correspond to the three levels of the chariot: *Elohim* (1:1–2:3), YHVH *Elohim* (2:4–3:24) and YHVH (4:1–6:8).[45] Ibn Kaspi takes this a step further and argues that the third of divisions can be divided again into yet another threefold division: Genesis 4:1–26 which recounts the birth of Cain and Abel, Genesis 5:1–31 which deals with Seth and his children, and Genesis 5:32–6:8 which tells of Noah and the evil of his generation.[46] Here again, Ibn Kaspi hints that there is some significance in threefold divisions, but what this may be is unknown because it is explained, he claims, only in *Mizraq Kesef*, which is no longer extant.

## Internal Biblical Contradictions

According to Jewish tradition, the Hebrew Bible is artfully constructed to convey hidden meanings. One method it employs is the deliberate placement of two statements that explicitly contradict each other in the same work. This is a risky strategy since the existence of contradictions in a holy scripture could undermine the authority of the text, and raise serious theological issues. When there is a contradiction between two verses, one of them is liable to be considered false. Early midrashic commentary noticed many internal contradictions, both within and between biblical texts, in some of which God seems to contradict himself. For example, did God say at Sinai to "remember the Sabbath day and keep it holy" (Exod. 20:8) or to "observe the Sabbath day and keep it holy" (Deut 5:12)? How can a man obey God's command to marry his deceased brother's wife (Deut 25:5), if it is forbidden to "uncover the nakedness of thy brother's wife" (Lev. 18:16)? How can a worshiper bring a sacrifice and burn it on the Sabbath (Num. 28:9–10) if kindling a fire on the Sabbath is forbidden (Exod. 35:3)?[47]

One of the central works that strives to explain the existence of contradictions is Maimonides' *Guide*, where he notes that many of the great writings of the past have featured contradictions that have puzzled readers and scholars alike, including the *Guide* itself. There, Maimonides distinguishes seven different reasons for contradictions in a text:[48]

1. *multiple authors*: two contradictory positions because they are written by different authors, but not cited as such

2. *development*: two contradictory positions because they represent earlier and later views of a single author, but are not indicated as such

3. *parable*: two contradictory positions either because (a) one is a parable with an internal meaning that is different from its external meaning and the other is not a parable and thus has only an external meaning or (b) two parables with external meanings that contradict, but internal meanings that do not

4. *context*: two positions that merely appear to be contradictory because they are not fully explained in both places

5. *pedagogy*: two contradictory positions that represent different stages in a pedagogical process, where not everything is revealed at first in order not to confuse the student

6. *error*: two contradictory positions because the author did not realize there was a mistake in his logic

7. *protection*: because one presents an easily grasped but false position, and the other presents a true position that is hidden from the masses in order to protect them from a philosophical truth that would harm them.[49]

Maimonides advertises, intriguingly, that his own work, the *Guide*, contains contradictions of the fifth kind (pedagogy) and seventh kind (protection), forcing his readers to search out and interpret its contradictions. Moreover, Maimonides also indicates that the books of the Hebrew Bible contain contradictions of the third kind (parables) and fourth kind (context), and potentially of the seventh kind (protection), as well. Interestingly, Maimonides does not explain in the *Guide* how to decipher such contradictions in the Bible, leaving this, instead, as a conundrum for later interpreters to unravel.

Ibn Kaspi takes up this challenge. He approves Maimonides' brilliant analysis explaining the reasons for contradictions in great works of art, and applies it to his own interpretation of the Bible. In *Maṣref la-kesef* he writes, "when we find contradictions among verses, Maimonides shows us the way [to resolve] them in the Torah and Scriptures."[50] In fact, this art was already being developed, according to Ibn Kaspi, by Solomon, in Proverbs and Ecclesiastes, who placed purposefully contradictory verses beside each other.[51] As such, he explains the comment of the rabbis in the Talmud that Ecclesiastes should not be included in the holy cannon because "of its contradictory sayings" (*devarim soterim ze et ze*) as in fact a sign of its philosophic strength in that Solomon intentionally contradicted himself in the work.[52]

Ibn Kaspi develops Maimonides' unexplored thesis that the Bible contains contradictions, and he explores the possibility of contradictions of the first (multiple authors), third (parable), fourth (context), and seventh (protection) kinds in the Bible. Looking at these four kinds of contradictions, Ibn Kaspi comes to the conclusion that contradictions created by multiple authors, parables, or context (the first, third, and fourth kinds) are only *apparent* contradictions. Upon careful examination, seemingly contradictory passages that can be explained by these kinds of contradictions, turn out not to be contradictions at all, since they were not created intentionally as such by by their author or authors.

He considers only the seventh (protection) kind of contradiction to be true contradictions, because only they were created by their author with intent. Maimonides' fifth type of contradiction, which is also made deliberately but for pedagogical reasons, is dismissed by Ibn Kaspi with respect to biblical interpretation, arguing that it is "not in the writings of the prophets, but only in books of the philosophers, of which the *Guide* is one, praise God."[53]

## THE FIRST CONTRADICTION: MULTIPLE AUTHORSHIP OF THE BIBLE

The first kind of contradiction in Maimonides' list occurs when a work has contradictions because it is a compilation of different authors and perspectives that were edited and put together in the same book (looking upon the Bible, here, as a "book" instead of a canon containing many different books).[54] Ibn Kaspi's response is twofold. First, he makes the point in *Maskiyot Kesef* that this kind of contradiction is not the primary intention of biblical prophets. However, he admits that it does exist when "they are engaged in explaining the difference [of subjects] among various speakers or time periods."[55] Ibn Kaspi notes in many of his biblical commentaries that the account of events in Samuel and Kings differs from that in Chronicles, Ezra, and Nehemiah as do events described in Isaiah and Ezekiel. The same is true of events described in the Bible as compared to how they are described in *Sefer Josipon*.[56] Second, Ibn Kaspi seems to imply that these contradictions are nothing more than different ways of describing the same event and thus are all true, for he writes in *'Adnei Kesef* that one should ". . . not be surprised that there are differences between the authors of the biblical books because many people wrote down the events, as is explained in *Sefer Josipon*."[57] Here, he makes the case that different people see things differently, and argues that this is true of biblical authors, as well.

Later, in *'Adnei* he also makes the small point that "every author adds or deletes what he chooses [in his book]."[58] Ibn Kaspi takes, as an example of this, David's attack on the Jebusites, which he notes is reported only very briefly in II Samuel 5:6, but is described in much greater detail in I Chronicles 11:4–6.[59] Ibn Kaspi points out that I Chronicles 20:1 entirely fails to mention the story of David and Bathsheba, which is crucial in II Samuel 11, where it is presented as David's great sin.[60]

Ibn Kaspi's application of the first type of contradiction, caused by multiple authors, to interpret the Bible is a subtle, but significant addition to Maimonides' suggestion about the nature of biblical contradictions. Maimonides only lists the *Mishna*, the *Baraita*, and the *Talmud* as examples of this kind of contradiction, since the authorship of these works is clearly attributed to different rabbis. By adding the Bible to Maimonides' list, Ibn Kaspi attributes a human and subjective element to biblical prophecies and to the accounts of the events given by different biblical prophets. As a result, he seems to take the role of the imagination in all the prophets except for Moses, to its logical and historical conclusion.

As was discussed above, the theology behind this can be brought into clearer focus by looking at a key argument in Ibn Kaspi's writings, that God, not Moses, is the sole author of the Pentateuch. He insists on this in order to maintain and convey what he considers to be the knowledge that God is the first and final cause of everything: the creator of all of nature, as described in Genesis 1, and the the source of ideas at the core of the Pentateuch that, Ibn Kaspi argues, are written in imitation of nature. By holding fast to this dogma, Ibn Kaspi ingeniously makes room for multiple biblical writers by turning God into an ultimate cause who is the First Cause of the universe, but not directly involved in the actual writing of the stories contained within the Bible.

THE THIRD CONTRADICTION: RESURRECTION OF THE DEAD

Maimonides' third kind of contradiction has to do with parables. Parables complicate matters because they have both a surface narrative and an inner meaning. This opens up two possibilities: a parable's surface meaning, but not its inner meaning, may contradict a more straightforward statement in the Bible; or there may be two parables with contradictory surface meanings, whose internal meanings are in agreement. Ibn Kaspi, like Maimonides, considers both of these cases to be apparent contradictions, because, if their inner meaning is understood correctly, they do not really contradict at all. The example that Ibn Kaspi gives of this is resurrection of the dead.[61] This is a notable example since it was one of the controversies in which Maimonides found himself embroiled because he was accused of not supporting the bodily resurrection of the dead in the *Guide* and in his *Mishneh Torah* despite the fact that resurrection is one of the thirteen principles listed in his *Commentary on the Mishna*. In commenting on the word "living" (*ḥay*) in Guide I 42, Maimonides suggests that the acquisition of knowledge is often called "life" and in support of this, quotes the Talmud saying, "the righteous even in death are called living,"[62] hinting, therefore, that the righteous live immortally *only* through the knowledge they have acquired.[63] To respond to the charge that he did not support the physical resurrection of the dead, Maimonides wrote the *Letter on Resurrection* to defend his belief in bodily resurrection, but nevertheless scholars have debated his true position on this matter ever since.[64]

Ibn Kaspi examines the question of physical resurrection of the dead by looking closely at apparent contradictions between biblical verses dealing with resurrection. He suggests that there are some verses that deny the physical resurrection of the dead like Psalm. 88:11, while there are others that support the physical resurrection of the dead such as Ezekiel 37, with the vision of the dry bones coming to life. Ibn Kaspi suggests in *Maskiyot Kesef* that this contradiction could be reconciled by taking Ezekiel's vision to be a parable. He does not explain what he thinks the difference is between the external and internals meaning of this parable, but appears to be hinting that its external meaning teaches the physical resurrection of the dead, but its internal meaning is that the righteous live immortally through the knowledge they have acquired.[65] If this position embroiled Maimonides in controversy, it is easy to see why Ibn Kaspi leaves this at a hint. If, indeed, this is his meaning, it would reconcile the apparent contradiction between these two passages, with the external meaning of Ezekiel's vision providing the popular teaching for the masses, while the inner meaning of Ezekiel's vision like Psalm. 88 provides the Bible's true teaching on resurrection. This type of reading is supported by Ibn Kaspi's explanation of the purpose of the third contradiction (parables) later in his Introduction to *Maskiyot Kesef*:

> [Maimonides] says that the third and the fourth [contradictions] are found in books and purposefully inserted by the author, so that the vulgar will accept things in the way the Teacher describes above: *in accord with the capacity of their understanding and the weakness of their representation*, etc. This means a notion devoid of truth—which is indeed what the author intends—since the vulgar cannot bear the matter as it truly is without losing their mind, behaving disorderly and becoming completely unraveled.[66]

## The Fourth Contradiction: Are Children Punished for Sins of Parents?

Maimonides' fourth kind of contradiction occurs when two similar passages in different parts of a text seem to contradict, but only because one is fully explained, and the other is not. The lack of explanation is what causes the apparent contradiction. Ibn Kaspi argues that this does "not amount to a factual contradiction, though it may seem contradictory to us."[67] Ibn Kaspi gives two reasons why such statements appear to contradict one another. The first is because they actually refer to different subjects, but this is not made clear because of the lack of detail in one of the statements. What we have here is the kind of contradiction that occurs when there is a clear affirmation in one statement, and a clear denial of the same thing in another statement. An example of this would be if one passage says (a) "Reuben walks" and another says (b) "Reuben does not walk." On the face of it, this is obviously a contradiction, but if, in fact, these passages refer to two different people named Reuben, it turns out that they do not contradict after all. The second reason of why two such statements can appear contradictory is because one or both do not stipulate the time or place in what they describe is happening, creating the false impression that they are occurring at the same time or in the same location.[68] For example, take two obviously contradictory statements: (a) Reuben eats and (b) Reuben does not eat. Add to these statements, however, the *time* when they occurred, and you could get: (a) Reuben eats today and (b) Reuben does not eat tomorrow. Obviously, if the time frame is different in these statements, they are not contradictory, after all. The same thing happens if you add the detail of *where* they occurred. If this turns out to be in different locations, you could get: (a) Reuben eats at home and (b) Reuben does not eat in the field. Again, it turns out that there is no contradiction after all.

The most prominent example Ibn Kaspi gives of this kind of apparent contradiction is in *Maskiyot Kesef*, where he compares biblical texts that say that children *are* punished for the sins of their parents (such as Exodus 20:5, 34:7, Numbers 14:18, and Isaiah 14:21), while other biblical texts say that children are *not* punished for the sins of the parents (such as Deuteronomy 24:16 and Ezekiel 18:20).[69] This is an apparent example of a contradiction between passages which say that something is so, and passages that say it is not so. Although Ibn Kaspi raises this contradiction in *Maskiyot Kesef*, he does not attempt to resolve it there, but chooses, instead, to do so in many of his other writings. His way of resolving this problem is to argue that the later statement, that children are *not* punished for the sins of their parents, must be understood as contingent, depending on whether the parents repent and embrace worthy actions. If they do not do this, however, the problem remains that delaying punishment of the parents, in hopes of their reform, could end up inflicting punishment on their children, instead. Ibn Kaspi sees this not as overcoming punishment, but as *possibly* overcoming it and, if not, there is a delay in punishment.[70] However, the statement in this passage, that children *are* punished for the sins of the parents refers to a future event that Ibn Kaspi argues will necessarily happen at some point in the future. At the same time, the parents are still the efficient cause for the sins of the sons.[71] He justifies the apparent injustice of punishing children for their parents' sins in his *Commentary on Proverbs*, where he explains that this arises naturally from the way children are raised and the habits they are given, which he sees as decisive factors in character development of one's offspring. This is based on the premise that most people continue in the customs and ways of their parents and society, so, he speculates, if the parents sin, so will their children. Since he implies that the origin of sin is an unbalanced character, it follows that if the parents sin as a result of their own character, then they will pass on those habits and unstable character traits to their own children.[72] In other words, sinful parents raise sinful children who are likely, at some time in the future, to commit sins deserving punishment. Ibn Kaspi argues that this overcomes the seeming contradiction in later passages in the Bible that say that children are *not* punished for the sins of the parents. For, according to this argument, the children are actually punished for their own sins, even though the fault lies partly with their parents for the way they were raised. Ibn Kaspi is uncomfortable with the implication that by delaying punishment, God allows the wicked to prosper, but claims that in fact this is not true, since it is merely a question of when the punishment will actually take place.[73] God may delay punishment of the parents' sins in the hope that they might reform, and may in fact delay so long that they get away without being punished at all, but this does not mean that God will not punish their children for the same sins, the children being liable to commit such sins because they likely have been raised by their parents to have the same bad character traits.

## The Seventh Contradiction: Human Freedom vs. God's Determinism

Ibn Kaspi finds examples in the Bible of Maimonides' seventh contradiction, particularly when it comes to the tension in the Bible between God's determinism and human freedom. The seventh contradiction is one that is created deliberately for the sake of protecting the masses from dangerous ideas. Maimonides argues that even its existence must be hidden. Maimonides is ambiguous, however, as to whether the seventh contradiction exists in the Bible. He raises this possibility but leaves it to others to resolve it, saying only that "whether contradictions due to the seventh cause are to be found in the books of the prophets is a matter for speculative study and investigation."[74] In 'Amudei Kesef, Ibn Kaspi shows no such restraint. He argues explicitly that the seventh contradiction is indeed to be found within the Hebrew Bible, and he seeks to reconcile such contradictions within and between biblical works:

> It seems to me, furthermore, that this [cause] is found in the Torah and prophetic books concerning the question of whether an individual's actions are determined by God or whether that individual chooses freely. The first view is established occasionally so that the vulgar will suppose that God creates and exercises action over every instance, while the second view aims to make clear to them that they freely choose to act and repent from every action. Averroes has written on this subject, namely, that within religions one will find contradictions concerning this notion.[75] This will suffice here as an interpretation according to our intention for this book which can be transmitted to all.[76]

Ibn Kaspi explores this possibility in his analysis of the relationship between the three opinions offered by Maimonides on the origin of the universe in *Guide* II 13 and II 25. Maimonides clearly contradicts himself in these two chapters as to whether the Platonic model of creation is closer to the Torah's model, in which everything is determined by the will of God, or closer to Aristotle's model, in which God creates the laws of nature but leaves humans free to act as we choose. In *Guide* II 13, Maimonides presents the Platonic position as being equivalent to the Aristotelian position, but in *Guide* II 25, he presents the Platonic position as being potentially reconcilable with the Torah's position.[77] Ibn Kaspi attempts to reconcile this contradiction by arguing that it is as an example of Maimonides' seventh kind of contradiction. He writes about *Guide* ll 13 in '*Amudei Kesef*:

> "And there is, in our opinion, no difference between those who believe that heaven must necessarily be generated from a thing and pass away into a thing or the belief of Aristotle who believed that it is not subject to generation and corruption" (*Guide* II 13, p. 285). *Guide* II 25 and II 13 are [an example of] the seventh cause [for contradiction], where it is possible to say that there is a slight change in language between the two [chapters]. Here [Maimonides] is less concerned about how people's belief in the fundamentals of the Torah and miracles could be overturned.[78]

According to Ibn Kaspi, Maimonides' claim in II 25 that there is common ground between the Torah's superficial position and Plato's position is a false presentation of the popular view that God's determinism is reconcilable with human freedom. Maimonides' true position, Ibn Kaspi argues, is in II 13 when he equates Plato's position to Aristotle's position, which supports human freedom.

Ibn Kaspi also sees the seventh contradiction at work in Maimonides' unique, threefold division of opinions on prophecy: the pagan's, the philosopher's, and the Torah's. The pagan opinion is that prophecy is an act of God alone without any human involvement; the philosopher's opinion is that prophecy is a consequence of the natural perfection of the prophet's understanding, or potential for understanding, that is actualized by human initiative alone; and the Torah's opinion agrees with the philosophers, that prophecy is a form of natural perfection, but with the proviso that God can withhold prophecy.[79] Ibn Kaspi comments explicitly about this in *Maskiyot Kesef*:

> The third opinion that he postulates is "the opinion of our Law and the foundation (*yesod*) of our [religious] doctrine." . . . But [if it is] so that it is "the opinion of our Law and the foundation (*yesod*) of our doctrine," why is it not included in the Laws of the Foundations of the Torah [in the *Mishneh Torah*] in enumerating the foundations? And so

> it says in Chapter 7 of the Laws of the Foundations of the Torah "it is one of the foundations of our religious doctrine that God inspires men with the prophetic gift, but the spirit of prophecy only rests upon the wise man who is distinguished by great wisdom and strong moral character, whose passions never overcome him in anything whatsoever." He did not say that this particular foundational principle is separate from the opinion of the philosophers. And further, where does one find in the Torah and the prophetic writings this condition [that God withholds prophecy] and only some biblical verses can be interpreted in this way and it is possible to interpret them otherwise, as he himself does in undermining all [that he said here]. Thus, it seems to me that all this language, was written by Maimonides using the seventh contradiction.[80]

According to Ibn Kaspi, Maimonides uses the seventh contradiction in the case of the different views of prophecy to falsely present the Torah's view that human beings are deterministically influenced by God. He thus reads Maimonides as delivering a covert message: asserting that God miraculously intervenes to prevent potential prophets from actualizing their natural potential for understanding, while hinting that the Torah's *true* position is equivalent to that of the philosopher, that people have the freedom to achieve natural perfection, and thereby the capacity for prophecy, by their own unaided effort.

For Ibn Kaspi, it is not necessary to study the *Guide* in order to see that the Torah's esoteric view comes down on the side of freedom, but its exoteric view comes down on the side of determinism. Indeed, Ibn Kaspi sees a glaring dichotomy within the Hebrew Bible because later biblical books contradict and correct the teachings of earlier books. For example, in Genesis punishment is described as being deterministically caused by God. This is true of both the Flood and God's punishment of Sodom. In both cases, God imposes a terrible punishment on human beings without giving them the opportunity or freedom to change and repent, in order to avert God's punishment. In later books, however, this changes drastically, and the role of human freedom and initiative becomes the focus.

Ibn Kaspi points to an example of the later view, supporting human freedom, which is taken from the Book of Jonah. At first, God proclaims Nineveh's destruction through Jonah—"yet forty days, and Nineveh shall be overthrown"[81]—but later, He accepts the people's repentance and agrees to partially reverse His decision: stating "and God saw their works, that they turned from their evil way; and God repented of the evil, which He said He would do unto them; and He did it not."[82] The problem is that if everything is already determined according to God's plan, as it says in Genesis, how can human freedom be possible, and how is it possible for human action to change God's plan? According to Ibn Kaspi, the source of this change is revealed in the statement in the next verse that "God repented"[83] and changed His mind, which he treats as a prime example of the seventh contradiction, because of a rule of interpretation that he sets out in *Maskiyot Kesef*: When there are two conflicting premises, one of which presents God as directly involved and cancelling a decree, that premise can always be taken to be an exoteric account intended for the masses, because the true view of God is that he does not intervene in human affairs. His only role is that of a remote cause.[84] The leaders of Nineveh came to understand this truth, he writes, and thus saved themselves—unlike those at the time of the flood and Sodom who were doomed to destruction. The conclusion to which the king and nobles came is expressed in the declaration: "who knoweth whether God will not turn and repent, and turn away from His fierce anger, that we perish not?"[85] Ibn Kaspi interprets this statement in *Shulḥan Kesef* to mean that they discovered that God's decree (at Jonah 3:4) is contingent upon repentance and prayer. However, they were not sure if the contingency of God's promise of destruction referred only to the people, so that the city itself would necessarily be destroyed but that they could escape the physical location, or whether the contingency of the decree applied to both the city and the people.[86] Ibn Kaspi, accordingly, interprets the statement in Jonah by highlighting human freedom as being the true position, while he interprets the statement in Jonah predicting God's plan to destroy the city as being the surface or exoteric statement meant for the masses. Ibn Kaspi thus sees the human freedom as the Bible's true view and the divine determinism as the false view needed for the masses during an earlier time.

## Dispersal

When looking at the structure of the Hebrew Bible, Ibn Kaspi argues that many of its teachings are not placed in a rationally ordered location, but are dispersed throughout. In fact, in *Tirat Kesef*, he he goes so far as to say that the Bible was written "in an illogical structure in a very incoherent manner."[87] Ibn Kaspi's explanation of this is to take Maimonides' method of deliberately dispersing his ideas throughout the *Guide*, often placing them strategically where they have no bearing, and project this strategy onto Moses and other authors of the Bible. Maimonides uses this strategy to force his readers to seek out these scattered pieces and put them together like a jigsaw puzzle in order to discover his true meaning.[88] Attributing this same strategy to the biblical authors allows Ibn Kaspi to insist on the rationality of comments that are placed out of order in the Bible. He justifies this in *Tirat Kesef* by saying that if a matter is 'taken out of its natural place and placed outside its natural context, there must be a reason if placed there by a wise sage."[89]

He gives a couple of examples in *Maṣref la-Kesef* and *Tirat Kesef* of passages that are taken out of their natural place, but appear instead in an unlikely context in the Bible. He argues that this was done deliberately, in order to make a philosophic point. His first example of a passage that is out of context is the statement that Sarah was not only Abraham's wife, but also his half-sister, sharing the same father but not the same mother. Ibn Kaspi wonders why this is not said in its more natural location in the genealogy of Terach and Abraham in Genesis 11:26–32, but instead inserts this piece of information in an ungenealogical context of explaining why Abraham did not reveal to King Abimelech that Sarah was his wife in Genesis 20:12, saying "she is indeed my sister, the daughter of my father, but not the daughter of my mother; and so she became my wife."[90] His second example of a similar dispersal of information in the Bible is the example of the introduction of Moses' parents. At first, their relationship is left hidden, the Bible saying only that "and there went a man of the house of Levi, and took to wife a daughter of Levi." Only later is it revealed, and in a different context, that Moses' father, Amram, married his aunt Yochebed.[91] Ibn Kaspi sees no reason why the authors of these examples of biblical dispersals did not reveal the missing pieces of information from the outset. The best he can do is to argue that there was indeed, a deliberate choice to artificially separate and disperse information on some small and mundane points in order to train readers to collect and piece together scattered hints. The reason for this, he hazards, is to prepare them to collect dispersed details with respect to the great secrets of the "Account of the Beginning" and the "Account of the Chariot" that he claims are dispersed throughout biblical texts.[92] In support of this claim, he quotes Maimonides: "nothing has been mentioned out of its place, save with a view to explaining some matter in its proper place."[93]

Maimonides often says, after a passage that he has placed out of context in the *Guide*, some such phrase as, "let's now return to our purpose."[94] He uses this expression or a similar expression in different contexts in the *Guide*. For example, he says this after putting a political interpretation of Jacob's ladder that explains the nature of prophecy in the middle of a chapter explaining the meaning of the words "to stand erect."[95] He also uses a similar phrase after teaching a lesson on how to read the Midrash, which he inserted into a discussion on the purpose of the four species (of the Feast of Tabernacles) in the chapter dealing with the reason behind different holidays.[96] The biblical prophets do not use a similar phrase to mark a dispersal, but Ibn Kaspi argues that the intention was the same.[97] Another example of dispersal is the insertion of the story of Judah and Tamar in Genesis 38 into the consecutive narrative story of Joseph's life in Genesis 37 and 39. Ibn Kaspi suggests that the phrase "And Joseph was brought down to Egypt," at Genesis 39:1, after the chapter of Judah and Tamar is equivalent to when Maimonides says in the *Guide* "let's now return to our purpose."[98] Ibn Kaspi further adds, in commenting on this story in *Ṭirat Kesef*, that "if you understand this, you will understand most of the secrets of the Torah, which are God's secrets."[99]

But what does Ibn Kaspi think is so important about the story of Judah and Tamar that it had to be inserted, out of place, in the middle of Joseph's story? Ibn Kaspi has gone out of his way to advertise its importance, but then leaves his readers to figure out its meaning for themselves. He says very little about this in *Ṭirat Kesef* and *Maṣref la-Kesef*, so I will try to piece together his dispersed comments from his other writings to explain the significance he assigns to this chapter. Judah's first mistake, according to Ibn Kaspi, was his desire to be like the Canaanites. This is represented symbolically by his marriage to a Canaanite woman. The Canaanites, it will be remembered, are the descendants of Noah's son, Ham, who was cursed by Noah for mocking his father's naked drunkenness. Noah's curse included the prediction that Ham's descendants would become slaves. If we put together Ibn Kaspi's justification for God's punishment of children for their parents' sins—because sinful parents will raise sinful offspring who will sin like themselves—then Ham was at fault for focusing only on the body. It may be that Ibn Kaspi thinks that Ham would have raised his children to be concerned purely with the body, like him. The result, presumably, would be the political weakness of his descendents. So the reason that Ibn Kaspi thinks Judah's three sons died could be because of their Canaanite mother's miseducation of her children to a focus purely on the body and its weakness. For Ibn Kaspi, the statement that "God slew him" at Genesis 38:7, 10 is a first cause and not the proximate cause.

This fits with Ibn Kaspi's observation that the names of each of these three children are etymologically rooted in physical weakness, which he thinks hints at the future political weakness of the Jews. This is appropriate as the kingship belongs to Judah and his descendants. The name of Judah's first son, *Er*, hints at the prediction of God's punishment of the Israelites, "May the LORD cut off to the man that doeth this, him that called (*er*) and him that answered out of the tents of Jacob, and him that offered an offering unto the LORD of hosts."[100] According to the Talmudic section Ibn Kaspi cites in this context, *er* refers to lacking of education by the Sages and lacking their wisdom.[101] The name of the second son, *Onan*, hints at sorrow, Ibn Kaspi argues, citing as comparisons "she called his name Ben-oni [son of my sorrow],"[102] and "his mother called his name Jabez, saying: 'Because I bore him with pain.'"[103] The name of the third son, *Shelah*, comes from *sh.l.h* and refers to a mistake, but its usage with respect to worldly matters has to do with being at rest. So Ibn Kaspi draws a causal link between making a mistake and being at rest, seeing one as the efficient cause of the other. In our examples in political history, when one makes a mistake because of the competitive nature of the world, making a mistake can lead to one being overcome by a stronger party and put to rest. In other words, being no longer in motion, when applied to politics, means political failure. Ibn Kaspi explicitly says that *true* intention of using Shelah as the name of one of Judah's sons explains the meaning of "The scepter shall not depart from Judah, nor the ruler's staff from between his feet, *ad ki yavo shilo, ve-lo yekehat amim*."[104] The contrast between children that Judah has with the Canaanite woman and those with Tamar is instructive. The etymology of the names of his Canaanite children carry the meanings of lack of education and wisdom, increase in sorrow, political failure, and they all die. Tamar's children, however, seem much tougher, for they are born in competition over who can emerge from the womb first. The point of this seems to teach Judah that his descendants will possess the mantle of kingship. To succeed, therefore, they must be more like the children of Tamar and less like the Canaanite's children.

For Ibn Kaspi, the earlier rabbis were already aware of the method of deliberate dispersal of key passages in the biblical text, for they wrote about it, using the expression "there is no chronological order in the Torah" (*'ayn muqdam u-me'uḥar ba-torah*), pointing out that many narratives in the Bible are not presented in their proper chronological order. This expression is frequently used by Rashi, for example, to make the case that events narrated in the Bible were not written according to a linear historical chronology. For example, Rashi says in multiple contexts that the patriarchs kept the six hundred and thirteen commandments, and claims that they actually practiced later laws from the Torah at a time *before* Moses revealed the Torah at Mount Sinai.[105] Ibn Kaspi does not go as far as Rashi in dismissing any historical chronology, but argues that the expression "there is no chronological order in the Torah" is meant to show that chronology is not the *only* principle at work in the Torah, and that many parts of the text are taken out of chronological sequence in order to point to a hidden meaning that should not be stated explicitly.

## Empty Spaces

Another literary device used throughout the Hebrew Bible is the strategic placement of empty spaces in the text. While these may appear to be errors of editors or copyists, Ibn Kaspi argues that, in *Shulḥan Kesef*, empty spaces are strategically placed to convey a message. As evidence, he points to fourteen strange breaks in the Hebrew Bible, five in the Pentateuch and nine in the Prophets.[106] Ibn Kaspi argues that yet another defect of translating the Bible into another language is that such literary features such as the empty spaces, can easily be lost. Ibn Kaspi compares himself favorably with Ibn Ezra who also noticed these strange breaks in the text, but could not give a reason for them.[107] Ibn Kaspi, in contrast, often gives two reasons for each break in the text, one exegetical and one philosophical.[108] The exegetical reason, he argues, is to show that just because something comes earlier or later in the text does not mean that what comes earlier is the cause of what comes later or even that it precedes the latter in time. In other words, the purpose of the break in the text is to show that there is no causal or linear connection between what comes before and what comes after the break. Of course, this reinforces the view that there is no chronological order in the Torah.[109] The philosophic reason for the break, he argues, is that it conceals a hidden matter that the author does not want to reveal explicitly, but wants to hint at, to those who can understand.

For example, there is a dramatic break in the text at Genesis 35:22 between "And it came to pass, while Israel dwelt in that land, that Reuben went and lay with Bilha his father's concubine; and Israel heard of it" and "Now the sons of Jacob were twelve."[110] Ibn Kaspi rejects Rabbi Jonathan's interpretation of this in the Babylonian Talmud that these two passages are put beside each other in order to show that Reuben did not actually sin, since the statement "the sons of Jacob were twelve" implies that they were all equal in righteousness.[111] Ibn Kaspi differs from the Talmud in this instance. He agrees with the plain meaning of the text, that Reuben sinned in committing adultery with Bilhah, and argues that an empty space was placed after "Israel heard of it" to emphasize Israel's silent and hidden response.[112] In other words, the text specifies that "Israel heard of it" and does *not* say that "Israel heard of it and responded in some way to his son." Ibn Kaspi pushes this further by speculating that this is why Jacob is referred to by two different names in this passage. With regard to Reuben's sin, it refers to Jacob as "his father" (*'aviv*) to emphasize Rueben's sin—it was considered a sin to sleep with one's father's concubine—but calls Jacob "Israel" when he hears of his son's transgression. Ibn Kaspi takes this to mean that because Jacob is called Israel here, this must mean that he overcame his emotional response, just as he overcame the angel he wrestled with, who then said, "Thy name shall be called no more Jacob, but Israel; for thou hast striven with God and with men, and hast prevailed."[113] If Ibn Kaspi's interpretation of this is correct, the question still remains: why is Jacob's silent and restrained response to Reuben's behavior so significant that it requires an empty space to hide it? It seems that the significance of empty space, for Ibn Kaspi, is to emphasize Jacob's controlled response, reacting without anger and with restraint.[114] According to Ibn Kaspi, Jacob waited until he was on his deathbed to punish Reuben by prophesying that although Reuben has the prerogative to inherit everything from his father, Jacob predicts that this will be of no advantage to him.[115] In *Maṣref la-Kesef*, Ibn Kaspi links this prediction, in Genesis 49:3–4, to a law in Deuteronomy 21:15–17 that says that if a man has two wives one of whom is loved and the other hated, and the eldest son is the son of the hated wife, he will receive a double portion of the inheritance. Ibn Kaspi argues that Jacob's prediction is meant to suggest that although Reuben may be about to inherit and has the right to claim Jacob's concubines as his own, based on the above law of inheritance, he claimed this right prematurely with Bilhah, thus, Jacob predicts that it will do Reuben no good, and will lead to his downfall.[116]

Another example of an empty space that Ibn Kaspi points to comes is the space between "And it came to pass on the day when the LORD spoke unto Moses in the land of Egypt" and "that the LORD spoke unto Moses, saying: 'I am the LORD; speak thou unto Pharaoh king of Egypt all that I speak unto thee.'"[117] Ibn Kaspi argues that this empty space is meant to draw the reader's attention to the significance of this day for Moses, for this is when Ibn Kaspi argues that Moses achieved knowledge of God and nature greatly surpassing that attained by his brother.[118] Surpassing Aaron is important, Ibn Kaspi argues, because Aaron is given precedence over Moses in the genealogy of the twelve tribes, presumably because he was Moses' older brother. This reading is supported by the fact that Aaron comes first in two other passages: "she bore him Aaron and Moses"[119] and "These are that Aaron and Moses, to whom the LORD said: 'Bring out the children of Israel from the land of Egypt according to their hosts.'"[120] In the next verse, however, after the empty space, this order is reversed and Moses takes precedence over Aaron: "These are they that spoke to Pharaoh king of Egypt, to bring out the children of Israel from Egypt. These are that Moses and Aaron."[121] From this point on, Moses is the central figure in liberating the Israelites and giving them the Torah, even if he is younger in years than Aaron.[122] Thus the point of the empty space was to hint to the significance of that day in Moses' attaining a higher intellectual level and superior knowledge of God and nature. The chapter where this empty space occurs leads up to this transition, Ibn Kaspi argues, by contrasting two different forms of priority: priority of time, and priority of rank, thus educating the reader about the superiority of priority of rank because Moses' superior knowledge gives him priority of rank over Aaron's priority of time, based on being Moses' elder brother.

Another interesting empty space that Ibn Kaspi analyzes in *Shulḥan Kesef* comes between the statement "And it came to pass after the plague," immediately followed by, "the LORD spoke unto Moses and unto Elazar the son of Aaron the priest, saying: 'Take the sum of all the congregation of the children of Israel, from twenty years old and upward, by their fathers' houses, all that are able to go forth to war in Israel.'"[123] Ibn Kaspi argues that an the empty space separates these two discussions so that the reader will not assume that the plague necessarily preceded the war in time or that the plague is the cause of the war. As evidence,

Ibn Kaspi points to the first word in the first clause quoted above, *va-yehi*, which is translated here as "and it came to pass." Ibn Kaspi argues that this indicates that the end of the plague is related to the previous chapter (Numbers 25) where it says that the Israelites began to commit harlotry with the daughters of Moab (reported at Numbers 25:1). He argues that God sent this plague as a punishment for their harlotry. The command to go to war is unrelated to this, Ibn Kaspi argues, because it marshals the next generation of Israelites for war, as they prepare to invade Canaan. The empty space, therefore, is meant to keep the reader from thinking that there is some direct temporal or causal link between the plague and the war, as if one must go to war because of the plague or that the command to war happened exactly after the plague.[124]

Another empty space, Ibn Kaspi points to teaches a lesson about the nature of prophecy: "And when David rose up in the morning" and "the word of the LORD came unto the prophet Gad, David's seer."[125] Ibn Kaspi argues that the point of there being an empty space in between these two phrases is to indicate that there is no causal link between waking up early and receiving prophecy. Prophecy, he argues, does not usually come to a prophet in the morning, but is more likely to come during an afternoon nap or in the evening. Without this empty space readers could easily make the mistake of thinking the opposite.[126] Ibn Kaspi's position, here, is challenged by examples in the Bible of other prophets who did receive prophecies in the morning. A case in point is Ezekiel's vision in Ezekiel 12:8.[127] Ibn Kaspi answers this challenge by interpreting Ezekiel's morning vision as a very low-level prophecy, corresponding to the two lowest levels, the first and second lowest levels of the eleven levels of prophecy delineated by Maimonides (of *Guide* II 45). Ibn Kaspi argues that only these two lowest levels of prophecy can be received in the morning. The reason Ibn Kaspi gives for Ezekiel having received such a low-level prophecy in the morning is that he was weak from having received a higher level prophecy the night before. God merely confirmed in the morning, Ibn Kaspi argues, what he told Ezekiel at night. In other words, prophecies received in the morning do not contain new predictions, but merely confirm what was prophesied at night. The purpose of morning prophecies, therefore, is to convey to Israel the higher-level evening prophecies.[128] This fits Maimonides' description of the first and second levels of prophecy at *Guide* II 45, even though Maimonides does not explicitly mention this particular example at Ezekiel 12:8. Maimonides' first level of prophecy is "a divine help that moves and activates him to a great, righteous and important action" and his second level of prophecy is when "an individual finds that a certain thing has descended upon him and that another force has come upon him and has made him speak."[129]

My final example of an empty space, interpreted by Ibn Kaspi, occurs between Jeremiah's speech saying "Whether it be good, or whether it be evil, we will hearken to the voice of the LORD our God, to whom we send thee; that it may be well with us, when we hearken to the voice of the LORD our God" and the report that, "it came to pass after ten days, that the word of the LORD came unto Jeremiah."[130] The context, here, is a consultation between Jeremiah and the survivors of Nebuchadnezzar's onslaught against Egypt. The surviving Jews ask Jeremiah what God wants them to do in response to this calamity. Jeremiah 42:7 may give the impression that Jeremiah's prophecy comes after the destruction of the temple, but Ibn Kaspi argues that the empty space between Jeremiah 42:6 and 42:7 indicates that this is *not* a new prophecy, but an application of an earlier prophecy.[131] Ibn Kaspi comes to this conclusion on the basis that this could not have been a new prophecy because, after the destruction of the temple, Jeremiah was in a state of mourning, crying, and lamentation and did not endeavor to isolate his mind to prophesize.[132] Here Ibn Kaspi is building on Maimonides' argument that a stable political environment is necessary for a prophet to focus his mind adequately to receive a prophecy. If one is in mourning and sadness over destruction, one cannot achieve prophecy.[133] Ibn Kaspi argues that Jeremiah 42, therefore, is not making a new prophesy, but merely restating what he had already prophesied before the destruction of the temple, that all of Egypt would be destroyed by Nebuchadnezzar and the Babylonians. Ibn Kaspi supports this with the argument that this was the point of the two parables, of the wine and the rods, both of which Jeremiah presented before the temple was destroyed.[134] Jeremiah, he argues, was therefore aware that Nebuchadnezzar would destroy Egypt, but did not know how it would affect the surviving remnants of the Jews.

## Repetitions

One of the arguments underlying modern source criticism of the Bible is based on the many repetitions within the text. These arguments are taken to be evidence that the Bible is a compilation of multiple sources, each of which contained a different author's account of biblical events: often these accounts were of the same event, but described from different perspectives.[135] When these accounts were compiled, the argument goes, multiple versions of the same narrative were synthesized in such a way that both versions were jumbled together in the same text, without being fully harmonized. The repetitions within the text were taken to be evidence of multiple sources. There are two different accounts of the creation, for example, and two different accounts of the flood.[136] The fact that these accounts can be disentangled and read independently is taken as further evidence that they come from multiple sources. Some modern literary critics, however, have criticized this theory, arguing that it ignores the artfulness of biblical repetitions. Robert Alter, for example, writes that what "in biblical scholarship were long deemed sure signs of a defective style, may be perfectly deliberate components of a literary artwork and recognized such by the audience it was intended for."[137]

Ibn Kaspi is also very interested in highlighting places where the Bible repeats itself, but for a very different reason. He does not think that most of the repetitions in the Bible are accidental, in fact, he thinks they are deliberate. He gives three different reasons for thinking that they are purposeful, because he discerns three different types of repetition.

The first type of repetition is pedagogical, intended to fix an important matter in the reader's memory. He writes that often the Bible repeats a matter to emphasize its importance since repetition helps to solidify a memory. He praises this tactic in *Maṣref la-Kesef* where he says: "the honoured custom of our holy Torah is to repeat a matter many times in order that we remember it constantly."[138] Ibn Kaspi lists multiple examples that fall into this category. One, the announcement of Isaac's birth, not once, but four times: "And Sarah conceived, and *bore* Abraham a son in his old age," "And Abraham called the name of his son that was *born* unto him, whom Sarah *bore* to him, Isaac," "And Abraham was a hundred years old, when his son Isaac was *born* unto him."[139] A second example of repetition in order to solidify a memory is the announcement that God is speaking to Moses, which is repeated a remarkable six times in Exodus at 6:1, 6:2, 6:10, 6:13, 6:28, and 6:29. Ibn Kaspi comments that "the way of all the philosophers and the sages in their books, like Aristotle and his followers, is to repeat matters even if they have already been stated, in order to propose and instill the matter in the heart of the observers."[140] A third example listed by Ibn Kaspi is the description introducing the different stages of the journey of the

Israelites in the desert, which is repeated no fewer than three times: "These are the *stages* of the children of Israel, by which they *went forth* out of the land of Egypt" and "And Moses wrote their *goings forth, stage by stage*, by the commandment of the LORD; and these are their *stages* at their *goings forth*."[141]

The second type of repetition is also pedagogical, but in a different way. Each repetition emphasizes a different step in the development of a point. He says that this can also be found in the works of the philosophers, indicating, for example, that there are numerous repetitions that take the form of constant reminders of what was said earlier in Aristotle's works, such as in the *Physics*, in *On the Heavens*, and in the *Meteorology*, which, he argues are there to help guide the reader through the argument in what amounts to being a gradual process of education.[142] Ibn Kaspi has one stipulation, however, with respect to this comparison: he argues that it is the philosophers who are imitating the Bible.

Ibn Kaspi gives, as an example of this type of repetition, Genesis 6:1–12 which begins with a statement about the evil of man and the introduction to Noah. This is a repetition of what can be found in previous chapters, but is restated here, Ibn Kaspi argues, in order to expand on principles already explained in previous chapters and to connect it to the current discussion.[143] This is also how he explains why Exodus begins by repeating some of the events of Genesis in summary.[144] This can be seen also in the multiplicity of repetitive prophecies attributed to a single prophet, Abraham, for example, in Genesis 12, 15, 17, or Ezekiel in Ezekiel 1, 10. The repeated material in these versions serves Ibn Kaspi's first reason for repetition, because they help explain and strengthen the memory of earlier passages.[145] But they also mark the development of different stages in Abraham's prophecy, for example, with repeated or interchangeable terms in God's statements to Abraham: "Get thee out of *thy country*, and from *thy kindred*, and from thy *father's house*."[146] Ibn Kaspi notes that repetition can also mark development from one philosophic work to another, for example, when a philosopher repeats himself in multiple works on the same topic. An example is Averroes' long, middle, and short commentaries on Aristotle's writings.[147] Ibn Kaspi finds this in the Bible, as well. For example, Moses repeats in Deuteronomy matters already described in the earlier books of the Pentateuch in order to build on what was previously taught and add further material, in this case, for a new generation.[148]

Ibn Kaspi's third type of repetition is done for the sake of showing increased intensity. He argues, for example, that the founders of the Hebrew language often repeated the same thing first in a positive way, then in a negative way, and the two beside each other in order to emphasize a point. Examples include: Jacob's command that his sons go to Egypt to get food "that we may live, and not die" to emphasize Jacob's strong command to his sons to go to Egypt and obtain food due to the famine;[149] Rebecca is described as, "a virgin, neither had any man known her" to emphasize the virginity of Rebecca;[150] "yet did not the chief butler remember Joseph, but forgot him" to emphasize the extent to which the chief butler forgot Joseph;[151] Isaiah's prophecy to Hezekiah that "for thou shalt die, and not live," and Jeremiah's critique of the people as "foolish . . .and they have no understanding."[152]

Ibn Kaspi is critical of other interpreters who attempt to find a hidden meaning in such a stylistic repetition, saying that "whoever innovates in these explanations give purposes to what those who said it did not intend."[153] He is likely thinking of Rashi, for example, who finds in repetition "a virgin, neither had any man known her"[154] quoting *Genesis Rabba* 60:5 that these two expressions refer to two kinds of virginity, the first in procreative sexual relations and the second in alternative forms of sexual relations that the Bible condemns.[155] To his credit, Ibn Kaspi, finds such attempts to read hidden messages into these sorts of repetitions problematic. Even God employs repetition for the sake of emphasis in repeating the command for Moses to go, to return to Egypt after Moses already received permission to do this from his father-in-law in order to underline the importance of Moses going on this journey.[156]

## Selectivity and Absence

Another principle that Ibn Kaspi employs in interpreting the Hebrew Bible is looking at its selectivity in disclosing information.[157] Certain sections of the Bible are flush with detail, but others have sparse or missing details. For example, the details of the wives of some biblical characters are given, but others are left out entirely. Why? Why are the meanings of certain biblical names given, but not others? Why are all the steps of conception and birth gone through in great detail in some cases, but not in others? The approach of the Midrash to these questions is to look, in each case, for the significance of either giving or omitting such detailed information. According to the tradition, the written Torah was accompanied by an oral Torah, which contained hidden interpretations. Ibn Kaspi differs, to some extent, from this approach, by arguing in *Masref la-Kesef* that the Torah is a microcosmic portrait of nature's laws. This being so, it must be selective for the sake of brevity:

> If God had written all He knew, these books would not be able to contain it all, so He shortened it for us in giving us the Ten Commandments, and if He had intended or desired to teach to us everything He knew or half of it, He would still be sitting on the mountain teaching. This is every author and teacher's method. Our Torah limited itself in order to lead us to perfection in all the truths of the perfect sciences.[158]
>
> Had Moses, our teacher, wanted to write the Pentateuch with everything that he knew that is necessary and useful it would be double or a thousandfold in length, and he chose brevity keeping in mind [only] what is necessary and useful.[159]

Fitting the important truths into a book meant for everyone, not just philosophers, Ibn Kaspi argues, requires a highly selective use of detail.

Ibn Kaspi frequently points out the Bible's selective reporting and absences in his biblical commentaries. For example, he draws attention to the Bible's lack of detail with respect to Cain's wife, stating only, "And Cain knew his wife," yet goes into much greater detail when it comes to the marriages of other biblical characters like Aaron and Eliezer.[160] The reason Ibn Kaspi gives for this is that if Seth's wife, for example, gets little mention, and Seth is the ancestor of Noah, then a fortiori Cain's wife deserves no detail which, he speculates, is because Cain was a murderer.[161] Another example he gives is in the genealogy of Noah's children (at Genesis 10), where most of Noah's descendants are named, without comment, except for Peleg, about whom it says, "the name of the one was Peleg, for in his days was the earth divided (*niflega*)."[162] Ibn Kaspi comments that all names in the Bible are there for a reason, but not all were chosen to be written about in the text, presumably because they have no relevance for the narrative, whereas Pereg apparently does. Another place Ibn Kaspi points to where the text is silent is that it does not give the reason why Terah and Abraham migrated from Ur of the Chaldees. His answer as to why is that the Bible cannot give the reason for every event it recounts. He speculates, however, that it was in response to a conflict that we know of only because of God's promise that "him that curseth thee will I curse."[163] Ibn Kaspi lists all kinds of other possible sources of conflict that may have caused their departure, but ultimately does not decide upon the exact cause.[164]

Ibn Kaspi notes that brevity is a frequent characteristic of biblical accounts of conception and birth, except when it comes to certain important biblical characters for whom it sets out the entire chain of events leading to their birth. Take, for example, the events leading to the birth of Isaac in Genesis 21.[165] There we are told about God remembering (*paqad*), God doing (*va-ya'as*), Sarah conceiving (*va-tahar*), and the baby being born (*va-teled*).[166]

Another case that Ibn Kaspi points to where part of a narrative is missing is in the biblical account of Simeon and Levi's murder of the tribe of Shechem. The Bible says only that "Simeon and Levi, Dinah's brethren, took each man his sword, and came upon the city unawares, and slew all the males."[167] The Bible is silent as to whether they alone killed all the males, or whether all their brothers, children, and servants participated in this slaughter. We know only that Simeon and Levi were the instigators. Ibn Kaspi raises this question, but observes that the Bible often describes a military commander as fighting a battle, obviously meaning that he led an entire army into battle, not that he did *all* the fighting himself.[168]

Ibn Kaspi also points out that there is a special selectivity used to describe Moses. The genealogy of the Israelites at Exodus 6:13–25 is meant to lead to Moses and Aaron, according to Ibn Kaspi, who explains its selectivity here in detail. He argues that it begins with Reuben and Simeon merely because they are Levi's older siblings, but notes that it does not include Levi's younger siblings. It also gives a much more detailed account of Moses' and Aaron's line descending from Levi than it gives of Gershom's and Merari's lines. Ibn Kaspi notes that the Bible does not go into much detail about Moses' wife and children, partly, he acknowledges, because they were mentioned previously at Exodus 2:21–22 and 4:20–26, but he thinks the more important reason is because she was not an Israelite and, therefore, her children were not destined for the priesthood, as were Aaron's children.[169]

Ibn Kaspi insists in *Shulḥan Kesef* that we cannot assume that a prophet's miracles were solely those reported in the text. Ibn Kaspi is troubled that, although the Bible reports that Elijah and Elisha revived the dead, it gives no report of Moses performing such impressive miracles. This bothers him because he ranks Moses as the greatest of all the prophets. Ibn Kaspi's way of dealing with this is to reject the notion that this means that later prophets were able to perform miracles that Moses did not or even could not perform. Ibn Kaspi uses the principle of selectivity to argue against this, saying that the Bible does not report every single thing Moses did. Moreover, since Moses is the most perfect prophet, it follows that he must have performed such miracles even if they were not reported in the Bible, perhaps because they were not relevant to the accounts of Moses' life and activities that were selected for the Bible.[170] Ibn Kaspi takes the Bible's brevity and selectivity to heart, for he writes, in *Tirat Kesef*, that his own books imitate the Bible in this respect. To achieve this goal he informs his readers that he employs two strategies. The first is to omit what others have already said, including the views of his predecessors. He says he will present only his own innovations. The second strategy is to avoid lengthy discussions even of his own innovations.[171] Ibn Kaspi is unique in applying the maxim to "walk in His ways" to God's way of writing in the Pentateuch which Ibn Kaspi interprets as meaning that he should imitate God's brevity in his own writings.[172]

## Historical Conventions and the Relationship to Surrounding Cultures

The last part of this study of Ibn Kaspi's heremeneutics of the Hebrew Bible is his explanation of many ambiguous or obscure statements, which he accounts for by the context of their original location, time, and cultural milieu. Interestingly, he applies this even to his own time. In his youth, Ibn Kaspi traveled to Egypt to meet the descendents of Maimonides and observe Egyptian culture, mores, politics, and religion, in the same spirit as an anthropologist. As far as we know, he did not write his observations down in a travel journal, but he did incorporate them into his biblical exegesis.[173]

He often justifies his explanation of biblical passages as reflecting the context of their time, place, or cultural milieu by quoting the Talmudic phrase "the Torah speaks in the language of the sons of men" (*dibra Torah kileshon bnei 'adam*).[174] In the Talmud, this phrase was used by different rabbis to limit attempts to derive legal conclusions from the duplication of words in biblical verses. They argued that since the Bible was written for a large audience, such duplications were incorporated for the masses but are not meant to convey some deeper meaning.[175] This expression was adopted by Maimonides and other medieval Jewish thinkers to explain why an eternal God without material form is described in anthropomorphic terms in the Bible.[176] Maimonides argues that although the true teaching of the Bible embraces a non-anthropomorphic conception of God, it describes God in corporeal terms as a concession to human weakness:

> The meaning of this is that everything that all men are capable of understanding and representing to themselves at first thought has been ascribed to Him as necessarily belonging to God, may He be exalted. Hence attributes indicating corporeality have been predicated to Him in order to indicate that He, may He be exalted, exists, inasmuch as the multitude cannot at first conceive of any existence save that of a body alone.[177]

Maimonides makes the case that in order to understand the meaning of many obscure statements in the Bible, one has to read ancient pagan writings, such as *The Nabatean Agriculture*, to understand the context of the Bible's polemic against ancient idolatry.[178] In other words, Maimonides implies that not every word in the Bible is an "eternal truth": to the contrary, many of its passages are polemical, aimed at a specific historical practice, such as idolatry, that was prevalent in the historical context in which the Bible was written.[179]

Isadore Twersky was the first to note that Ibn Kaspi is unique in expanding Maimonides' point that the Bible contains concessions to the masses, not merely with respect to its description of God, but also to the social and historical context with respect to all kinds of matters. Twersky writes that Ibn Kaspi tries to solve many problems in the Bible by explaining them away as concessions to errors, superstitions, popular conceptions, local mores, folk beliefs, and customs.[180] Twersky is right to point out the similarities of Ibn Kaspi's approach to modern historicism, as "in embryo a general historicistic position." This has been noted by other scholars, as well, who have referred to him as a predecessor of modern biblical criticism.[181]

Ibn Kaspi writes that he discovered these myriad applications of this principle in Egypt, where he met Maimonides' descendants. He reports that he was disappointed, presumably with their lack of knowledge of philosophy and the sciences,[182] but he found a silver lining to the trip, in his discovery of new ways to apply the principle that "the Torah speaks in the language of the sons of men" to understand the historical context of the Bible.[183] He argues that this is a key to understanding the Bible that previous interpreters lacked. He writes in *Tirat Kesef*:

> Had I wanted to mention all the matters in the [holy] writings that you will not understand unless you know the custom of these lands, it would lengthen their telling, but most will be clarified in the course of our book.[184]

Being in Egypt allowed him to study the culture and practices of Egypt, which he thought helped explain many parts of the Hebrew Bible that a reader living in Europe would not appreciate.

Ibn Kaspi's observations in Egypt led to some intriguing interpretations of the Bible. When the text says that God commanded Moses to "Go to Pharaoh in the morning as he goes out to the river,"[185] he observed, for example, that the Sultan went out to the Nile twice a week to play with a small ball. Ibn Kaspi speculates that this may explain why God commanded Moses to "Go to pharaoh in the morning as he goes out to the river."[186] He suggests that Moses may have arranged to go out in a small boat and wait for him there.[187] Another observation he makes is that Egyptians treat their slaves badly, like animals, and attributes this to Egyptian culture. He thinks this may explain why Joseph did not contact his father, Jacob, when he was a slave in Egypt, thinking this would not help free him but would only serve to cause his father more pain.[188]

Ibn Kaspi derives an important lesson on Egyptian religious belief, based on Pharaoh granting Moses' request to allow all of Egypt's Jewish slaves to depart for three days to worship God in the wilderness.[189] Ibn Kaspi argues that this shows that Pharoah was not afraid that the reach of the God of Israel could extend to punishing him or other Egyptians, but that he respected each nation's unique relationship with their God, and thought that the Jewish God might be able to punish his worshipers, if they displeased him. This would be bad for Egypt, as well, if he should harm or even kill all of Egypt's Jewish slaves.[190]

Some of Ibn Kaspi's other observations apply to the behavior of the Egyptians and their manner of dress. He notes that beating slaves and throwing blood at them were customary practices in Egypt in his day, and takes this as confirmation of biblical reports of an Israelite being treated in like fashion.[191] He makes other negative comments about the behavior of Muslims in his commentary on a statement in Isaiah: "For all tables are full of filthy vomit and no place clean." He claims, in confirmation of this, that leaving excrement and vomit on the table until it is full of vomit, is the way some Muslims behaved in his own time. Presumably, this was something he observed in Egypt.[192] He also comments on forms of sexual behavior that are forbidden by the Bible, which he claims were prevalent in Egypt and practiced by Muslims in his time, for he had observed groups of prostitutes in public markets, offering homosexual as well as heterosexual prostitution, even extending to sexual relations between one man and two women.[193] He disputes, however, the biblical verse "And according unto thy word shall all my people be kissed," saying that it is not the custom in Egypt to kiss on the mouth directly.[194] Ibn Kaspi observes that the Egyptian custom of removing shoes when entering a mosque explains God's command to Moses, "Draw not nigh hither; put off thy shoes from off thy feet, for the place whereon thou standest is holy ground." He explains that this is the custom because Egyptian sandals are so hard that when they are removed, they fall off.[195]

Of course, Ibn Kaspi is operating on the assumption that the Egyptians continued to follow in his own day the same practices that they followed in the biblical era, enabling him to use Egyptian customs of his own era to shed light on the the Bible. This is highly questionable and was, in fact, challenged on two different grounds. Kalonymous ben Kalonymous attacked this assumption in his letter of critique, arguing that since customs depend on religion, and since Egyptian religion has changed since the biblical era, their customs have probably changed, as well.[196] Ran Ben-Shalom challenges Ibn Kaspi's argument on an entirely different basis by raising the question of whether Ibn Kaspi's view of Egyptian society is not colored with certain orientalist assumptions that look down upon the Muslims as primitive and amoral. Nevertheless, Ibn Kaspi's study of Egyptian culture has inspired a whole new approach to biblical scholarship that seeks to understand how the Bible's surrounding culture can help us better understand the Bible.

# Conclusion

Ibn Kaspi interprets the Hebrew Bible as presenting two interdependent models of history which are both separate and concurrent. The first is a secular political history that is defined by power and competition between kingdoms. The second is a history of the progressive accumulation and dissemination of the secrets of the divine chariot, inspiring an increase in love and compassion for the lower parts of nature. Although the advocates of political realism are often opponents of those who defend moral and intellectual progress, Ibn Kaspi thinks this is a false dichotomy. To him, both are essential elements of history, as is made clear in the Hebrew Bible. Ibn Kaspi argues that the success of each nation depends in part on its progress with respect to knowledge, and its progress with respect to knowledge depends in on its political strength. To put it more simply, power needs progress and progress needs power.

This is illustrated, Ibn Kaspi argues, by failures of the Jewish kingdoms during the First and Second Temple periods. These failures were largely the fault of kings whose refusal to listen to the guidance of wise prophets brought their kingdoms to ruin. These kings often had weak intellects and were driven by their physical passions. Knowledge of the art of war is important for a ruler, but it is not enough to ensure a nation's success or survival. The advanced knowledge of empires, history, and the contingent nature of the world that Ibn Kaspi attributes to prophets is also necessary for success in a dangerous world. According to Ibn Kaspi, this is the reason for the command in Deuteronomy 18:15 to listen to the prophet. Ibn Kaspi argues, the Hebrew Bible shows that ignoring the words of the prophets was an important cause of the destruction of the Jewish temples and the loss of political power.

However necessary progress in intellectual knowledge may be, it cannot stand alone, but needs political stability. Ibn Kaspi illustrates this with his argument that although the secret knowledge of the divine chariot was originally a Jewish teaching, it was lost to the Jews, and absorbed into Greek and Roman philosophy after Israel was conquered by the Greeks and later by the Romans. Ibn Kaspi gives three reasons for loss of knowledge. The first is that conquering armies have the power to take knowledge by force, along with everything else. He argues that the Greeks and Romans not only stole this wisdom from the Jews, but claimed it as their own. Right or wrong, this is the way of the world: history is written by the conqueror. The second reason Ibn Kaspi gives is that losing their kingdom puts the survivors into a desperate state of political instability and insecurity. Lacking a stable political environment makes it difficult, if not impossible, for a prophet to focus his mind sufficiently to achieve prophecy. Add to this a state of mourning over their loss and their ensuing struggle for survival in a hostile land, and it is not surprising that this knowledge was lost to the Jews. The third reason Ibn Kaspi gives for their loss of knowledge is that the secrets of the divine chariot are embedded in the very structure of the Hebrew language. This, too, was lost by the Jews as they were forced, in exile, to adopt the languages of other nations. Succeeding generations forgot Hebrew and thus lost access to the deeper truths in the Bible. This made the survival of the Jewish religious and intellectual heritage even more problematic, because the Bible was never intended to transmit all knowledge of Hebrew, but relied on the continuation a living and fluid Hebrew language.

Beyond the problem of recovering the Hebrew language, Ibn Kaspi's two-pronged approach to biblical history requires the correct method of reading the Bible. First, it must be understood that the Bible is written for multiple audiences and imparts a level of knowledge suitable to each. This is in keeping with its goal, which is to improve its readers by guiding each of them to a higher intellectual and moral level: different readers to different levels, depending, of course, on the level they have already attained. Ibn Kaspi contrasts this disparagingly with the New Testament which, he says, reserves deeper knowledge for the few, but leaves the uneducated with false imaginative teachings. He argues that in order to accomplish the difficult task of imparting different lessons to different people, the Hebrew Bible contains intentional contradictions corresponding to the seventh kind of contradiction described by in Maimonides. This is a contradiction that occurs between a statement that is easily understood but false and another statement that is hidden but true. This type of contradiction is created deliberately, Maimonides argues, in order to shield the unphilosophical masses from philosophical truths that would harm them. But deep philosophical truths are also hidden by other methods as well: by structuring the text in such a way that it has different, contradictory parts; by dispersing ideas throughout the Bible, and out of logical order; by leaving empty spaces in the text, but indicating to careful readers that something has been left out, or hidden; by repetition of key phrases either for emphasis, or in order to fix them in the reader's memory; and finally, by selectively revealing or concealing important information. These methods reveal and conceal simultaneously, providing direction to serious students of the Bible, assisting the student while preventing profound truths to those who are not ready to receive them.

The second thing that Ibn Kaspi thinks a serious student of the Hebrew Bible must understand is that the God of the Bible is the first cause of existence, but He is not a proximate cause of events in the sublunar world. This means that He does not know all particular future contingencies. This is why Ibn Kaspi refers to God as the "Lord of intellectual divination" (*'adon ha-shi 'ur ha-sikhli*) who knows all the future possibilities, but does not know with any certainty which of these possibilities will actually occur. In other words, He portrays God as being something like an expert "investor" who understands the stock market and can predict the success or failure of a particular stock, but cannot know for certain how all the different factors that can affect it will actually work out. If, as Ibn Kaspi argues, God does not directly intervene in human affairs, this means that our fate is not already determined by divine ordinance, which of course means that we are partially on our own. But it also means that we have human freedom to act for good or ill. This also means we have human freedom to accumulate and disseminate knowledge. God's non-interference in human affairs does not take away from the Bible's status, as a divine document, Ibn Kaspi argues. He sees it as a text whose divinity rests, not in God having written every line, though he sometimes makes this argument, but in its being written in Hebrew. Hebrew is the only language that mirrors nature, Ibn Kaspi argues, and to such a degree that he thinks it is possible to understand all the secrets of both natural and divine science simply through the study of the Hebrew language. This is because, he also argues, each Hebrew root expresses a phenomenon or principle in the natural world and all the different words deriving from each root reflect, in some way, that same, which in turn corresponds to a natural truth.

In all of this, Ibn Kaspi presents a remarkable vision of the Bible. He sees it as able to guide the simple and the wise alike to higher intellectual and moral levels, able to unite political realism with moral and intellectual progress, and contains all knowledge of natural and divine science.

# Notes

## Preface

1. Alexander Green, *The Virtue Ethics of Levi Gersonides* (New York, 2016).

2. Leopold Zunz, "On Rabbinical Literature (1818)," in *A Jew in the Modern World*, eds. Paul Mendes Flohr and Jehuda Reinharz (Oxford, 1995), p. 222.

3. Abraham Geiger, "Excerpts from Geiger's Works," in *Abraham Geiger and Liberal Judaism: The Challenge of the Nineteenth Century*, ed. Max Wiener (Philadelphia, 1962), pp. 155–57, 178.

4. Heinrich Graetz, *The Structure of Jewish History and Other Essays*, trans. Ismar Schorsch (New York, 1975), pp. 74–124.

5. Eliezer Schweid, "The Rejection of the Diaspora in Zionist Thought: Two Approaches," *Studies in Zionism* 5, no. 1 (1984), pp. 43–70.

6. Yitzhak F. Baer, *Galut* (New York, 1947), p. 118.

7. Yehezkel Kaufman, *Exile and Alienation*, vol. 1–2 (Tel-Aviv, 1929–1930) and Schweid, "The Rejection of the Diaspora," p. 50.

8. Yoav Gelber, "The History of Zionist Historiography," in *Making Israel*, ed. Benny Morris (Michigan, 2007), p. 50, and David Myers, "History as Ideology: The Case of Ben-Zion Dinur, Zionist Historian 'Par Excellence,'" *Modern Judaism* 8, no. 2 (1988), pp. 167, 176–77.

9. Nathan Rotenstreich, "Gershom Scholem's Conception of Jewish Nationalism," in *Gershom Scholem: The Man and His Work*, ed. Paul Mendes-Flohr (Albany, 1994), p. 113: "the central theme in Scholem's discussions of Zionism is not the return of the nation to the land, but its return to the plan of history which means the acceptance of the responsibility for itself."

10. Cf. For alternative readings of Scholem on the demonic, see: David Biale, *Gershom Scholem: Kabbalah and Counter-History* (Cambridge, 1982), p. 4; Moshe Idel, *Old Worlds, New Mirrors* (Philadelphia, 2010), pp. 102–05 ("Scholem's Reading of Jewish History as Demonic"); and Vivian Liska, *German-Jewish*

*Thought and its Afterlife* (Indiana, 2017), pp. 112–22 ("Reading Scholem and Benjamin on the Demonic").

11. Gershom Scholem, "Reflections on Modern Jewish Studies (1944)," in *On the Possibility of Jewish Mysticism in Our Time and Other Essays*, ed. Avraham Shapira and trans. Jonathan Chipman (Philadelphia, 1997), p. 53.

12. Ibid., pp. 63–64.

13. Ibid., pp. 57–58.

14. For an extended discussion of this comparison, see: Warren Zev Harvey, "Two Jewish Approaches to Evil in History," in *Wrestling with God: Jewish Theological Responses during and after the Holocaust*, eds. Steven Katz, Shlomo Biderman and Gershon Greenberg (Oxford, 2007), pp. 326–31.

15. Scholem, *Major Trends in Jewish Mysticism* (New York, 1946), pp. 35–37.

16. Scholem, "Against the Myth of the German-Jewish Dialogue," in *On Jews and Judaism in Crisis: Selected Essays* (New York, 1976), pp. 61–64.

17. For Scholem's response to Jabotinsky, see: Biale, "Gershom Scholem on Nihilism and Anarchism," *Rethinking History* 19, no. 1, pp. 66–67.

18. Scholem, "Ha-Matara ha-Sofit," *She'foteinu* 2 (August 1931), p. 156. English translation from Biale, *Gershom Scholem: Kabbalah and Counter-History*, p. 104.

19. Scholem, "Redemption Through Sin," in *The Messianic Idea and Other Essays in Jewish Spirituality* (New York, 1971), pp. 95–96: "Whether or not Jewish history will be able to endure this entry into the concrete realm without perishing in the crisis of the Messianic claim which has virtually been conjured up—that is the question which out of his great and dangerous past the Jew of this age poses to his present and to his future."

20. Gershom Scholem, *Explications and Implications: Writings on Jewish Heritage and Renaissance* (Tel-Aviv, 1989), p. 81. Translation by Nitzan Lebovic, "Finally, This Author Puts the Great Gershom Scholem in Context," *Haaretz* May 2, 2015.

# Introduction

1. This brief biography of Ibn Kaspi is based on the scholarship of the last hundred years which has worked to uncover and piece together the various details of Ibn Kaspi's life that he hints to in his writings. See: Ernest Renan, *Les Écrivains Juifs Français du XIVe Siècle* (Paris, 1893), pp. 131–36; Heinrich Gross, *Gallia Judaica* (Paris, 1897), pp. 67–71; Richard Emery, "Documents Concerning Jewish Scholars in Perpignan in the 14th and 15th Centuries," *Michael* 4 (1976), pp. 27–48; Ram Ben-Shalom, "The Unwritten Travel Journal to the East of Joseph Ibn Caspi," *Pe'amim* 145 (2016), pp. 143–146; Moshe Kahan, "Joseph Ibn

Kaspi—New Biographical Data," *Pe'amim* (forthcoming); and Adrian Sackson, *Portrait of a Hebrew Philosopher in Medieval Provence* (Leiden, 2017), pp. 24–56.

2. Ibn Kaspi's attempt to synthesize Maimonides and Ibn Ezra has been discussed by both Hannah Kasher and Yechiel Tzeitkin. See: Hannah Kasher, *Joseph Ibn Caspi as a Philosophical Exegete* (Bar-Ilan University, 1982), p. 19; Ibid., "Joseph Ibn Kaspi's Aristotelian Interpretation and Fundamentalist Interpretation of the Book of Job," *Daat* 20 (1988), p. 119; Yechiel Tzeitkin, *The Characteristics of Biblical Exegesis in the Works of Peshat Commentators of the Maimonidean School of Provence in the 13th and 14th Centuries* (Bar-Ilan University, 2011), pp. 143–53. This point fits well with Tamas Visi's thesis that the conflict between Maimonideans and anti-Maimonideans was articulated in the defense of either Rashi or Ibn Ezra as the more authoritative biblical commentator. See: Tamas Visi, "Ibn Ezra, a Maimonidean Authority: The Evidence of the Early Ibn Ezra Supercommentaries," in *The Cultures of Maimonideanism: New Approaches to the History of Jewish Thought*, ed. James T. Robinson (Leiden, 2009), p. 94.

3. SHK, p. 133.

4. Sackson, *Portrait of a Hebrew Pholosopher*, p. 32.

5. TIK, p. 8.

6. AS II. P. 87.

7. TIK, p. 95, 118. Abraham Grossman, "A Social Controversy in Biblical Commentaries of Rabbi Joseph Ibn Kaspi," in *Studies in Hebrew Poetry and Jewish Heritage*, eds. Ephraim Hazan and Joseph Yahalom (Ramat Gan, 2006), pp. 103–24; and Ibid., "Contempt for Women on Philosophical Grounds: Joseph Ibn Kaspi," *Zion* 68 (2003), pp. 41–67. However, Sackson's recent study of Ibn Kaspi's *Terumat Kesef* challenges Grossman's conclusion that Ibn Kaspi held mysoginistic opinions. See: Sackson, *Portrait of a Hebrew Philosopher*, pp. 211–18.

8. The theory that Ibn Kaspi's marriage dissolved arises from very negative statements he makes about women and marriage in his writings. Ibn Kaspi surprisingly praises Christian scholars for appreciating the *Guide*. See YD, pp. 149–50: "So it is recorded of Rabbi Meir: he ate the kernel, and threw away the husk. This is the method pursued nowadays by Christian scholars. They highly esteem the *Guide*, although it contains certain passages opposed to the Christian faith."

9. The translations of the titles of Ibn Kaspi's works follows that of Barry Mensch in QK, pp. 9–10. The thesis of this book is that the order that Ibn Kaspi wrote his many books is not important for the argument being developed here. But there are discussions about the order that Ibn Kaspi composed these works. See: See Kasher. "Introduction," in SK, pp. 16–27.

10. The two manuscripts of QK, p. 10 describe the title differently, one describing the basin in the singular, the other the basins in the plural.

11. This was a point of discussion among nineteenth-century scholars. See: Renan, *Les Écrivains*, pp. 477–78 and Gross, *Gallia Judaica*, pp. 70. The scholarly

consensus was that Ibn Kaspi was born in Argentière until recent findings by Kahan questioning that conclusion and proposing that Argentière may refer to the family's place of origin. See: Kahan, "New Biographical Data," pp. 12–13.

12. QK, p. 9. This is a reference to Gen. 37:28.
13. Gen. 44:2 and QK, p. 26.
14. Gen. 42:35.
15. QK, p. 38 and TAK, pp. 41–47.
16. *Guide* III 32.
17. This point may be reinforced by Ibn Kaspi's interpretation of God's command to Moses to "let them make Me a sanctuary, that I may dwell among them. According to all that I show thee, the pattern of the tabernacle, and the pattern of all the furniture thereof, even so shall ye make it" (Exodus 25:8–9). At *Menorat Kesef* (AS II, p. 98), he argues that the verse indicates that Moses saw the divine chariot which is the three realms of nature, referred to as "the heavenly sanctuary," and used that as a model in constructing the tabernacle and its vessels, so that Moses or a high priest could imagine the secret of the three realms of the Divine Chariot through carrying out the ritual practices there.
18. Exod. 28:43, 29:30.
19. QK, p. 9.
20. I Kings 8:13.
21. QK, p. 40.
22. Exod. 26:19.
23. Ibid. 26:32.
24. I Chron. 28:16.
25. Ibid. 28:15.
26. Esth. 1:7 and QK, p. 19.
27. Esther Rabba 2:1, 2:11 and Targum Rishon 1:7. For a longer discussion, see: Aaron Koller, *Esther in Ancient Jewish Thought* (Cambridge, 2014), pp. 182–83.
28. Isadore Twersky phrases it well in stating that "his name was mentioned in standard works and histories accompanied by encyclopedia-like blurbs, bibliographical summations, or stereotype characterizations—varying in length from a few lines to a few pages." See: Isadore Twersky, "Joseph Ibn Kaspi—Portrait of a Medieval Jewish Intellectual," in *Studies in Medieval Jewish History and Literature*, ed. Isadore Twersky (Cambridge, 1979), p. 231.
29. Gross, *Gallia Judaica*, pp. 67–69; Renan, *Les Écrivains*, pp. 131–201; and Moritz Steinschneider, "Josef Caspi," in *Gesammelte Schriften*, eds. Heinrich Malter and Alexander Marx (Berlin, 1925), pp. 89–135.
30. For Husik, "none of these men stands out as an independent thinker with a strong individuality, carrying forward in any important and authoritative degree the work of the great Maimonides" and for Guttmann, the only mention of Ibn Kaspi is that "he repeatedly attempted to interpret Maimonides' devia-

tions from Aristotelianism, especially his polemic against the doctrine of the eternity of the world, as a mere accommodation on the part of the master to conventional religious views." See: Isaac Husik, *A History of Mediaeval Jewish Philosophy* (New York, 1940), p. 329 and Julius Guttmann, *Philosophies of Judaism: A History of Jewish Philosophy from Biblical Times to Franz Rosenzweig* (New York, 1973), p. 223.

31. Colette Sirat, *A History of Jewish Philosophy in the Middle Ages* (Cambridge, 1985), pp. 322–30 and Eliezer Schweid, *The Classic Jewish Philosophers*, trans. Leonard Levin (Leiden, 2010), pp. 318–19. Schweid summarizes his reading of Ibn Kaspi in one succinct sentence: "If we could characterize his approach in one sentence, it would be striving to break the tension that accumulated around Maimonides' teachings by spilling its secrets and revealing Maimonides' views on dangerous topics as he understood them, so that they would be obvious to any reader of the *Guide*." This is a surprising conclusion since Ibn Kaspi appears to hide many of his ideas as much as he reveals others.

32. Hannah Kasher, "Joseph Kaspi," *Stanford Encyclopedia of Philosophy*. October 16, 2013. Web. http://plato.stanford.edu/entries/kaspi-joseph/

33. Adrian Sackson frames Ibn Kaspi's originality nicely in stating "Ibn Kaspi may not have written a comprehensive philosophical or theological book; but, as I will argue, he attempted to mould an ambitious philosophical *curriculum*" (Sackson, *Portrait of a Hebrew Philosopher*, p. 7).

34. Shlomo Pines, "On the Probability of the Re-Establishment of a Jewish State according to Ibn Kaspi and Spinoza," *Iyyun* 14 (1963), pp. 289–317 and Twersky, "Joseph Ibn Kaspi," pp. 238–42.

35. It is very useful to speak of his view of history as accidental to contrast this model with Hegel's teleological philosophy of history. Hegel argued that history is rational and purposeful, while Ibn Kaspi held that it is accidental. Since *anything* can happen, it is also possible that the Jews will re-establish their polity in the Land of Israel. For a recent critique of the proto-Zionist reading of Ibn Kaspi, see: Sackson, *Portrait of a Hebrew Philosopher*, pp. 236–42.

36. BT Yebamot 71a.

37. Salo Baron, "The Historical Outlook of Maimonides," *Proceedings of the American Academy of Jewish Research* 6 (1934–1935), pp. 5–113; J. J. Ross, "Maimonides and Progress—Maimonides' Concept of History," in *Hevrah vi-Historia*, ed. Yehezkel Cohen (Jerusalem, 1980), pp. 529–42; David Novak, "Does Maimonides have a Philosophy of History?" *Proceedings of the Academy for Jewish Philosophy* 4 (1983), pp. 397–420; Amos Funkenstein, *Perceptions of Jewish History* (Berkeley, 1993), pp. 131–68; Kenneth Seeskin, "Maimonides' Sense of History," *Jewish History* 18, no. 2/3 (2004), pp. 129–45; and Micha Goodman, "History and Meta-History in the Posture of Maimonides," in *Bedarkhey Shalom: Studies in Jewish Thought Presented to Shalom Rosenberg*, eds. Benjamin Ish-Shalom and Amichai Bernholz (Jerusalem, 2007), pp. 243–53.

38. *Guide* I 2, p. 24. Maimonides makes a similar comment in the *Mishnah*, *'Im Perush Mosheh ben Maimon* [*Commentary on the Mishna*], trans. Joseph Qafiḥ (Jerusalem, 1965), vol. ii, p. 140 where he compares heretical works to "those found among the Arabs: books of chronicles, on the government of kings, genealogies of the Arabs, and books of songs, and similar books which have no wisdom and material purpose, but are only a waste of time" (English translation of Abraham P. Socher, "Of Divine Cunning and Prolonged Madness: Amos Funkenstein on Maimonides' Historical Reasoning," *Jewish Social Studies* 6, no. 1 [1999], p. 9).

39. Baron. "The Historical Outlook of Maimonides," p. 11. Though Baron speculates at pp. 8 and 10 that the Arab historical works Maimonides was reading were aimed at a popular audience containing stories of love affairs and hatred of Jews, Maimonides would have appreciated some Arab historians who were more philosophically inclined. Novak, "Does Maimonides have a Philosophy of History?" p. 398 sharply undermines the foundations of Baron's critique of Maimonides in pointing out how "Maimonides does have a philosophy of history, but one that Baron has missed because of his peculiarly modern, post-Hegelian, assumptions about history. History, for a pre-Hegelian, medieval thinker like Maimonides has its ontological foundation in a theory of nature with which a theory of time is inextricably linked."

40. Aristotle, *Poetics*, trans. Seth Benardete and Michael Davis (Indiana, 2002), p. 26 (1.9, 1451a36–1451b10).

41. MT I Idolatry 1.2, p. 63.

42. *Guide* III 29.

43. Ibid., III 32.

44. Ibid., I 36.

45. Novak, "Does Maimonides have a Philosophy of History?" p. 412 and Moshe Halbertal. *People of the Book: Canon, Meaning and Authority* (Cambridge, 1997), pp. 59–63.

46. MT I Intro, pp. 3–6.

47. Another way of framing this point is to state as Sackson does that "Ibn Kaspi's orientation with respect to these matters is, unsurprisingly, heavily influenced by the writings of Maimonides, although Ibn Kaspi is often explicit about matters regarding which Maimonides is silent" (Sackson, *Portrait of a Hebrew Philosopher*, p. 220).

48. TIK, pp. 64–65.

49. One could respond that the entire *Guide* is an interpretation of biblical parables and Midrash. See: James Diamond, *Maimonides and the Hermeneutics of Concealment: Deciphering Scripture and Midrash in the* Guide of the Perplexed (Albany, 2002). What differentiates Ibn Kaspi's project, as I discuss below, is his analysis of the range of hermeneutical tools of biblical narrative.

50. SHK, p. 57.

51. It was often assumed that Samuel Ibn Tibbon merely translated Maimonides into Hebrew, while more recent scholarship has also shown that he was the first interpreter of Maimonides. Maimonides' thought in the *Guide* contains a tension between an Orthodox Aristotelian (or proto-Averroistic) science that emphasizes God as the first cause of the laws of nature and a Neoplatonic Avicennian skepticism about the ability to know God's nature and providence. Ibn Tibbon interprets Maimonides following the former approach and believed this was Maimonides' true position, as he articulated to him in a famous letter. See: Steven Harvey, "Did Maimonides' Letter to Samuel Ibn Tibbon Determine Which Philosophers Would Be Studied by Later Jewish Thinkers?" *Jewish Quarterly Review* 83, no. 1/2 (Jul.–Oct., 1992), pp. 51–70 and Aviezer Ravitzky, "Samuel Ibn Tibbon and the Esoteric Character of the *Guide of the Perplexed*," *AJS Review* 6 (1981), pp. 87–123.

52. Carlos Fraenkel, *From Maimonides to Samuel Ibn Tibbon: The Transformation of the* Dalalat al Ha'irin *into the* Moreh ha-Nevukhim (Jerusalem, 2007).

53. Rafael Jospe, "Rejecting Moral Virtue as the Ultimate Human End," in *Studies in Islamic and Judaic Traditions*, ed. William Brinner and Stephen Ricks (Denver, 1986), pp. 185–204 and Yehuda Halper, "*Da'at Harambam* and *Da'at* Samuel Ibn Tibbon: on the Meanings of the Hebrew Term *Da'at*, and their Relationship to the Central Questions of the *Mishneh Torah* and the *Guide of the Perplexed*," *Daat* 83 (2017), pp. 47–68.

54. Nonetheless, Gersonides too is interested in history, but primarily as material for stories with morals, which have pedagogic value, e.g., to teach moral virtues.

55. This model is similar to the paradigm articulated by Augustine in the *City of God* that distinguishes between the history of the "City of Man" as represents the endless competition of states and empires driven by a lust for glory, and the history of "City of God," which represents the cumulative historical process of educating humanity about the teachings of Christ. See: Augustine, *City of God*, trans. Marcus Dods (Peabody, MA, 2009), p. 430 (14.28) where the two cities are contrasted. The City of Man is well explicated in 4.4 entitled "How Like Kingdoms Without Justice are to Robberies" (p. 101) and in 10.14 where he develops the historical evolution of the City of God that "the education of the human race. represented by the people of God, has advanced, like that of an individual, through certain epochs, or, as it were, ages, so that it might gradually rise from earthly to heavenly things, and from the visible to the invisible" (p. 285). While there is no evidence that Ibn Kaspi read Augustine's writings directly, Augustine's philosophy of history permeated all later Christian thinking, such that later Christians utilize his paradigm without needing to have been directly quoting with Augustine or agreeing with him on all points.

56. Ibn Kaspi never explicitly reveals if he actually read works of Christian philosophy or theology or which ones or if his knowledge of Christianity is

based purely on oral conversations. If the latter, he does not reveal the depth of the conversations he had. He does tell us that he has respect for the Christian scholarship on the Hebrew Bible and the *Guide*. Isaiah Dimant suggests that "In spite of Christian polemics, Caspi holds a lot of respect for Christain scholars and Christan scholastics. He admits that many Christian scholars apprehend the deeper philosophic meaning of Scripture. He further argues that some Christian scholars know Maimonides' teachings better than some Jewish scholars and make better use of these teachings to support religious doctrines." See: Isaiah Dimant, *Exegesis, Philosophy and Language in the Writing of Joseph Ibn Caspi* (Dissertation, University of California, Los Angeles, 1979), p. 114. While Ibn Kaspi may not have received these two models of history directly from reading Augustine's *City of God*, Augustine's theology permeated Christian thought. See M. W. F. Stone "Augustine and Medieval Philosophy" in *The Cambridge Companion to Augustine*, eds. Eleonore Stump and Norman Kretzmann (Cambridge, 2006), pp. 253–66.

# Chapter 1

1. *Politics*, 1.2, p. 37. Aristotle's *Politics* does not appear to have been translated into Arabic and therefore was not available to Jewish thinkers living in the Christian world until at least the fifteenth century, so Aristotle's political ideas were available to medieval Jewish thinkers only indirectly through statements in Aristotle's *Nicomachean Ethics* and in the works of Islamic philosophers such as Al-Farabi, Ibn Bajja, and Averroes. Shlomo Pines, "Aristotle's Politics in Arabic Philosophy," *Israel Oriental Studies* 5 (1975), pp. 150–60; Abraham Melamed, "Aristotle's *Politics* in Medieval and Renaissance Jewish Thought." *Peamim* 51 (1993): 27–69; Muhsin Mahdi, *Alfarabi and the Foundation of Islamic Political Philosophy* (Chicago, 2001), pp. 34–39; and Remi Brague, *The Law of God: The Philosophical History of an Idea* (Chicago, 2007), pp. 115–17. A version of this statement appears at Aristotle, *NE* 1.7 (1097b11) and 9.9 (1169b19). It seems very likely that Maimonides had an Arabic copy of the *Nicomachean Ethics* by the time he wrote the *Guide* in Egypt. See: Steven Harvey, "The Source of Quotations from Aristotle's *Nicomachean Ethics* in Maimonides' *Guide of the Perplexed* and Shem Tov Ibn Falaquera's *The Guide to the Guide*," *Jerusalem Studies in Jewish Thought* 14 (1998), pp. 87–102. This statement also appears in Abu Nasr Al-Farabi, *On the Perfect State (Mabadi' Ara Ahl al-Madina al-Fadila)*, trans. Richard Walzer (Oxford, 1985), p. 229 (15.1).
2. *Guide* II 40, p. 381.
3. Ibid., p. 382.
4. Ibid., pp. 383–84.
5. Eccles. 3:16.
6. Gen. 31:25.

7. Exod. 1:8.
8. AS I, p. 199.
9. Averroes, Averroes on Plato's Republic, trans. and ed. Ralph Lerner (Ithaca, 1974), p. 72 (61.14–15).
10. Adrian Sackson organized a critical edition of Ibn Kaspi's epitome on Averroes' Commentary on Plato's Republic. Terumat Kesef. See: Sackson, Joseph Ibn Kaspi: Portrait of a Hebrew Philosopher, pp. 263–94. He also dedicates his fourth chapter ("The Republic in Hebrew: Ibn Kaspi and Platonic Political Thought") to analyzing the significance of Kaspi's epitome. See: Ibid., pp. 170–219.
11. Compare Al-Farabi, On the Perfect State, pp. 237–43 (15.6–8) to Ibn Bajjah, "Rule of the Solitary (Tadbīru'l-Mutawaḥḥid)" in D. M. Dunlop, "Ibn Bājjah's Tadbīru'l-Mutawaḥḥid (Rule of the Solitary)," Journal of the Royal Asiatic Society of Great Britain & Ireland (New Series) 77, no. 1–2 (1945), pp. 77–78. For a comparison, see: Lawrence Berman, "The Ideal State of the Philosophers and Prophetic Laws," in A Straight Path: Studies in Medieval Philosophy and Culture. Essays in Honor of Arthur Hyman, ed. Ruth Link-Salinger (Washington, 1988), pp. 11–15, and Steven Harvey, "The Place of the Philosopher in the City According to Ibn Bājjah," in The Political Aspects of Islamic Philosophy: Essays in Honor of Muhsin S. Mahdi, ed. Charles E. Buttersworth (Cambridge, 1992), pp. 199–233.
12. Sackson, Joseph Ibn Kaspi, p. 190: "Ibn Kaspi's purpose in summarising the Republic (and the Ethics) thus seems to be primarily educational: His intention was to transmit knowledge rather than to formulate new philosophical arguments."
13. Ralph Lerner, "Introduction," Averroes on Plato's Republic, p. xv: "it is no simple matter to tell in every instance whether Averroes is speaking in his own name. The gentle glidings from 'he says' to 'we say' and back again (with variations en route) lull the senses of the good-natured reader who nods along as Averroes repeats whatever Plato 'says' or 'asserts' or 'holds' or 'explains.'"
14. TEK, pp. 288–93 and Averroes, Averroes on Plato's Republic, pp. 75–94. A summary of the end of the second treatise and a summary of the third treatise are missing. While this may be coincidental (perhaps this is simply the parts of the manuscript he had access to), it seems too coincidental that he very poetically ends with a critique of philosophic politics and a defense of theoretical wisdom, while missing everything more political that follows.
15. Averroes, Averroes on Plato's Republic, pp. 75–78 (63.5–64.28).
16. TIK, p. 8.
17. AS I, p. 125. Grossman, "A Social Controversy," pp. 110–11.
18. Gen. 41:45.
19. MK, p. 83.
20. Gen. 44:15.
21. MK, p. 97.

22. TIK, p. 132.

23. SHK, 42, p. 102. Averroes' position is summarized in Howard Kreisel, *Prophecy: The History of an Idea in Medieval Jewish Philosophy* (Dordrecht, 2001), pp. 340–46. Averroes' commentary on Aristotle's *Parva Naturalia* (*ha-Ḥush ve-ha-Muḥash*) was translated into Hebrew by Moses Ibn Tibbon in 1254 and has been edited and translated by Harry Blumberg. See: Averroes, *Epitome of Aristotle's Parva Naturalia*, trans. to Hebrew Moses Ibn Tibbon and ed. Harry Blumberg (Cambridge, 1954) and *Epitome of Aristotle's Parva naturalia*, trans. to English Harry Blumberg (Cambridge, 1961).

24. Ibn Kaspi expicitly references the *Parva Naturalia* (*ha-Ḥush ve-ha-Muḥash*) in his writings, such as in AM ('*Amudei Kesef*), p. 44 and AS II (*Menorat Kesef*), p. 93.

25. Deut. 18:18–22; Quoted in SHK, 41, pp. 101–02.

26. SHK, 42, p. 102.

27. Ibid., 65, p. 122.

28. Ibid., 70, p. 130; 75, pp. 137–38.

29. The language of "necessary future" and "contingent future" appears similar to language used in Christian debates during Ibn Kaspi's life over God's knowledge of future events rooted in how to interpret Aristotle's *On Interpretation*, Ch 9. Pines points this out, but does not feel he could prove a direct scholastic source that influenced Ibn Kaspi. See: Pines, "On the Probability," p. 295. Likewise, here I am not aiming to prove whether Ibn Kaspi was influenced by Christian scholastics, but instead to piece together the different facets of his overall system that he is building.

30. SHK., 63, p. 118; 65, p. 122.

31. Pines drew this connection which is not explicit at Pines, "On the Probability," pp. 309–10 referencing Aristotle, *On the Heavens*, 1.12.

32. *Guide* II 1, p. 247.

33. SHK, 65, p. 122.

34. GK, 9, p. 186.

35. Gen. 15:13. This point is explicated in full detail in GK, pp. 177–93, though one can find a shorter version as well in TIK, pp. 80–82.

36. GK, 9, pp. 189–90.

37. Ibid., p. 191.

38. In TAK, p. 21, Ibn Kaspi interestingly adds that God knew that the nation that would enslave the Israelites would be Egypt, but he did not want to reveal that secret to Abraham in Gen. 15:13 for whatever reason that was known to Him. Is this to teach Abraham that the event to occur to the Israelites in Egypt is a reflection of a necessary process in nature and is not *really* about the specifics of Egypt?

39. TAK, 8, p. 45. Sackson translation in Adrian Sackson, "Rationalistic Messianism and the Vicissitudes of History: The Final Chapter of Joseph Ibn Kaspi's *Tam ha-kesef*," *Zutot* 12 (2015), p. 11.

40. Gen. 25:23.

41. Gerson D. Cohen, "Esau as a Symbol in Early Medieval Thought," in *Jewish Medieval and Renaissance Studies*, ed. Alexander Altmann (Cambridge, 1967), pp. 19–48.

42. TAK, 5, p. 31.

43. There has not been much scholarly discussion of Ibn Kaspi's interpretation of the Book of Esther until recently where, in a series of articles by Robert Eisen and Hannah Kasher, they have debated Ibn Kaspi's intention in this text. See: Robert Eisen, "Joseph Ibn Kaspi on the Secret Meaning of the Scroll of Esther," *Revue des Études Juives* 160, no. 3–4 (2001), pp. 379–408; Hannah Kasher, "On the Book of Esther as an Allegory in the works of Joseph Ibn Kaspi: A Response to Robert Eisen in REJ 160/3–4," *Revue des Études Juives* 161, no. 3–4 (2002), pp. 459–64; Eisen, "Kaspi on Allegory in the Book of Esther: A Rejoinder to Hannah Kasher," *Revue des Études Juives* 163, no. 1–2 (2004), pp. 289–93.

44. For the different places where Ibn Kaspi subtly suggests this, see: Eisen, "Joseph Ibn Kaspi on the Secret Meaning of the Scroll of Esther," pp. 386–87. I will provide only one example here since Eisen goes into all the sources in his article. While Kasher challenges Eisen's thesis, they do come to some agreement by the end.

45. AS II, p. 39.

46. In the next section we will deal with the question of God's providence and how that related to political history.

47. Esth. 3:13.

48. Ibid. 8:11–12.

49. Eisen also fits Ibn Kaspi's reading of the Book of Esther into this category of prophecy. He says that "[Ibn] Kaspi views the story of Esther as an allegory showing how human beings can overcome negative prophetic predictions that reflect the changeless will of God by understanding the unstated conditions of those predictions" (Eisen, "Joseph Ibn Kaspi on the Secret Meaning of the Scroll of Esther," p. 401). I think Kasher is correct that we should not assume that this necessarily is related to the messianic era as these categories of prophecy are pretty consistent throughout Ibn Kaspi's writings (Kasher, "A Response to Robert Eisen," p. 464).

50. AS II, p. 32.

51. AS II, pp. 34–35.

52. Charles Manekin presents various solutions for how to reconcile freedom and determinism in Ibn Kaspi's thought: libertarian/incompatibility, determinist/compatibilist, libertarian/compatibilist, traditional and moderately esoteric. Perhaps an easier solution would be that Ibn Kaspi has two models of prophecy and those prophecies predicting a contingent future work within the libertarian model while prophecies predicting a necessary future work within the determinist model. See: Charles Manekin, "Ambiguities of Scriptural Exegesis:

Joseph Ibn Kaspi on God's Foreknowledge," in *Philosophers and the Jewish Bible*, eds. Charles Manekin and Robert Eisen (Maryland, 2008), pp. 97–111.

53. TAK, p. 20. English translation of this article and quotation is from *The Collected Articles of Shlomo Pines on Spinoza*, ed. Warren Zev Harvey (unpublished).

54. Pines, "Jewish Philosophy," in *Studies in the History of Jewish Thought: The Collected Works of Shlomo Pines*, vol. v, eds. Warren Zev Harvey and Moshe Idel (Jerusalem, 1997), p. 28. There is a similar statement and more detailed description in Hebrew in "On the Probability," p. 294.

55. Kasher, *Joseph Ibn Caspi as a Philosophical Exegete*, pp. 64–66; Eisen, "Joseph Ibn Kaspi on the Secret Meaning of the Scroll of Esther," p. 391n47; and Manekin, "Ambiguities of Scriptural Exegesis," pp. 79–81. Kasher proposes an alternative analogy: the prophet is more like a psychologist who can predict how an individual will act with more certainty by understanding the workings of their inner psyche.

56. GK, 23, pp. 274–75.

57. Gen. 34:30.

58. NE 6.11, 1143b, p. 130: "One ought to pay attention to the undemonstrated assertions and opinions of experienced and older people, or of the prudent, no less than to demonstrations, for because they have an experienced eye, they see correctly." Ibn Kaspi would have read it through Averroes' commentary. See: Averroes, *Averroes' Middle Commentary on Aristotle's Nicomachean Ethics in the Hebrew Version of Samuel ben Judah*, ed. Lawrence V. Berman (Jerusalem, 1999), pp. 218–19.

59. GK, 23, p. 276.

60. Ibid.

61. NE 6.9, 1142a12–16.

62. Esth. 1:13.

63. Ibn Kaspi, "Additions to Esther Commentary," in *Recensionen, Varianten und Ergänzüngen zu der Edition ['Aśarah kele kesef]*, ed. Isaac Last (Pressburg, 1904), p. 22. The quote is very similar to the previous line in *Gevia Kesef*: This point is discussed in Barry Walfish, *Esther in Medieval Garb: Jewish Interpretation of the Book of Esther in the Middle Ages* (Albany, 1993), p. 46.

64. Esth. 1:19.

65. Ibid. 1:20.

66. Here I am building on how Kasher reads the different pieces of the Esther story as metaphors in Ibn Kaspi's interpretation, though I am drawing a different conclusion. See: Kasher, "A Response to Robert Eisen," pp. 463–64.

67. Jon. 4:5.

68. GK, 17, p. 251.

69. Ibn Kaspi discusses the Book of Jonah in *'Adnei Kesef* (ADK II, pp. 102–03) and *Shulchan Kesef* (SHK, 69, p. 127) in terser fashions than he does

in *Gevia Kesef* and as a result does not reveal in the former two the process of how Jonah came to learn of the contingency of the prophecy.

70. AS II, pp. 91, 94 and AM, pp. 31–32.

71. Gen. 28:12.

72. *Guide* I 15, p. 41.

73. Ibn Kaspi focusses on how Jacob's ladder represents the threefold division of nature, while Maimonides hints that the parable should be divided into seven segments in *Guide* Intro, pp 12–13. James Diamond unpacks the possibility of what the division into seven segments would entail in Diamond, *Maimonides and the Hermeneutics of Concealment*, pp. 85–130.

74. This is referring to Exodus 33 and is not prohibiting Moses, at a later point in life such as before his death, from predicting the future.

75. AS II, pp. 93–94.

76. Michael Marmura, "Some Aspects of Avicenna's Theory of God's Knowledge of Particulars," *Journal of the American Oriental Society* 82, no. 3 (1962), pp. 299–311.

77. Maimonides lays out the differences between Moses and other prophets in the *Commentary on the Mishna* when expanding on the seventh of the thirteen principles of faith and in the *Mishneh Torah*, *Laws of the Foundations of the Torah* 7.2–6 and expands upon it further in the *Guide*. See: *Mishnah, 'Im Perush Mosheh ben Maimon* [Commentary on the Mishna], vol. iv, pp. 213–14; MT, pp. 41–42; *Guide* II 35, pp. 367–69.

78. TAK, 3, p. 21.

79. For a similar conclusion, see: Shalom Sadiq, "Natural Law and the Law of Moses in the Thought of R. Josef Ibn Kaspi," *Daat* 83 (2017), pp. 169–70. Sadiq writes in the English abstract: "In [Ibn] Kaspi's opinion, for if the masses were to understand that the Law of Moses constantly adjusts to circumstances, they would choose to change the law according to their corporeal temptations. This is the reason that Moses wrote in Deuteronomy (4:2) 'Ye shall not add unto the word which I command you, neither shall ye diminish from it.'"

80. *Guide* II 48, pp. 409–12. The influence of *Guide* II 48 on Ibn Kaspi has been discussed in Sackson, *Portrait of a Hebrew Philosopher*, pp. 156–69.

81. AS II, pp. 87–90.

82. TAK, 3, 20.

83. Gen. 6:1–22.

84. Ibid 18:16–33.

85. BT Shabbat 55a.

86. ADK II, p. 102.

87. Gen. 6:5.

88. TIK, p. 62.

89. Ibid.

90. Ibid., p. 63.

91. MK, p. 57.
92. Gen. 13:13.
93. Ibid. 19:25.
94. ADK II, p. 36.
95. Ezek. 16:49–50.
96. ADK II, p. 37.
97. Jon. 3:4.
98. Ibid. 3:10.
99. Ibid. 3:5–9.

100. Ehud Benor analyzes Maimonides' model of prayer across his different writings and concludes that "he saw it as an act that brings a person to realize the true nature of God, to experience God's presence, and to inculcate this realization in all dimensions of life." See: Ehud Benor, *Worship of the Heart: A Study in Maimonides' Philosophy of Religion* (Albany, 1995), p. 1. We see this approach to prayer echoed across Ibn Kaspi's writings. For example, MK, p. 49 on Genesis 13:4 where he says that prayer educates us in the two first laws of Maimonides *Mishneh Torah*—to know there is a first existent and that He is one.

101. Jon. 3:9.
102. SHK, 69, p. 128.
103. AM, p. 10.

104. The history of the interpretation of Genesis 49:10 specifically has been delved into by scholars. See: Adolf Posnanski, *Shiloh: Ein Beitrag zur Geschichte der Messiaslehre—Downloaded; i. Theil, Die Auslegung von Genesis c. 49, v. 10 im Altertum bis zu Ende des Mittelalters.* Leipsig, 1904; Robert Chazan, *Fashioning Jewish Identity in Medieval Western Christendom* (Cambridge, 2009), pp. 181–97; Ibid., "Genesis 49:10 in Thirteenth-Century Christian Missionizing," in *New Perspectives on Jewish-Christian Relations: In Honor of David Berger* (Leiden, 2012), pp. 93–108; and Shaye Cohen. "Does Rashi's Torah Commentary Respond to Christianity? A Comparison of Rashi with Rashbam and Bekhor Shor," in *The Idea of Biblical Interpretation: Essays in Honor of James L. Kugel*, eds. Hindy Najman and Judith H. Newman (Leiden, 2004), pp. 452–59.

105. Gen. 49:8–10. Here I am following Robert Chazan (*Fashioning Jewish Identity*, p. 186) in leaving the last line in transliterated Hebrew since the debate between Jews and Christians arises from how one understands the meaning and grammar of these words.

106. Christian sources that read Genesis 49:10 as predicting Christ include Augustine, *City of God*, p. 561 (18.6) and Justin Martyr, *The First Apology*, Chapters 32 and 54.

107. BT Sanhedrin 5a.
108. MK, p. 105.
109. Ibid.

110. Gen. 49:9.
111. MK, p. 105.
112. Gen. 49:10.
113. SAK, p. 654.
114. MK, p. 105. The Vulgate translation of Genesis 49:10 is "*non auferetur sceptrum de Iuda et dux de femoribus eius donec veniat qui mittendus est et ipse erit expectatio gentium.*" The Kings James translation reads "the sceptre shall not depart from Judah, nor a lawgiver from between his feet, until Shiloh come; and unto him shall the gathering of the people be."
115. See: SHK, 1-9, pp. 57-66. This will be discussed further in chapter 3.
116. Lam. 1:5.
117. Ibid. 1:5.
118. AS II, p. 12. The evidence he gives that the transgressions were an error is Deuteronomy 32:28: "For they are a nation void of counsel, and there is no understanding in them." This will be discussed in greater detail in "Destruction of the First Temple" below.
119. This translation is based on Ibn Kaspi's definition of the other words: *ad ki yavo*: *ad* refers to a curtailment (MK, p. 105), *ki* refers to giving reason or cause (SHK, pp. 665-66); and *yavo* as presence where entering and leaving metaphorically refers to presence and absence (MK, p. 105).
120. MK, p. 106.
121. Ibid., p. 107.
122. *Guide* II Intro, p. 236.
123. Aristotle argues in *Physics* Book 7 that no motion is possible without force acting on the moving object, suggesting that there can be absence of motion if there is absence of force. This appears in Maimonides' twenty-five premises for the existence of God in premise numbers 8, 9, 13, and 17 (*Guide* II Intro, pp. 236-37).
124. BT Sanhedrin 5a.
125. MT XIV-E, p. 15. *Laws of Sanhedrin* 4:13: "The exilarchs of Babylon stand in the place of the king. They exercise authority over Israel everywhere and sit in judgment over the people, with or without the consent of the latter, as it is said: 'The scepter shall not depart from Judah' (Gen 49:10). This refers to the exilarchs of Babylon."
126. MK, p. 107.
127. *Sifra Deuteronomy 17*, 156 in *The Jewish Political Tradition*, vol. 1: Authority, eds. Michael Walzer, Menachem Lorberbaum, Noam J. Zohar (Yale, 2000), pp. 147-48.
128. MT, p. 1233-234 and Maimonides, *The Commandments (Sefer Ha-Mitzvoth)*, vol. i, trans. Charles B. Chavel (London, 1976), pp. 182-83, Positive Commandment #173.

129. Ibid., pp. 1243–1245.

130. Ibid., pp. 1234–1235. See: James Diamond, *Converts, Heretics, and Lepers: Maimonides and the Outsider* (Notre Dame, 2007), pp. 79–106 (Chapter 4: The King: The Ethics of Imperial Humility).

131. Leo Strauss pointed this out in an early unpublished piece in Leo Strauss, "On Abravanel's Critique of Monarchy (1937)," trans. Martin D. Yaffe, in *Reorientation: Leo Strauss in the 1930s*, eds. Martin D. Yaffe and Richard S. Ruderman (New York, 2014), pp. 267–68.

132. MK, p. 284.

133. ADK I, p. 15.

134. GK, 15, pp. 240–41.

135. Prov. 6:6–8.

136. AS I, pp. 24, 92. He would have been reading *De Animalibus* through Jacob ben Machir ibn Tibbon's 1302 Hebrew translation of Averroes' commentary translated into Hebrew as *Sefer Ba'alei Ḥayyim*. In Aristotle's *History of Animals*, trans. D'Arcy Wentworth Thompson, 1.1, he states that "social creatures are such as have some one common object in view; and this property is not common to all creatures that are gregarious. Such social creatures are man, the bee, the wasp, the ant, and the crane. Again, of these social creatures some submit to a ruler, others are subject to no governance: as, for instance, the crane and the several sorts of bee submit to a ruler, whereas ants and numerous other creatures are every one his own master." He argues that the Talmudic story at BT Hulin 57b comes to the same conclusion that Aristotle does.

137. Isa. 5:29.

138. ADK I, p. 92.

139. SAK, p. 682.

140. Prov. 23:1.

141. AS I, p. 111.

142. Prov. 30:32.

143. AS I, p. 128.

144. TAK, 8, p. 42. Sackson translation in "Rationalistic Messianism," p. 6.

145. Hannah Kasher proposed that Ibn Kaspi began to write a commentary on Daniel and stopped in the middle, since in *Tam ha-Kesef* he points to Ibn Ezra's commentary on Daniel and writes that there is no reason to write a commentary in addition, which is merely extraneous.

146. ADK I, pp. 141–42.

147. Dan. 7:3–7.

148. Ibid. 7:23.

149. Ibid. 7:24.

150. Genesis Rabba 42:2, Leviticus Rabba 13:5 and 29:2.

151. For a discussion of the rabbinic scholarship surrounding Daniel 7, see: Rivkah Raviv, "The Talmudic Formulation of the Prophecies of the Four Kingdoms in the Book of Daniel," *Jewish Studies, an Internet Journal* 5 (2006), pp. 1–20.

152. Maimonides expounds his reading of Daniel 7 in his famous "Epistle to Yemen" where he says "from the prophecies of Daniel and Isaiah and from the statements of our sages it is clear that the advent of the Messiah will take place some time subsequent to the universal expansion of the Roman and Arab empires, which is an actuality today . . . The statement *horsemen in pairs* (Isaiah 21:7) refers to the two empires Edom and Ishmael. A similar interpretation of Daniel's vision concerning the image and the beasts is correct beyond doubt" (Maimonides, "The Epistle to Yemen," in *Epistles of Maimonides: Crisis and Leadership*, trans. Abraham Halkin and ed. David Hartman [Philadelphia, 1985], p. 121 and in *Iggerot*, trans. Joseph Qafi [Jerusalem, 1972], p. 48).

153. Ibn Ezra identifies the fourth animal as Islam in his commentary on Daniel 7:14. He criticizes those who want to predict Christianity's oppression of the Jews in the medieval period from God's statement about Jacob and Esau. Instead, he read Edom as simply an ancient people that was conquered in the time of the first animal and sees the Romans and Christians as a continuation of the Greeks (*yavan*) in the third animal. In his commentary to Genesis 27:40, he writes there that "and the sleepers who have not awoken from their foolish sleep will think that we are in the exile of Edom, but this is not so. Edom (Esau) was subject to Judah" (Abraham ibn Ezra, *Ibn Ezra's commentary on the Pentateuch*, vol. i, trans. H. Norman Strickman and Arthur M. Silver [New York, 1988], p. 270). He makes a similar point in commenting on Psalm 137:7 and Zechariah 11:15.

154. Moses Nahmanides, *Commentary on the Torah*, vol. i, trans. Charles Chavel (New York, 2005), Genesis 14:1 but in greater detail in "The Book of Redemption," in *Writings of the Ramban*, vol. ii, trans. Charles B. Chavel (New York, 1978), pp. 576–90. Especailly p. 690: "Even if there [were or] will be other empires in the world contemporaneously with those [four] kingdoms, Scripture does not consider them. He did not show their appearance to Daniel, for it was not necessary for Daniel to see them in order to know the duration of exile. It is well known that it was the Romans who exiled us in the days of Titus and Vespasian, not the Ishmaelites [Arabs]. Therefore, wherever we are, we are in the exile of Rome. . . ."

155. ADK I, p. 79, II, pp. 1, 25, 78, 100, 102, 113, 117.

156. ADK I, pp. 108, 160, II, pp. 25, 75, 100, 117, 124, 130, 139.

157. ADK II, 106–08, 124, 129, 139, 148–49. Ibn Kaspi follows Ibn Ezra in not differentiating between Greece and Rome as part of the third animal and sees Christianity as a continuation of it. He describes Rome as "of the organs of

Greece." See: TAK, 8, p. 42 (Sackson translation in "Rationalistic Messianism," p. 7) and *Menorat Kesef*, AS II, p. 131. *Sefer Yosipon* was the main historical source for medieval Jews, written by Joseph ben Gorion, a Jew living in southern Italy in either the 9th or the 10th century, claiming to be the Jewish-Roman historian Flavius Josephus. The work was a unique compilation of the *Book of Maccabees*, Josephus' *Jewish War*, and Pseudo-Hegesippus' *De excidio urbis Hierosolymitanae*.

158. TAK, 8, p. 42. Sackson translation in "Rationalistic Messianism," pp. 6–7.

159. Gen. 12:6.

160. TIK, p. 73. Ibn Kaspi's supercommentary on Ibn Ezra's *Commentary on the Torah* is only in manuscript form (Ms. Vatican 151). Visi notes that Ibn Kaspi does not comment on Genesis 12:6 in *Parshat Kesef*. There is another work entitled *An Explanation of Ibn Ezra's Secrets* that scholars doubt the authenticity of being written by Ibn Kaspi. See: Tamas Visi, *The Early Ibn Ezra Supercommentaries: A Chapter in Medieval Jewish Intellectual History* (PhD Thesis, Budapest, 2006), pp. 123, 279, and Hannah Kasher, "On the Question of the Authorship of the *Explanation of Ibn Ezra's Secrets* attributed to Joseph Ibn Kaspi," in *Alei Shefer: Studies in the Literature of Jewish Thought: Presented to Rabbi Dr. Alexander Shafran*, ed. Moshe Hallamish (Ramat-Gan, 1990), pp. 97–108.

161. MK, p. 47.

162. Ibid., pp. 67–68.

163. Ibid., p. 73.

164. TAK, 8, p. 42. Sackson translation in "Rationalistic Messianism," p. 6.

165. Tosefta 13:22, BT Yoma 9a–b, BT Baba Metzia 30b, BT Shabbat 119b.

166. Hannah Kasher looks at the influence of Maimonides' naturalistic and political approach to the destruction of the temples among Maimonides' medieval philosophic interpreters in Kasher, "'Why is the Land in Ruins?' (Jeremiah 9:11): Religious Transgression versus Natural Historical Process in the Writing of Maimonides and His Disciples," *Hebrew Union College Annual* 69 (1998), pp. 143–56.

167. Maimonides, "Letter on Astrology," in *A Maimonides Reader*, ed. Isadore Twersky (Springfield, NJ, 1972), p. 465.

168. Prov. 11:14.

169. AS I, p. 41.

170. TIK, p. 15.

171. TAK, 2, p. 10.

172. Ibid., 2, pp. 8–10.

173. Ibid., 2, p. 10 and ADK I, pp. 35–36.

174. II Sam. 12:10.

175. TAK, 2, p. 17.

176. Ibid., 7, p. 36.
177. Ibid., p. 47.
178. TIK, pp. 29–30; TAK, 7, pp. 37–40.
179. It is important to note that Ibn Kaspi does list other causes of the destruction mentioned by Jeremiah, such as breaking the sabbath (Jer. 17:21–26) and failure to execute justice and righteousness (Jer. 22:3–4) and sees them as all contributing to the destruction in relation to ignoring the words of the prophet, but not as direct as the actions of Zedekiah and the problematic actions of the kings preceding him (TAK, 7, p. 38).
180. ADK I, p. 79.
181. Ibid., p. 107.
182. MT, pp. 1243–245.
183. ADK I, p. 79.
184. MT, pp. 1244–245.
185. ADK I, p. 107.
186. Ibid., pp. 79–80.
187. Ibid., p. 95.
188. Ibid., p. 101.
189. Ibid., p. 102.
190. Ibid., p. 162.
191. Ibid., p. 167.
192. Ibid., p. 166. Aristotle's term for practical wisdom (alternatively translated as prudence or practical wisdom) is *phronēsis*. It was translated into Arabic as *ta'aqul* and into Hebrew by Samuel ben Judah of Marseilles as *ha-heskel*. See: Averroes, *Averroes' Middle Commentary on Aristotle's Nicomachean Ethics*, pp. 208–10 and 377.
193. In the 1263 Barcelona Disputation between Naḥmanides and Pablo Christiani, each cites one of the interpretations in the Midrash of the Suffering Servant, Naḥmanides that it refers to the people of Israel and Christiani that it refers to the Messiah. See: Naḥmanides, "The Disputation at Barcelona," in *Writings of the Ramban*, vol. ii, pp. 734–45. Hyam Maccoby writes: "it must certainly be said in favor of this approach that there are certain aspects of Aggadah of both Talmud and Midrash which tended to be ignored by Medieval Jews because they were felt to be something of a handicap in Jewish-Christian controversy . . . Naḥmanides, in the disputation, did not deny the existence of such an interpretation in Midrashic sources, but said he preferred the alternative interpretation that the passage refers to the sufferings of the people Israel, the servant of mankind. Naḥmanides added that even if one accepts the Messianic interpretation, the passage has little application to Jesus, since it refers to suffering but not to death at the hands of enemies" (Hyam Maccoby, *Judaism on Trial: Jewish-Christian Disputations in the Middle Ages* [Rutherford, 1982], p. 42).
194. ADK I, pp. 100–01.

## Chapter 2

1. Mishna Hagiga 2:1.
2. AS II, p. 129.
3. Ibn Kaspi's analysis of the divine chariot is in his work *Menorat Kesef* and is summarized in Barry Mensch, *Studies in Joseph ibn Caspi: Fourteenth-Century Philosopher and Exegete* (Leiden, 1975), pp. 89–91. He argues there that Ibn Kaspi's metaphysics is a mixture of Al-Farabi's *Political Regime*, Al-Batalyawsi's *Book of Intellectual Circles*, and Maimonides' *Guide*.
4. AS II, p. 76.
5. Ibid., p. 79.
6. Ibid.
7. Moshe Halbertal, *Concealment and Revelation: Esotericism in Jewish Thought and its Philosophical Implications* (Princeton, 2007), pp. 9, 12.
8. *Guide* III Intro, pp. 415–16.
9. Ibid. I 71, pp. 175–76.
10. Ibid. III Intro, p. 416: "I shall interpret to you that which was said by *Ezekiel the prophet*, peace be on him, in such a way that anyone who heard that interpretation would think that I do not say anything over and beyond what is indicated by the text . . .On the other hand, if that interpretation is examined with perfect care by him for whom this Treatise is composed and who has understood all its chapters—every chapter in its turn—the whole matter, which has become clear and manifest to me, will become clear to him so that nothing in it will remain hidden from him."
11. Song of Songs Rabba 1:1:8. Translation of James Robinson in James Robinson, "Translator's Introduction" in *Samuel ibn Tibbon's Commentary on Ecclesiastes: The Book of the Soul of Man* (Germany, 2007), p. 60.
12. Samuel Ibn Tibbon, *Samuel ibn Tibbon's Commentary on Ecclesiastes: The Book of the Soul of Man*, trans. and ed. James T. Robinson (Germany, 2007), pp. 600–03 [Chapter 12, Paragraph 752–56].
13. Robinson, "Translator's Introduction," pp. 60–62. At p. 61 he argues that "in his [Samuel Ibn Tibbon's] opinion, the midrash points not only to the existence of secrets of the Torah, but of a literary-philosophical tradition devoted to the teaching and transmitting of these secrets."
14. Samuel Ibn Tibbon, *Ma'amar Yikavu Hamayim* (*Treatise of the Gathering of the Waters*), ed. Mordechai Bisliches (Pressburg, 1837), Chapter 22, pp. 173, 175. English translation thanks to Howard Kreisel in Howard Kreisel, "From Esotericism to Science: The Account of the Chariot in Maimonidean Philosophy till the End of the Thirteenth Century," in *Judaism as Philosophy: Studies in Maimonides and the Medieval Jewish Philosophers of Provence*, ed. Howard Kreisel (Boston, 2015), p. 247.
15. BT Gittin 60a.

16. Psalm. 119:126.

17. Ephraim E. Urbach, *The Sages: Their Concepts and Beliefs* (Jerusalem, 1975), pp. 341–42 and 836n93 and Menachem Elon, *Jewish Law: History, Sources, Principles*, trans. Bernard Auerbach and Melvin J. Skyes (Philadelphia, 1994) vol. ii, p. 503. In the modern period, this verse has been used by Reform Judaism to argue for liberal innovation in Jewish law and by Orthodox Judaism to argue for greater stringency in Jewish law.

18. *Guide* Intro, p. 16.

19. Ravitzky, "Samuel Ibn Tibbon and the Esoteric Character," pp. 114–16.

20. TIK, pp. 4, 49 and MK, p. 228.

21. Another possible reading: "all the books [of the world] could not contain it."

22. MK, p. 5.

23. The progressive relationship between the knowledge of the different prophets will be discussed further in "Biblical Characters as Historical Actors." He repeats the refrain often that "there is nothing in the Prophets that is not in the Torah [Pentateuch]" (MK, p. 40).

24. One difference between Maimonides and Ibn Kaspi here is that Maimonides speaks about scientific progress beyond the Bible, while Ibn Kaspi speaks about scientific progress already beginning within the Bible. For Maimonides position, see: Menachem Kellner, *Maimonides on the "Decline of the Generations" and the Nature of Rabbinic Authority* (Albany, 1996), pp. 76–78. Though Leo Strauss proposes that Maimonides may hint to a form of intra-biblical progress and if so, Ibn Kaspi works out the exact details in a way that Maimonides only hints. See: Leo Strauss. "How to Begin to Study the *Guide of the Perplexed*," in *Guide*, pp. xxxviii–xi.

25. AS II, p. 77.

26. YD, p. 154.

27. Abraham Melamed, *The Myth of the Jewish Origins of Science and Philosophy* (Jerusalem, 2010) traces the origin and history of this myth across the Jewish, Christian, and Islamic world. Maimonides' usage was discussed in Kellner, *Maimonides on the "Decline of the Generations,"* pp. 43–49.

28. AS II, p. 77, 85, 91–92, and AM, p. 84.

29. AS II, p. 85.

30. There is an interesting echo here to the Rabbi's argument in Judah Halevi's *Kuzari* 1:63 where he argues that all thinking is historical and thus no argument is independent of its historical tradition. There is no such thing as a universally true argument. Traditions succeed because of the military success of the state or empire that is using it. The Greeks did not discover the science of nature, but presented its universality because of their political victories, and when they lost, they lost their thinking. Ibn Kaspi does not mention Halevi or the *Kuzari* so we have no evidence that he read it and was influenced by it.

31. TIK, pp. 134–45.
32. Melamed, *The Myth of the Jewish Origins*, p. 100.
33. Gregg Stern, "Philosophic Allegory in Medieval Jewish Culture: The Crisis in Languedoc (1304–1306)," in *Interpretation and Allegory: Antiquity to the Modern Period*, ed. Jon Whitman. Leiden: Brill, 2003, pp. 189–209.
34. Abba Mari of Lunel, *Minhat Qena'ot*. In *Responsa of the Rashba to Rabbi Solomon ben Abraham ben Aderet*, ed. H. Z. Dimitrovsky (Jerusalem, 1990), pp. 316, 345–46, 575–86.
35. Kasher argues that Ibn Kaspi moderated his critique about the allegorical status of the Bible, strongly rejecting it in earlier work, while moderating his opposition to certain allegorists in later works (Kasher, *Joseph Ibn Caspi as a Philosophical Exegete*, p. 23). I do not think this changes my thesis here since Ibn Kaspi is consistent in his assertion of the inadequacy of ignoring the potential that the biblical characters were historical actors and the biblical narratives historically took place.
36. AS I, p. 19.
37. GK, pp. 164, 169–70, 254.
38. BT Baba Batra 15a and cited by Maimonides at *Guide* III 22, p. 486.
39. AS I, pp. 137–38.
40. BT Baba Batra 14b.
41. GK, p. 169.
42. AS I, p. 138. Translation of Robert Eisen in Robert Eisen, "Joseph Ibn Kaspi on the Book of Job," *Jewish Studies Quarterly* 13, no. 1 (2006), p. 61.
43. GK, p. 170.
44. Ibid., p. 266.
45. NE 2.1. Ibn Kaspi summarizes NE 2.1 in *Terumat Kesef* (M.S. Pococke 17, fol. 22v–23r).
46. It is important to note that Ibn Kaspi does not use the explicit language of progress in *Menorat Kesef* to describe this historical process. This reading is based on the fact that the work is divided into four sections (Moses, Isaiah, Ezekiel, and Zechariah), the first of which describes the process leading up to Moses and the latter three describe the continual description of greater details that were not discussed (at least openly) by their predecessors.
47. Alexander Altmann connects Ibn Tibbon and Ibn Kaspi on this point, noting that "He [Ibn Kaspi] too, then, follows the pattern introduced by Samuel Ibn Tibbon in trying to show that a vision of the Merkaba is alluded to already in the Tora, particularly in Jacob's dream" (Altmann, "The Ladder of Ascension," in *Studies in Mysticism and Religion, Presented to Gershom G. Scholem on His Seventieth Birthday*, eds. Ephraim Urbach, R. J. Zwi Werblowski, Chaim Wirszubski [Jerusalem, 1967], p. 22).
48. AS II, p. 85.
49. BT Yoma 28b.

Notes to Chapter 2 / 171

50. AS II, p. 86.

51. MT, p. 34. In YD, p. 132: "now, the knowledge of God is the primary precept of all our 613 laws, as may be seen from the texts enforcing this knowledge. It is the basis of the four precepts enumerated by Maimonides at the beginning of his Code. He specifically terms them the Foundations of the Torah . . .They are designated the Foundations of the Torah, for they are at once the purpose and the root of all the commandments, the observance of which is the whole end of man."

52. AS II, pp. 91–92.

53. Gen. 28:12.

54. Guide II 10, pp. 272–73 and AS II, p. 91.

55. AS II, p. 91.

56. Ibid., p. 92.

57. Exod. 25:8.

58. AS II, p. 98. Ibn Kaspi is building here on the Midrash that points out the linguistic similarities between the building of the tabernacle and the creation of the world in Genesis. For example: Exodus Rabba 34:2, Numbers Rabba 12:13. The literary structure of the biblical chapters are compared in Nahum Sarna, *Exploring Exodus: The Origins of Biblical Israel* (New York, 1986), p. 213.

59. AS II, p. 99. English translation of Mensch in *Studies in Joseph ibn Caspi*, p. 94.

60. These points are summarized well by Mensch in *Studies in Joseph ibn Caspi*, pp. 94–95.

61. AS II, p. 107.

62. Ibid.

63. Ibid.

64. Ibid., p. 104.

65. Ibid., p. 101.

66. Ibid., p. 102.

67. Ibid., p. 129.

68. Isa. 6:1–3.

69. AS II, p. 112.

70. *Guide* I 11, pp. 37–38.

71. AS II, p. 112.

72. Ibid., p. 113. This is a polemic against Samuel Ibn Tibbon, *Ma'amar Yikavu Hamayim*, Chapters 9 and 11, pp. 42–45 and 56–57.

73. AS II, p. 113.

74. *Guide* I 43, p. 94.

75. AS II, p. 114.

76. Ibid. and GK, p. 137.

77. AS II, p. 115.

78. BT Hagiga 13b quoted in *Guide* III 6, p. 427.

79. Rashi reads it in this way, explaining the statement in the Babylonian Talmud by adding to "Isaiah is like unto a city man who saw the king" on Hagiga 13b by saying Isaiah is like one "who is not compelled to report everything, for he was a descendent of kings and raised in a palace; accustomed to seeing royalty, he is not overwhelmed or astonished and therefore is not impelled to tell all."

80. *Guide* III 6, p. 427.

81. Different views of prophetic error in medieval Jewish philosophy is discussed in Charles Touati, "Le Problème de l'Inerrance Prophetique dans la Théologie Juive du Moyen Age," *Revue de l'Histoire des Religions* 174 (1968), pp. 169–87. For a critique of the perspective that the prophets made scientific mistakes, see: Isaac Abarbanel, *Commentary on the Guide of the Perplexed* III.1–7 under the heading "Me-ha-Abarbanel le-Heleq Shlishi me-ha-Moreh," in *Sefer Moreh Nevukhim 'im Arba'ah Perushim* (Jerusalem, 1960), pp. 71–73.

82. Ezek. 1:24.

83. These two mistakes are discussed in Shalom Rosenberg, "Bible Exegesis in the Guide," *Jerusalem Studies in Jewish Thought* 1 (1981), pp. 146–51; Warren Zev Harvey, "How to Begin to Study the *Guide of the Perplexed*, 1:1," *Daat* 21 (1988): 21–23; and Daniel Davies, *Method and Metaphysics in Maimonides' Guide for the Perplexed* (Oxford, 2011), pp. 136–39.

84. *Guide* II 45, p. 401.

85. MT, pp. 34–36. Harvey, "How to Begin to Study the *Guide of the Perplexed*, 1:1," pp. 146–51.

86. AM, II 8, p. 95.

87. Ibid., pp. 118, 120.

88. Ezek. 1:10.

89. AS II, p. 120.

90. Ezek. 1:6.

91. AS II, p. 118.

92. *Guide* I 49, p. 110 and II 10, p. 271.

93. Ezek. 1:9.

94. AS II, p. 120.

95. Ezek. 1:16 and AS II, p. 122.

96. Ezek. 9:2.

97. AS II, p. 127.

98. Ibid.

99. Ibid., pp. 126–27.

100. Ibid., p. 129. The other prophetic visions not discussed here (2, 3, and 4) deal with the subject matter of the first chapter of the book regarding political history and the future of the Israelite kingdom in relation to other kingdoms.

101. Zecha. 1:8.

102. Ibid., 1.8: "the greater the mass of fire or earth the quicker always is its movement towards its own place."

103. Aristotle, *On the Heavens*, 1.2: "Single thing has a single contrary; and upward and downward motion are the contraries of one another . . . for if the natural motion is upward, it will be fire or air, and if downward, water or earth."

104. *Guide* I 40, pp. 90–91 and II 32, p. 361.

105. Leviticus Rabba 30:12.

106. AS II, p. 129. Ibn Kaspi does not see the fact the spheres are divided up into different numerical categories as problematic, such as the faces of the four animals in Ezekiel and as three horses in Daniel, since they are done so for different reasons at different times (AS II, p. 130).

107. Zecha. 4:2–3.

108. AS II, p. 135.

109. *Guide* II Intro, p. 237.

110. AS II, p. 137.

111. Zecha. 5:9 and AS II, p. 138

112. Zecha. 5:3.

113. Ibid. 5:4.

114. *Guide* III 8, p. 431.

115. AS II, p. 137.

116. Zecha. 6:1–3.

117. AS II, pp. 141–42.

118. Aviezer Ravitzky refers to this as the "anthropological theory of miracles" and discusses its history as rooted in Neo-Platonism and Avicenna before being adopted by certain medieval Jewish philosophers before and after Ibn Kaspi. See: Aviezer Ravitzky, "The Anthropolgical Theory of Miracles in Medieval Jewish Philosophy," in *Studies in Medieval Jewish History and Literature*, vol. ii, ed. Isadore Twersky (Cambridge, 1984), pp. 231–72.

119. *Guide*, II 37 p. 374.

120. Maimonides introduces the seventh contradiction at *Guide* Intro, p. 18. For a full discussion of Ibn Kaspi's interpretation of Maimonidean contradictions, see Chapter 3, subsection 3: "Internal Biblical Contradictions."

121. *Guide* II 32, pp. 360–61.

122. AM, p. 113. Ibn Kaspi's text does not include this entire quote, but I included slightly more since it helps explain the context of his argument.

123. Ibn Kaspi explains *Guide* II 32 in *Maskiyot Kesef*, but already hints to this problem in *Tirat Kesef*. See: TIK, pp. 25–26. Ibn Kaspi points out there the contradiction in Maimonides' evidence in that he himself contradicts in other places the biblical verses he quotes.

124. SHK, p. 170

125. AM, p. 94.

126. Ibid., p. 99.

127. Amira Eran traces the history and reception of Avicenna's model of "intuitive prophecy" (*ḥads*) within medieval Jewish philosophy in Amira

Eran, "Intuition and Inspiration—The Causes of Jewish Thinkers' Objection to Avicenna's Intellectual Prophecy" (Ḥads)," *Jewish Studies Quarterly* 14, no. 1 (2007), pp. 39-71.

128. The summary is thanks to Eran, "Intuition and Inspiration," p. 39. A collection of Avicenna's texts in English translations from his different writings where he discusses intuitive prophecy can be found in Dimitri Gutas, *Avicenna and the Aristotelian Tradition*, second edition (Leiden, 2004), pp. 179-200.

129. *Guide* I 34, p. 75.

130. Ibn Kaspi appears to have adopted Avicenna's view through Falaquera's commentary on the *Guide* since both are discussing intutitive prophecy in commenting on *Guide* I 34 and Falaquera makes very similar comments in his commentary. See: Shem Tov Ibn Falaquera, *Moreh ha-Moreh*, ed. Yair Shiffman (Jerusalem, 2001), pp. 18-19.

131. SHK, pp. 172-73.

132. Averroes, *Epitome of Aristotle's Parva Naturalia*, p. 52.

133. Ibid. This is pointed out by Kasher in *Joseph Ibn Caspi as a Philosophical Exegete*, pp. 85-86.

134. Avicenna, "Healing: Metaphysics X," trans. Michael E. Marmura in *Medieval Political Philosophy: A Sourcebook*, eds. Ralph Lerner and Muhsin Mahdi (Ithaca, 1963), p. 110 [Part 4, Book 10, Chapter 5]. Ibn Kaspi does not quote this specific quote from Avicenna, but it is fitting in comparison to the quote he does bring in from Averroes' *Epitome of Aristotle's Parva Naturalia*.

135. Ravitzky, "The Anthropolgical Theory of Miracles," pp. 231-32.

136. Kalonymos ben Kalonymos, *ha-Teshuvah le-Yosef Kaspi*, ed. Joseph Perles (Munich, 1879), p. 4. Translation in Ravitzky, "The Anthropolgical Theory of Miracles," p. 244.

137. AS I, pp. 126-27. The English translation is thanks to Ravitzky in Ibid., p. 244.

138. Maimonides, *Iggerot*, pp. 98-100 and English translation: "Letter on Resurrection," in *Crisis and Leadership*, pp. 231-32.

139. Exod. 7:9-12, 14:21, 3:14-17 and Num. 26:10.

140. TIK, p. 3. Some of this translation is adapted from Ravitzky, "The Anthropolgical Theory of Miracles," p. 244.

141. Exod. 7:20.

142. MK, p. 172.

143. Ibid., p. 173.

144. Ibid., p. 174.

145. Ibid., p. 175.

146. Ibid., p. 176.

147. SHK, p. 205.

148. Michael Fishbane, "Inner-Biblical Exegesis" in *Hebrew Bible, Old Testament: The History of Its Interpretation*, Vol. 1, ed. Magne Saebo (Germany,

1996), pp. 33–49, and Judy Klitsner, *Subversive Sequels in the Bible: How Biblical Stories Mine and Undermine Each Other* (Jerusalem, 2011).

149. AS II, p. 77.

150. MK, p. 6. Though Ibn Kaspi is clear to remind and repeat to the reader here that he is not suggesting the prophets innovated, but merely explained their message in greater detail. He says that there is nothing new in the prophets that is not already in Torah, except for the teaching about the coming of Messiah (MK, pp. 39–40).

151. AS II, pp. 77–78.

152. Ibid., p. 88.

153. Ibid.

154. Aristotle, *On the Heavens*, 1.4–5 and MK, p. 3.

155. Isa. 51:13, 51:16.

156. ADK I, p. 164 on Isa. 51:16.

157. Gen 1:6–7.

158. Guide II 30, pp. 352–53 and ADK I, p. 164.

159. Guide II 30, p. 353.

160. Jer. 10:13.

161. ADK II, p. 7.

162. Isa. 51:16.

163. ADK I, p. 164.

164. Gen 1:2.

165. MK, p. 6.

166. Isa. 45:18–19.

167. Ibid. 45:19.

168. ADK, pp. 157–58.

169. Guide III 37, p. 542.

170. Guide I 36, p. 83. Moshe Halbertal and Avishai Margalit, *Idolatry*, trans. Naomi Goldblum (Cambridge, 1998), pp. 108–09.

171. MT, pp. 62–64.

172. Guide III 32.

173. Naḥmanides, *Commentary on the Torah*, vol. iii, 18–20 (or Lev. 1:9–2:11). Abel's sacrifice is at Gen. 4:3–5, while Noah's sacrifice is at Gen. 8:20–21.

174. MT, p. 646.

175. AS II, p. 85.

176. Gen. 4:4–5.

177. Lev. 1:3.

178. Gen. 8:21.

179. MK, pp. 23–24.

180. Gen. 8:20.

181. MK, p. 34.

182. Gen. 31:54.

183. Ibid. and MK, p. 77.
184. Gen. 46:1.
185. MK, p. 99 and Kasher, *Joseph Ibn Caspi as a Philosophical Exegete*, p. 30.
186. Gen. 12:8 and 13:4 and MK, p. 49.
187. MK, p. 47.
188. MT, pp. 94–95.
189. *Guide* III 32, pp. 527–529.
190. MK, p. 49.
191. Gen. 22.
192. Ibn Kaspi's interpretation of the binding of Isaac is analyzed by Hannah Kasher in "'How Could the Lord Command Such an Abomination to Be Done?'—Rabbi Joseph Ibn Caspi's Critics on the Binding of Isaac," in *'Et Ha-Da'at* 1 (1997): 38–46 and sharply criticized by Isaac Abarbanel for the charge of portraying it as a dream and denying the historicity of the event. See: Moses Maimonides, *Sefer Moreh Nevuḥim le-ha-Rav Moshe ben Maimon ha-Sefardi; be-ha'ataqat Shmu'el ibn Tibbon 'im Arba'ah Perushim: Efodi, Shem Ṭov, Ibn Qresqas, Abarbanel* (Jerusalem, 1959), p. 1:25b. Abarbanel's interpretation of the binding of Isaac and its relationship to Maimonides is discussed in detail in James Diamond, "Abarbanel's Exergetical Subversion of Maimonides' *'Aqedah*: Transforming a Knight of Intellectual Virtue into a Knight of Existential Faith," in *The Hebrew Bible in Fifteenth Century Spain: Exegesis, Philosophy, Literature, and the Arts*, eds. Jonathan Decter, Aturo Pratis Olivan (Leiden, 2012), pp. 75–100.
193. GK, p. 219.
194. Ibid., p. 229.
195. Gen. 22:1 and TIK, pp. 46–47.
196. Gen. 22:2 and GK, p. 218.
197. Gen. 22:4.
198. GK, p. 228.
199. Ibid., p. 229.
200. Gen. 22:2 and GK, p. 231.
201. GK, p. 219.
202. Compare Gen. 22:1 to Gen. 22:11.
203. Ibid. and GK, p. 230.
204. Gen. 22:18 and MK, p. 63.
205. GK, p. 220.
206. Deut. 12:31 and MK, p. 282.
207. MK, p. 229.
208. NE 5.10, pp. 111–13.
209. *Guide* III 34, pp. 534–35.
210. AM, III 41, p. 137.
211. *Guide* I Intro, p. 9. It is interesting to compare Ibn Kaspi to Strauss on this issue as Strauss saw the sevenfold division as the key to unpacking the

structure of the Guide, where the work is actually divided into seven sections, most of which themselves can be divided into seven. One can see his division in Strauss, "How to Begin," pp. xi–xiii. He writes there that "the Guide consists then of seven sections or of thirty-eight subsections. Wherever feasible, each section is divided into seven subsections; the only section that does not permit of being divided into subsections is divided into seven chapters" (p. xiii).

212. MK, pp. 14–15, 23.
213. Guide I 14, p. 40.
214. Ibid. I 2, pp. 24–25.
215. Ezek. 1:26 and AM, p. 30.
216. AM, p. 30.
217. Ibid., p. 31.
218. Guide I 4, p. 27.
219. AM, pp. 14–15.
220. Ibid., p. 85.
221. Guide II 13, pp. 280–85 and II 32, pp. 360–61.
222. Ibid., II 32, p. 360.
223. Lawrence Kaplan, "Maimonides on the Miraculous Element in Prophecy," Harvard Theological Review 70, no. 3–4 (1977), pp. 233–56; Herbert Davidson, "Maimonides' Secret Position on Creation," in Studies in Medieval Jewish History and Literature, ed. Isadore Twersky (Cambridge, 1979), pp. 16–40; and Warren Zev Harvey. "A Third Approach to Maimonides' Cosmogony-Prophetology Puzzle," Harvard Theological Review 74, no. 3 (1981), pp. 287–301.
224. Harvey summarizes these three positions in "A Third Approach," pp. 288–89.
225. Guide, II 13 p. 285 and II 25, p. 329.
226. AM, p. 99.
227. Ibid., p. 113.
228. In defending the structure of 1:1, 2:3, 3:2, Ibn Kaspi, Abarbanel and Davidson each view a different matching pair as Maimonides' true position. For Abarbanel 1:1 is the true view, for Davidson 2:3 is the true view, and for Ibn Kaspi 3:2 is the true view.
229. This interpretation differs from that of Hannah Kasher who argues that Ibn Kaspi is an exponent of rational egoism. See: Kasher, Joseph Ibn Caspi as a Philosophical Exegete, pp. 98–101. The sources for Kasher's argument in this section rely heavily on Ibn Kaspi's commentary on Proverbs, while my argument here is rooted in Maṣref la-Kesef and Ṭirat Kesef.
230. MK, p. 294. Translation of Nehama Leibowitz, Commentary on Devarim (Deuteronomy), trans. Aryeh Newman (Jerusalem, 1993), p. 221. I made one change to the translation, translating 'anava as humility and not modesty.
231. MK, p. 293.
232. Ibid.

233. Deut. 21:11–12 and MK, p. 293.
234. Lev. 19:18 and MK, p. 293.
235. Lev. 18:18.
236. Ibid.
237. MK, p. 230. I am uncertain where Ibn Kaspi is drawing this from in the Aristotelian corpus. In the *Rhetoric*, which was not translated into Hebrew at this point, in discussing the emotion of envy, he quotes the line "kinship, too, knows how to envy." See: Aristotle, *On Rhetoric*, trans. George A. Kennedy (Oxford, 1991), p. 159 (2.10).
238. Deut. 22:6–7 and MK, p. 293.
239. MK, p. 294. The connection between the dietary laws and mercy is already suggested by Maimonides in *Guide* II 48, but is used for different purposes. This will be discussed further in the next subsection.
240. TIK, p. 35.
241. Deut. 20:19.
242. MK, p. 294.
243. Immanuel Kant, *Metaphysics of Morals*, trans. Mary Gregor (Cambridge, 1996), 6:387, 443 and Mary Leukam, *Dignified Animals: How "Non-Kantian" is Nussbaum's Conception of Dignity?* MA Thesis, Georgia State University, 2011, p. 16.
244. Nussbaum, "The Future of Feminist Liberalism," *Proceedings and Addresses of the American Philosophy Association* 74, no. 2 (2000), p. 50 and Leukam, *Dignified Animals*, p. 21.
245. MT, pp. 45–47. The centrality of humility in Maimonides' thought has been studied in contemporary scholarship. See: Daniel Frank, "Humility as a Virtue: A Maimonidean Critique of Aristotle's *Ethics*," in *Moses Maimonides and His Time*, ed. Eric L. Ormsby (Washington, 1989), pp. 89–99; Raymond Weiss, *Maimonides' Ethics: The Encounter of Philosophic and Religious Morality* (Chicago, 1991), pp. 38–46, 102–15; and Diamond, *Converts, Heretics, and Lepers*, pp. 79–106 (Chapter 4: The King: The Ethics of Imperial Humility).
246. Num. 12:3.
247. *Guide* III 27, p. 510.
248. MK, p. 294.
249. Deut. 21:10–11 and BT Kiddushin 21b.
250. *Guide* III 41, p. 567.
251. MK, p. 293.
252. EC, IV, pp. 26, 64–65; *Guide* III 35, p. 537.
253. *Guide* III 48, p. 600.
254. Lev. 11:7–8; Deut. 14:8 and *Guide* III 48, p. 598.
255. Gen. 9:3–4; Lev. 17:10–14; Lev. 22:8 and *Guide* III 48, p. 598.
256. There has been much scholarship written on the contradiction between sending away the mother bird (*shiluach ha-ken*) in the *Mishneh Torah* and the *Guide*, where in the *Mishneh Torah* he writes that the reason of this

command is *not* mercy, while in the *Guide* he writes that it *is* mercy. For the sake of this discussion, I am following the *Guide*, as it appears that Ibn Kaspi, who was likely aware of this contradiction, appears to have followed the reasoning of the *Guide* over that of the *Mishneh Torah*, while also going beyond it. See: Jacob Levinger, "Abstinence from Alcohol in the Guide of the Perplexed," *Bar Ilan University Annual: Decennial Volume* 1955–65, pp. 299–305; Roslyn Weiss, "Maimonides on *Shiluah Ha-Qen*," *Jewish Quarterly Review* 79 (1989), pp. 345–66; Josef Stern, *Problems and Parables of Law: Maimonides and Nahmanides on Reasons for the Commandments (Ta'amei Ha-Mitzvot)* (Albany, 1998), pp. 49–66; Edward Halper, "Maimonides and Nachmanides on Sending Away the Mother Bird," in *Thinking about the Environment: Our Debt to the Classical and Medieval Past*, eds. Thomas Robinson and Laura Westra (Lanham, 2002), pp. 185–202.

257. Lev. 22:28; Deut. 22:6–7 and *Guide* III 48, pp. 599–600.
258. *Guide* III 48, p. 599.
259. Ibid. Intro, p. 15.
260. Ibid. III 35, p. 537.
261. Ibid. I 54, p. 125.
262. Ibid., p. 126.
263. Ibid. III 17, p. 471.
264. Ibid., p. 473. Many of the commentators have drawn the connection between III 17 and III 48. See: Weiss, "Maimonides on *Shiluah Ha-Qen*," p. 356; Stern, *Problems and Parables of Law*, p. 54; Halper, "Maimonides and Nachmanides on Sending Away the Mother Bird," p. 190.
265. MK, pp. 293–94.
266. Deut. 20:19–20.
267. Ibid. 20:19.
268. MK, p. 294.
269. MT, p. 1238.
270. MK, p. 294.
271. EC, IV, pp. 26, 65.
272. *Guide* III 39 p. 553.
273. MK, p. 254.
274. MK, p. 257. Ibn Kaspi humorously plays on the expression "the actions of the fathers are a sign for the children" (*ma'ase 'avot siman le-banim*, BT Yebamot 121b), writing instead "the actions of the fathers produced children" (*ma'ase 'avot ya'asu banim*).
275. MK, p. 256.
276. *Guide* III 8, p. 431 and AM, pp. 122–23.
277. TIK, pp. 67–68.
278. Gen. 9:22.
279. Ibid. 9:24–25.
280. BT Sanhedrin 70a; TIK, p. 68.

281. TIK, p. 69.
282. Gen. 19:31.
283. TIK, p. 95; MK, p. 58.
284. Gen. 29:11.
285. MK, p. 72.
286. Gen. 29:30–31.
287. MK, p. 73.

288. Unlike a common trope in medieval Jewish-Christian philosophical polemics, Ibn Kaspi is not arguing that Judaism is rational and Christianity is irrational. See: Daniel Lasker, *Jewish Philosophical Polemics Against Christianity in the Middle Ages* (London, 2007), pp. 25–43. I do not think it is important to identify which historical Christianity Ibn Kaspi was refering to since both the Judaism and Christianity that Ibn Kaspi discusses are philosophical constructions. Adrian Sackson articulates this well in stating that "owing to the fact that Ibn Kaspi is convinced that 'philosophical religion' is the authentic version of Judaism—and of (at least some) other religious traditions—he conceives of the difference between Judaism and other religions as consisting in the difference between Judaism *as understood by Jewish philosophers*, especially Maimonides, and other religious traditions (especially Islam) *as understood by their philosophers*" (Sackson, *Portrait of a Hebrew Philosopher*, pp. 113–14).

289. GK, p. 136.
290. Ibid., p. 156.
291. Ibid., p. 137.

292. Isa. 6:3 and GK, p. 138. Kasher, *Joseph Ibn Caspi as a Philosophical Exegete*, pp. 50–52. Kasher notes that Ibn Kaspi's argument is similar to that of Isaac Albalag. See: Lasker, Ibid., pp. 78–79.

293. AM, p. 45. This English translation is partially based on Sackson, *Portrait of a Hebrew Philosopher*, pp. 114–15.

294. AM, p. 45. This citation of Avicenna appears to be taken directly from Falaquera's commentary on the same chapter in the *Guide* (I 35) in his commentary on the *Guide*, *Moreh ha-Moreh*. See: Falaquera, *Moreh ha-Moreh*, p. 20.

295. Kreisel, *Maimonides' Political Thought*, p. 197; and Pines, "The Philosophical Sources of the *Guide of the Perplexed*," in *Guide*, pp. cxviii–cxix. Kreisel writes that "The question raised by this point is why was Maimonides so insistent that Judaism reverse its pedagogical strategy in the area of beliefs about God to the point that he employed all the legal arsenal at his disposal to accomplish this end. Why risk disturbing the nairve faith of the masses . . .Such luminous Islamic philosophers such as Alfarabi, Avicenna and Averroes advised against it."

296. Ibn Kaspi's distinction between the two pedagogical approaches of the Islamic philosophers and Maimonides is an interesting way of answering a

problem that readers of medieval philosophy are often seeking an answer to: why does one finds little engagement with the Quran or references to Muhammed, such as when Al-Farabi discusses prophecy and divine law and likewise a strong separation between Averroes' religious and philosophical writings that one does not find in the writings of Maimonides? In contrast, Maimonides presents, at least on the surface, the Torah and philosophy as existing in a form of harmony.

## Chapter 3

1. BT Sanhedrin 90a.

2. Translation of Kellner in Menachem Kellner, *Dogma in Medieval Jewish Thought* (London, 1986), p. 14. For the Arabic, see Maimonides, *Mishna im Perush Rabbenu Moshe ben Maimon*, vol. 4, *Seder Nezikin* (Jerusalem, 1963), p. 214.

3. Marc Shapiro observes that the thirteen principles were never unanimously accepted and notes the different divergences from them in *The Limits of Orthodox Theology: Maimonides' Thirteen Principles Reappraised* (London, 2004).

4. BT Baba Batra 15a.

5. Gen. 12:6, Deut. 1:1, and Deut. 31:9. Ibn Ezra, *Ibn Ezra's Commentary on the Pentateuch*, vol. 1, p. 151 and vol. 5, pp. 1–2, 225, and Warren Zev Harvey, "Spinoza on Ibn Ezra's Secret of the Twelve," in *Spinoza's Theological-Political Treatise: A Critical Guide*, eds. Yitzhak Melamed and Michael Rosenthal (Cambridge, 2010), pp. 41–55.

6. BT Baba Batra 14b.

7. Exod. 34:1 and Deut. 10:2.

8. AS II, p. 87

9. Dimant, *Exegesis, Philosophy and Language*, pp. 71–73. This thesis is later expounded by Spinoza in his *Compendium of Hebrew Grammar (Compendium Grammatices Linguae Hebraeae)*. See: Warren Zev Harvey, "Spinoza's Metaphysical Hebraism," in *Jewish Themes in Spinoza's Philosophy*, eds. Heidi M. Ravven and Lenn E. Goodman (Albany, 2002), pp. 107–14.

10. Aristotle, *On Interpretation*, trans. E. M. Edghill, 1.1–2: "Spoken words are the symbols of mental experience and written words are the symbols of spoken words. Just as all men have not the same writing, so all men have not the same speech sounds but the mental experiences, which these directly symbolize, are the same for all, as also are those things of which our experiences are the images."

11. Harry Wolfson compares the approaches of Aristotle, Plato, and Epicurus on the nature of language "The Veracity of Scripture in Philo, Halevi, Maimonides, and Spinoza," in *Alexander Marx Jubilee Volume* (New York, 1950),

pp. 603-60. Mensch (*Studies in Joseph ibn Caspi*, p. 33n145) applies this to Ibn Kaspi and concludes that "Hebrew is the only language which according to Wolfson's analysis is both 'conventional' and 'natural.'"

12. QK, pp. 31-32. Ibn Kaspi emphasizes this point in MK, p. 212 (on Exodus 21:19) where he says: "Hebrew is the most perfect of the languages."

13. Translation and quote from Moshe Kahan, "Aspects of Medieval Lexicography—Between Jonah ibn Janāḥ's *Kitāb al-'Uṣūl* and Joseph Kaspi's *Šaršot Kesef*," *Revue des Etudes Juives* (forthcoming).

14. Moshe Kahan, "The Relationship of Synonyms in Kaspi's Sharshot Kesef," *Hebrew Linguistics* 69 (2014), pp. 87-105.

15. Isa. 33:9.

16. SAK, p. 655.

17. Ibid., p. 656.

18. Gen. 2:25.

19. Ibid. 3:1.

20. MK, pp. 21-22 and *Sharshot Kesef*, MS. Paris 1444 291b-92a.

21. SAK, p. 682.

22. Exod. 34:29.

23. SAK, p. 683.

24. SHK, pp. 57-59 and MK, p. 4.

25. MK, pp. 296-97 and AS II, p. 95.

26. SHK, p. 61.

27. Ibid., p. 62.

28. *Guide* I 67, p. 162.

29. MK, p. 116.

30. ADK I, p. 183.

31. Ibid., p. 83.

32. MK, p. 16.

33. Isa. 19:18.

34. ADK, p. 116.

35. MK, p. 14.

36. Martin Buber, *On the Bible: Eighteen Studies*, ed. Nahum Glatzer (New York, 1968), p. 24.

37. MK, p. 14.

38. Ibid.

39. Ibid., p. 82.

40. Ibid., p. 83.

41. Ibid., p. 232.

42. Ibid., p. 210.

43. MK, pp. 70, 112 and TIK, p. 121.

44. MK, p. 83.

45. MK, pp. 14-15, 23 and AS II, pp. 77-78.

46. MK, p. 23.

47. This is discussed in the Midrash on Psalm. 62:12 on "God hath spoken once, twice have I heard this" which deals with verses that contradict each other. Israel Knohl, *The Divine Symphony: The Bible's Many Voices* (Philadelphia, 2003), pp. xi–xii concludes on interpreting the Midrash that "the divine speech is one, but it has within it many voices. The human ear can only hear these voices separately . . . The human mind can't easily grasp this dichotomy, so it must seek to reconcile the contradictions."

48. *Guide* I Intro, pp. 17–20. Arthur Melzer in *Philosophy Between the Lines: The Lost History of Esoteric Writing* (Chicago, 2014) writes about the phenomenon of esoteric writing more generally across the history of Western thought. He divides esotericism into four categories. Maimonides' fifth contradiction would correspond to Melzer's "pedagogical esotericism" and his seventh contradiction would corresponds to Melzer's "defensive esotericism" and "protective esotericism."

49. Contemporary academic literature has been debating the extent and meaning of Maimonides' use of contradictions, especially surrounding the seventh contradiction. Is there a hidden Aristotelian system of nature or a hidden Socratic skepticism? According to the latter, the human mind is unable to achieve demonstrative certainty on certain questions. See: Leo Strauss, "The Literary Character of *The Guide of the Perplexed*," in *Persecution and the Art of Writing* (Chicago, 1952), pp. 60–78; Marvin Fox, "A New View of Maimonides' Method of Contradictions," *Annual of Bar-Ilan University* (1987), pp. 19–43; Yair Lorberbaum, "'The Seventh Cause': On the Contradictions in Maimonides' *Guide of the Perplexed*: A Reappraisal," *Tarbitz* 69 (1999–2000), pp. 212–37 and "On Contradictions, Rationality, Dialectics, and Esotericism in Maimonides' *Guide of the Perplexed*," *The Review of Metaphysics* 55, no. 4 (2002), pp. 711–50. For some sharp critiques, see: Kenneth Seeskin, *Searching for a Distant God: The Legacy of Maimonides* (Oxford, 2000), pp. 177–88 and Herbert Davidson, *Moses Maimonides: The Man and His Work* (Oxford, 2005), pp. 393–402. The "very obscure matters" (*umūr ghāmiḍa jiddan*) that are the content of the seventh contradiction are not identified there, but in I 35 seemingly they are identified as the deep philosophic matters of divine attributes, creation, God's governance, divine knowledge, providence and prophecy.

50. MK, p. 205.

51. AS I, p. 118.

52. Ibid.

53. AM, p. 9.

54. Ibid., p. 8. English translation from Igor Holanda de Souza, *Philosophical Commentaries on the Preface to the* Guide of the Perplexed, *c. 1250–1362* (University of Chicago, 2014), p. 442: "All our books of Torah and of Scripture constitute, in this instance, one single book, since the Torah is the head and

the rock whence all the other books of Scripture are hewn, and it is as if they were all given from one shepherd."

55. AM, p. 7. English translation from Souza, *Philosophical Commentaries*, p. 442.

56. Is the denial of the existence of the first contradiction in *Maskiyot Kesef* and the appearance of what appears to be examples of it in *'Adnei Kesef*, an example of the seventh contradiction?

57. ADK I, p. 32.

58. Ibid., p. 73.

59. Ibid., p. 32.

60. AS II, p. 52.

61. AM, p. 8.

62. BT Berachot 18a–b.

63. Maimonides, *Guide*, I 42, pp. 92–93.

64. Some of the contemporary scholarship that has discussed Maimonides' position on resurrection include: Albert Dov Friedberg, "Maimonides' Reinterpretation of the Thirteenth Article of Faith: Another Look at the Essay on Resurrection," *Jewish Studies Quarterly* 10, no. 3 (2003), pp. 244–57; Alexandra Wright, "Immortality and Resurrection: Maimonides and the Maimonidean Controversy," in *Aspects of Liberal Judaism: Essays in Honour of John D. Rayner*, eds. David J. Goldberg and Edward Kessler (London, 2004), pp. 159–69; Charles Manekin, "Possible Sources of Maimonides' Theological Conservatism in his Later Writings," in *Maimonides After 800 Years: Essays on Maimonides and His Influence*, ed. Jay M. Harris (Cambridge, 2007), pp. 220–28.

65. Confirmed in TIK, p. 18.

66. AM, p. 8. English translation from Souza, *Philosophical Commentaries*, p. 445.

67. Ibid., p. 442.

68. Ibn Kaspi is likely influenced by Aristotle's discussion of contradictions in his logical work, *On Interpretation*. Aristotle's *On Interpretation* was known in Arabic as *Kitāb al-'Ibāra* or in Arabic as *Sefer ha-Meliṣah*. An epitome of Averroes' commentary was translated into Hebrew in 1288 by Jacob b. Makhir as *Kol Melekhet ha-Higgayon*.

69. AM, p. 8.

70. TIK, pp. 151–52.

71. TAK, pp. 16–18.

72. AS I, p. 51.

73. QK, p. 23. Barry Mensch writes that Ibn Kaspi had multiple solutions to this problem in his writings at Mensch, *Studies in Joseph ibn Caspi*, p. 23n105. My answer here, I think, reconciles Ibn Kaspi's disparate discussions and unites into one unified solution.

74. *Guide*, I Intro, p. 19.

75. This is discussed in Averroes, *The Book of the Clarification of the Systems of Proof in the Beliefs of the Nation* (*Kitab al-Kashf'an Manahij al-Adilla fi 'Aqaid al-Mila*), Topic 5, Question 3. The English translation is in Averroes, *The Philosophy and Theology of Averroes*, trans. Mohammed Jamil-al-Rahman [Baroda, 1921], p. 260 "This is one of the most intricate problems of religion. For if you look into the traditional arguments about this problem you will find them contradictory; such also being the case with arguments of reason. The contradiction in the arguments of the first kind is found in the Quran and the Traditions. There are many verses of the Qur'an, which by their universal nature, teach that all the things are predestined and that man is compelled to do his acts; then there are verses which say that man is free in his acts and not compelled in performing them."

76. AM, p. 7. English translation from Souza, *Philosophical Commentaries*, p. 449.

77. *Guide* II 13, p. 285 and II 25, p. 329.

78. AM, p. 99.

79. *Guide* II 32, pp. 360–61.

80. AM, p. 113.

81. Jon. 3:4.

82. Jon. 3:10.

83. Ibid.

84. AM, p. 10.

85. Jon. 3:9.

86. SHK, 69, p. 128.

87. TIK, p. 49. English translation of Diment, *Exegesis, Philosophy and Language*, p. 28.

88. *Guide* I Intro, p. 15.

89. TIK, p. 159.

90. MK, p. 44.

91. Compare Exod. 2:6 to 6:20. MK, p. 44.

92. MK, p. 44.

93. *Guide* I Intro, p. 15.

94. MK, p. 87.

95. *Guide* I 15, p. 41.

96. Ibid. III 43, p. 573.

97. MK, p. 87.

98. Ibid.

99. TIK, p. 123

100. Mal. 2:12.

101. BT Shabbat 55b: "He shall have none awakening [i.e., teaching] among the Sages."

102. Gen 35:18.

103. II Chron. 4:9.

104. Gen. 49:8–10 and MK, p. 86.

105. One of the original sources of this concept is BT Yoma 28b where it is written that "our father Abraham kept the whole Torah." This point is employed by Rashi in his comments on Genesis 7:2, 25:27, 26:5, and 32:5. See: Menachem Kellner, "Rashi and Maimonides on the Relationship of Torah and Cosmos," in *Between Rashi and Maimonides: Themes in Medieval Jewish Thought, Literature and Exegesis*, ed. Ephraim Kanarfogel and Moshe Sokolow (New York, 2010), pp. 23–58.

106. SHK, pp. 66–67.

107. Ibid., p. 73. Ibn Ezra, *Ibn Ezra's commentary on the Pentateuch*, vol. ii, pp. 141–42 (on Exodus 6:28).

108. Hannah Kasher, "Introduction," p. 38.

109. SHK, pp. 69–70.

110. Gen. 35:22.

111. BT Shabbat 55b. BT Shabbat 55b argues that Jacob kept his bed in Rachel's tent when she was alive and moved it to the tent of Bilhah when Rachel died. Reuben, Leah's son, felt that it slighted his mother and moved Jacob's bed into his mother, Leah's, tent. For an expanded discussion of this issue, see: Steven Fraade, *Legal Fictions: Studies of Law and Narrative in the Discursive Worlds of Ancient Jewish Sectarians and Sages* (Leiden, 2011), pp. 423–24.

112. SHK, p. 70; TIK, p. 122.

113. Gen. 32:29.

114. SHK, pp. 71–72.

115. Gen. 49:3–4.

116. MK, p. 104.

117. Exod. 6:28–29 and SHK, p. 72.

118. MK, p. 150.

119. Exod. 6:20.

120. Ibid. 6:26.

121. Ibid. 6:27.

122. SHK, p. 74.

123. Num. 26:1–2.

124. Num. 25:17–18 and SHK, p. 76.

125. II Sam. 24:11.

126. SHK, pp. 79–80.

127. Ibid., p. 82.

128. Ibid., p. 83.

129. *Guide* II 45, pp. 396, 398.

130. Jer. 42:6–7.

131. SHK, pp. 88, 91.

132. Ibid., p. 88.
133. *Guide* I 71, p. 175 and II 37, p. 373.
134. Jer. 13:12–14, 28:10–14 and SHK, pp. 88–89.
135. Richard Elliott Friedman, *Who Wrote the Bible?* (New York, 1987), pp. 15–49.
136. Ibid., pp. 50–69.
137. Robert Alter, "Introduction to the Old Testament," in *The Literary Guide to the Bible*, ed. Robert Alter and Frank Kermode (Cambridge, 1987), p. 27.
138. MK, p. 60.
139. Gen. 21:2, 3, 5 and MK, p. 60.
140. MK, p. 151.
141. Num. 33:1–2 and MK, p. 60.
142. TIK, p. 63.
143. Ibid., pp. 63–64.
144. MK, p. 112.
145. MK, p. 29 and AS II, p. 125.
146. Gen. 12:1.
147. TIK, p. 64.
148. TIK, p. 109 and AS II, p. 125.
149. Gen. 42:2 and MK, p. 93.
150. Gen. 24:16.
151. Gen. 40:23.
152. Isa. 38:1, Jer. 4:22 and MK, p. 66.
153. MK, p. 66.
154. Gen. 24:16.
155. Genesis Rabba 60:5.
156. Exod. 4:18–19 and MK, p. 135.
157. Discussed briefly in Basil Herring, "Joseph Ibn Kaspi: An Introduction," in *Joseph Ibn Kaspi's* Gevia' Kesef: *A Study in Medieval Jewish Philosophic Bible Commentary*, ed. and trans. Basil Herring (New York, 1982), p. 60.
158. MK, p. 5.
159. Ibid., p. 216.
160. Compare: Gen. 4:17 to Exod. 14:23–25.
161. MK, p. 24.
162. Gen. 10:25.
163. Gen. 12:3.
164. MK, p. 44.
165. Ibid., p. 60.
166. Gen. 21:1–2.
167. Ibid. 35:24.
168. TIK, p. 119.

169. MK, pp. 148–49.

170. SHK, p. 205.

171. TIK, p. 4.

172. Deut. 28:9 and TIK, p. 69.

173. Ran Ben-Shalom attempts to reconstruct the details of Ibn Kaspi's journey through piecing together the details he gives across his different commentaries. See: Ben-Shalom, "The Unwritten Travel Journal," pp. 7–51.

174. Twersky, "Joseph Ibn Kaspi," pp. 238–42 and Dimant, *Exegesis, Philosophy and Language*, pp. 16–20.

175. For example, see: BT Baba Metziah 31b. The entire list of citations of this phrase in the Talmud is listed and discussed in Jay Harris, *How Do We Know This?: Midrash and the Fragmentation of Modern Judaism* (Albany, 1995), pp. 25–50 and analyzed within the context of this phrase's longer reception in Funkenstein, *Perceptions of Jewish History*, pp. 88–90 and Dimant, *Exegesis, Philosophy and Language*, pp. 16–17.

176. For an analysis of Maimonides use of the expression, see: Abraham Nuriel, *Concealed and Revealed in Medieval Jewish Philosophy* (Jerusalem, 2000), pp. 93–99 and Sara Klein-Braslavy, *Maimonides' Interpretation of the Story of Creation* (Jerusalem, 1987), pp. 24–27.

177. *Guide* I 26, pp. 56–57.

178. Ibid., III 29, pp. 514–22.

179. This is one the apparent contradictions between the *Guide* and the *Mishneh Torah*. In *Guide* III 29, Maimonides cites an idolatrous pagan book as a means to understand the Bible, while in the *Mishneh Torah*, *Book of Knowledge, Laws of Idolatry and Idolaters* 2:2 (MT, p. 64) Maimonides codifies the law forbidding the reading of works of idolatry! He says there: "Idolaters wrote many books about their worship, what the main part of their worship is, how it is done and what the related laws are. God commanded us not to read such books at all, and nor to think about them or any connected matter at all." The same alleged contradiction appears *within* the *Mishneh Torah*. Thus, in *Laws of Sanhedrin* 2:1, Maimonides states that judges must study "the superstitious practices of idolaters" (MT, p. 1176). Similarly, one might today be against the publishing, distribution, and reading of pornography, but still hold that judges, lawmakers, etc., should read it in order to know how to judge it. For a contempory application of the meaning of this tension within Maimonides' writings, see: Yehuda Parnes, "Torah u-Madda and Freedom of Inquiry," *The Torah U-Madda Journal* 1 (1989), pp. 68–71 and David Berger and Lawrence Kaplan, "On Freedom of Inquiry in the Rambam—And Today," *The Torah U-Madda Journal* 2 (1990), pp. 37–50.

180. Twersky, "Joseph Ibn Kaspi," p. 239.

181. Ibid., p. 240 and Moshe Weinfeld, "Bible Criticism," in *Contemporary Jewish Religious Thought*, eds. Arthur A. Cohen and Paul Mendes-Flohr (New York, 1972), p. 35.

182. TIK, pp. 18–19: "I stood in the study hall of Maimonides, may his memory be for a blessing, and there were his sons of the fourth and fifth generation to him. The reason for me going was based on what these without understanding told me that there were great sages there, but when I arrived, I did not find what I had hoped."

183. TIK, p. 19.

184. Ibid., p. 20.

185. Exod. 7:15.

186. Ibid.

187. MK, p. 155 and TIK, p. 19. To be exact, Ibn Kaspi does not use the term Sultan, but the "king of Egypt" (*melech miṣrayim*).

188. TIK, p. 123.

189. Exod. 5:3.

190. MK, p. 139.

191. Exod. 5:14 and 24:6, and MK, pp. 141 and 214.

192. Isa. 28:8 and ADK I, p. 129.

193. MK, p. 298; AM, pp. 135, 141 and AS I, p. 113.

194. Gen. 41:40 and MK, p. 92.

195. Exod. 3:5 and TIK, p. 19.

196. Kalonymos, *ha-Teshuvah le-Yosef Kaspi*, p. 15 and Ben-Shalom, "The Unwritten Travel Journal," pp. 22–23.

# Bibliography

## Primary Sources

Abarbanel, Isaac. "Me-ha-Abarbanel le-Ḥeleq Shlishi me-ha-Moreh," in *Sefer Moreh Nevukhim 'im Arba'ah Perushim*. Jerusalem: 1960), pp. 71–73.

Abba Mari of Lunel. *Minhat Qena'ot*. In *Responsa of the Rashba to Rabbi Solomon ben Abraham ber. Aderet*. Edited by H. Z. Dimitrovsky. Jerusalem: Mossad ha-Rav Kook, 1990.

Al-Farabi, Abu Nasr. *On the Perfect State (Mabadi' Ara Ahl al-Madina al-Fadila)*. Translated by Richard Walzer. Oxford: The Clarendon Press, 1985.

Aristotle. *History of Animals*. Translated by D'Arcy Wentworth Thompson.

———. *On Interpretation*. Translated by E. M. Edghill.

———. *On the Heavens*. Translated by J. L. Stocks.

———. *Nicomachean Ethics*. Translated by Robert C. Bartlett and Susan D. Collins. Chicago: University of Chicago Press, 2012.

———. *On Rhetoric*. Translated by George A. Kennedy. Oxford: Oxford University Press, 1991.

———. *Poetics*, Translated by Seth Benardete and Michael Davis. South Bend, IN: St. Augustine Press, 2002.

———. *Politics*. Translated by Carnes Lord. Chicago: University of Chicago Press, 1984.

Augustine. *City of God*. Translated by Marcus Dods. Peabody, MA: Hendrickson Publishers Inc., 2009.

Averroes. *Averroes' Middle Commentary on Aristotle's Nicomachean Ethics in the Hebrew Version of Samuel ben Judah*. Edited by Lawrence V. Berman. Jerusalem: The Israel Academy of Sciences and Humanities, 1999.

———. *Averroes on Plato's Republic*. Edited and translated by Ralph Lerner. Ithaca, NY: Cornell University Press, 1974.

———. *Epitome of Aristotle's Parva Naturalia*. Translated to Hebrew by Moses Ibn Tibbon and edited by Harry Blumberg. Cambridge, MA: Medieval Academy of America, 1954.

———. *Epitome of Aristotle's Parva Naturalia*. Translated to English by Harry Blumberg. Cambridge, MA: Medieval Academy of America, 1961.

———. *The Book of the Clarification of the Systems of Proof in the Beliefs of the Nation* (*Kitab al-Kashf'an Manahij al-Adilla fi 'Aqaid al-Mila*). Edited by al-Jabari. Beirut, 1998.

———. *The Philosophy and Theology of Averroes*. Translated by Mohammed Jamil-al-Rahman. Baroda: A. G. Widgery, 1921.

Avicenna, "Healing: Metaphysics X." Translated by Michael E. Marmura in *Medieval Political Philosophy: A Sourcebook*. Edited by Ralph Lerner and Muhsin Mahdi. Ithaca, NY: Cornell University Press, 1963: 98–111.

Falaquera, Shem Tov Ibn. *Moreh ha-Moreh*. Edited by Yair Shiffman. Jerusalem: World Union of Jewish Studies, 2001.

Geiger, Abraham. "Excerpts from Geiger's Works," in *Abraham Geiger and Liberal Judaism: The Challenge of the Nineteenth Century*. Edited by Max Wiener. Philadelphia: Jewish Publication Society, 1962: 147–246.

Ibn Bajjah. "Rule of the Solitary (*Tadbīru'l-Mutawaḥḥid*)" in D. M. Dunlop, "Ibn Bājjah's *Tadbīru'l-Mutawaḥḥid* (Rule of the Solitary)," *Journal of the Royal Asiatic Society of Great Britain & Ireland* (New Series) 77, no. 1–2 (1945): 72–81.

Ibn Ezra, Abraham. *Ibn Ezra's Commentary on the Pentateuch*, 5 volumes. Translated by H. Norman Strickman and Arthur M. Silver. New York: Menorah Publishing Company, 1988.

Ibn Kaspi, Joseph. *'Adnei Kesef*, vol. i–ii. Edited by Isaac Last. London: Narodiczky, 1911–1912.

———. *'Amudei Kesef Umaskiyot Kesef, Shnei Perushim al Sefer ha-Moreh le-ha-Rambam*. Edited by Solomon Werbluner. Frankfurt am Main: Baeck, 1848.

———. *'Asara Kelei Kesef*, vol. i–ii. Edited by Isaac Last. Presburg: Alkalay, 1905.

———. *Qevuṣat Kesef*. English Translation in Barry Mensch, *Studies in Joseph ibn Caspi: Fourteenth-Century Philosopher and Exegete*. Leiden: E. J. Brill, 1975: 7–42.

———. *Maṣref la-Kesef*. Edited by Isaac Last. Cracow: Fisher, 1906.

———. *Recensionen, Varianten und Ergänzüngen zu der Edition* ['Aśarah kele kesef]. Edited by Isaac Last. Pressburg: Alkalay, 1904.

———. *Sharshot Kesef*. Selection published in Isaac Last "Sharshoth Kesef. The Hebrew Dictionary of Roots, by Joseph Ibn Kaspi" *Jewish Quarterly Review* 19, no. 4 (1907): 651–87.

———. *Sharshot Kesef*. Ms. Paris—Bibliotheque Nationale, heb. 1244.

———. *Shulḥan Kesef*, Edited by Hannah Kasher. Jerusalem: Ben-Zvi Institute, 1996.

———. *Tam ha-Kesef*. Edited by Isaac Last. London: Narodiczky, 1913.

———. *Terumat Kesef*. Edited by Adrian Sackson. In *Joseph Ibn Kaspi: Portrait of a Hebrew Philosopher in Medieval Provence*. Leiden: Brill, 2017: 263–94.

———. *Ṭirat Kesef* or *Sefer ha-Sod*. Edited by Isaac Last. Presburg: Alkalay, 1905.

———. *Yore Deʻa* or *Sefer ha-Musar*. English Translation in *Hebrew Ethical Wills*. Edited and translated by Israel Abrams. Philadelphia: Jewish Publication Society, 1926: 127–61.

Ibn Tibbon, Samuel. *Ma'amar Yikavu Hamayim (Treatise of the Gathering of the Waters)*. Edited by Mordechai Bisliches. Pressburg: Anton Edlen v. Schmid, 1837.

———. "Preface to translation of Maimonides, Commentary on Avot." Translated by Menachem Kellner in Menahem Kellner, "Maimonides and Samuel Ibn Tibbon on Jeremiah 9:22–23 and Human Perfection," in *Studies in Halakhah and Jewish Thought Presented to Rabbi Professor Menahem Emanuel Rackman on His Eightieth Birthday*. Edited by M. Beer. Ramat-Gan: Bar-Ilan University Press, 1994: 49–57.

———. *Samuel ibn Tibbon's Commentary on Ecclesiastes: The Book of the Soul of Man*. Edited and translated by James T. Robinson. Germany: Mohr Siebeck, 2007.

Kalonymos ben Kalonymos. *ha-Teshuvah ṿe-Yosef Kaspi*. Edited by Joseph Perles. Munich, 1879.

Kant, Immanuel. *Metaphysics of Morals*. Translated by Mary Gregor. Cambridge, UK: Cambridge University Press, 1996.

Kimḥi, Joseph. *The Book of the Covenant*. Translated by Frank Talmage. Toronto: The Pontifical Institute of Mediaeval Studies, 1972.

Maimonides, Moses. *Mishnah, 'Im Perush Mosheh ben Maimon [Commentary on the Mishnah]*. Translated by Joseph Qafiḥ. 7 volumes. Jerusalem: Mossad Harav Kook, 1963–1969.

———. *Iggerot*. Translated by Joseph Qafiḥ. Jerusalem: Mossad Harav Kook Press, 1972.

———. "Letter on Astrology," in *A Maimonides Reader*. Edited by Isadore Twersky. Springfield, NJ: Behrman House, 1972: 463–73.

———. "Letter on Resurrection," in *Crisis and Leadership: Epistles of Maimonides*. Edited by Abraham Halkin and David Hartman. Philadelphia: Jewish Publication Society, 1985: 211–45.

———. *Mishneh Torah: The Book of Knowledge*. Translated by Moses Hyamson. Jerusalem: Feldheim Publishers, 1974.

———. *Mishneh Torah: The Code of Maimonides*. Edited by Yohai Makbili. Israel: Or Vishua Publications, 2009.

———. *Mishneh Torah: The Book of Judges*. Translated by Abraham M. Hershman. New Haven CT: Yale University Press 1949.

———. *The Commandments (Sefer ha-Mitzvot)*. Translated by Charles B. Chavel. London: The Soncino Press, 1976.

———. *The Eight Chapters of Maimonides on Ethics (Shemonah Perakim)*. Edited and translated by Joseph I Gorfinkle. New York: Columbia University Press, 1912.

———. *Mishna im Perush Rabbenu Moshe ben Maimon*, vol. 4, Seder Nezikin. Jerusalem: Mossad ha-Rav Kook, 1963.

———. "The Epistle to Yemen," in *Epistles of Maimonides: Crisis and Leadership*. Translated by Abraham Halkin and edited by David Hartman. Philadelphia: Jewish Publication Society, 1985: 93–149.

———. *Sefer Moreh Nevuḥim le-ha-Rav Moshe ben Maimon ha-Sefardi; be-ha'ataqat Shmu'el ibn Tibbon 'im Arba'ah Perushim: Efodi, Shem Ṭov, Ibn Qresqas, Abarbanel*. Jerusalem, 1959.

———. *The Guide of the Perplexed*. Translated by Shlomo Pines. Chicago: University of Chicago Press, 1963.

Naḥmanides, Moses. *Commentary on the Torah*, vol. i–v. Translated by Charles B. Chavel. New York: Shilo Publishing House, 1971–1976.

Naḥmanides, Moses. *Writings of the Ramban*, 2 volumes. Translated by Charles B. Chavel. New York: Shilo Publishing House, 1978.

## Secondary Sources

Alter, Robert. "Introduction to the Old Testament," in *The Literary Guide to the Bible*. Edited by Robert Alter and Frank Kermode. Cambridge, MA: Harvard University Press, 1987: 11–35.

Altmann, Alexander. "The Ladder of Ascension," in *Studies in Mysticism and Religion, Presented to Gershom G. Scholem on His Seventieth Birthday*. Edited by Ephraim Urbach, R. J. Zwi Werblowski, and Chaim Wirszubski. Jerusalem: Magnes Press, 1967: 1–32.

Armitage, J. Mark. "Aquinas on the Division of the Ages: Salvation History in the *Summa*," *Nova et Vetera* 6, no. 2 (2008): 253–70.

Baer, Yitzhak F. *Galut*. New York: Schocken Books, 1947.

Baron, Salo. "The Historical Outlook of Maimonides," *Proceedings of the American Academy of Jewish Research* 6 (1934–1935): 5–113.

Ben-Shalom, Ram. "The Unwritten Travel Journal to the East of Joseph Ibn Caspi," *Pe'amim* 124 (2010): 7–51.

Benor, Ehud. *Worship of the Heart: A Study in Maimonides' Philosophy of Religion*. Albany: State University of New York Press, 1995.

Berger, David, and Lawrence Kaplan, "On Freedom of Inquiry in the Rambam—And Today," *The Torah U-Madda Journal* 2 (1990): 37–50.

Berman, Lawrence. "Ibn Rushd's *Middle Commentary on the Nicomachean Ethics* in Medieval Hebrew Literature," in *Multiple Averroès: Actes du Colloque*

*International Organisé à l'occasion du 850e Anniversaire de la Naissance d' Averroès*. Edited by Jean Jolivet. Paris: Belles Lettres, 1978: 287–321.

———. "The Ideal State of the Philosophers and Prophetic Laws," in *A Straight Path: Studies in Medieval Philosophy and Culture. Essays in Honor of Arthur Hyman*. Edited by Ruth Link-Salinger. Washington, DC: Catholic University of America Press, 1988: 10–22.

Biale, David. *Gershom Scholem: Kabbalah and Counter-History*. Cambridge, MA: Harvard University Press, 1982.

———. "Gershom Scholem on Nihilism and Anarchism," *Rethinking History* 19, no. 1: 61–71.

Brague, Remi. *The Law of God: The Philosophical History of an Idea*. Chicago: University of Chicago Press, 2007.

Buber, Martin. *On the Bible: Eighteen Studies*. Edited by Nahum Glatzer. New York: Schocken Books, 1968.

Burger, Ronna. "Male and Female Created He Them: Some Platonic Reflections on Genesis 1–3," in *The Nature of Woman and the Art of Politics*. Edited by Eduardo Velasquez. Maryland: Rowman and Littlefield, 2000: 1–18.

Chazan Robert. *Fashioning Jewish Identity in Medieval Western Christendom*. Cambridge: Cambridge University Press, 2009.

———. "Genesis 49:10 in Thirteenth-Century Christian Missionizing," in *New Perspectives on Jewish-Christian Relations: In Honor of David Berger*. Leiden: Brill, 2012: 93–108.

Cohen, Gerson D. "Esau as a Symbol in Early Medieval Thought,' in *Jewish Medieval and Renaissance Studies*. Edited by Alexander Altmann. Cambridge, MA: Harvard University Pres, 1967: 19–48.

Cohen, Shaye. "Does Rashi's Torah Commentary Respond to Christianity? A Comparison of Rashi with Rashbam and Bekhor Shor," in *The Idea of Biblical Interpretation: Essays in Honor of James L. Kugel*. Edited by Hindy Najman and Judith H. Newman. Brill: Leiden, 2004: 449–72.

Davidson, Herbert. "Maimonides' Secret Position on Creation," in *Studies in Medieval Jewish History and Literature*. Edited by Isadore Twersky. Cambridge, MA: Harvard University Press, 1979: 16–40.

———. *Moses Maimonides: The Man and His Work*. Oxford: Oxford University Press, 2005.

Davies, Daniel. *Method and Metaphysics in Maimonides' Guide for the Perplexed*. Oxford: Oxford University Press, 2011.

Diamond, James. "Abarbanel's Exegetical Subversion of Maimonides' 'Aqedah: Transforming a Knight of Intellectual Virtue into a Knight of Existential Faith," in *The Hebrew Bible in Fifteenth Century Spain: Exegesis, Philosophy, Literature, and the Arts*. Edited by Jonathan Decter and Aturo Pratis Olivan. Leiden: Brill, 2012: 75–100.

———. *Converts, Heretics, and Lepers: Maimonides and the Outsider*. Notre Dame, IN: University of Notre Dame Press, 2007.

———. *Maimonides and the Hermeneutics of Concealment: Deciphering Scripture and Midrash in the* Guide of the Perplexed. Albany: State University of New York Press, 2002.

Dimant, Isaiah. *Exegesis, Philosophy and Language in the Writing of Joseph Ibn Caspi*. Dissertation. University of California, Los Angeles, 1979.

Eisen, Robert. "Joseph Ibn Kaspi on the Book of Job," *Jewish Studies Quarterly* 13, no. 1 (2006): 50–86.

———. "Joseph Ibn Kaspi on the Secret Meaning of the Scroll of Esther," *Revue des Études Juives* 160, no. 3–4 (2001): 379–408.

———. "Kaspi on Allegory in the Book of Esther: A Rejoinder to Hannah Kasher," *Revue des Études Juives* 163, no. 1–2 (2004): 289–93.

Elon, Menachem. *Jewish Law: History, Sources, Principles*, 4 vols. Translated by Bernard Auerbach and Melvin J. Skyes. Philadelphia: Jewish Publication Society, 1994.

Emery, Richard. "Documents Concerning Jewish Scholars in Perpignan in the 14th and 15th Centuries," *Michael* 4 (1976): 27–48.

Eran, Amira. "Intuition and Inspiration—The Causes of Jewish Thinkers' Objection to Avicenna's Intellectual Prophecy" (Ḥads)," *Jewish Studies Quarterly* 14, no. 1 (2007): 39–71.

Fishbane, Michael. "Inner-Biblical Exegesis," in *Hebrew Bible, Old Testament: The History of Its Interpretation, Volume 1*. Edited by Magne Saebo. Germany: Vandenhoeck and Ruprecht, 1996: 33–49.

Fox, Marvin. "A New View of Maimonides' Method of Contradictions," *Annual of Bar-Ilan University* (1987): 19–43.

Fraade, Steven. *Legal Fictions: Studies of Law and Narrative in the Discursive Worlds of Ancient Jewish Sectarians and Sages*. Leiden: Brill, 2011.

Fraenkel, Carlos. *From Maimonides to Samuel ibn Tibbon: The Transformation of the* Dalalat al Ha'irin *into the* Moreh ha-Nevukhim. Jerusalem: Magnes Press 2007.

Frank, Daniel. "Humility as a Virtue: A Maimonidean Critique of Aristotle's Ethics," in *Moses Maimonides and His Time*. Edited by Eric L. Ormsby. Washington, DC: Catholic University of America Press, 1989: 89–99.

Friedberg, Dov. "Maimonides' Reinterpretation of the Thirteenth Article of Faith: Another Look at the Essay on Resurrection," *Jewish Studies Quarterly* 10, no. 3 (2003): 244–57.

Friedman, Richard Elliott. *Who Wrote the Bible?* New York: Harper and Row, 1987.

Funkenstein, Amos. *Perceptions of Jewish History*. Berkeley: University of California Press, 1993.

Gelber, Yoav. "The History of Zionist Historipography," in *Making Israel*. Edited by Benny Morris. Michigan University Press, 2007: 47–80.

Goodman, Micha. "History and Meta-History in the Posture of Maimonides," in *Bedarkhey Shalom: Studies in Jewish Thought Presented to Shalom Rosenberg*. Edited by Benjamin Ish-Shalom and Amichai Bernholz. Jerusalem: Beit-Morasha Press, 2007: 243–53.
Graetz, Heinrich. *The Structure of Jewish History and Other Essays*. Translated by Ismar Schorsch. New York: Jewish Theological Seminary of America, 1975.
Green, Alexander. *The Virtue Ethics of Levi Gersonides*. New York: Palgrave Macmillan, 2016.
Gross, Heinrich. *Gallia Judaica*. Paris: Librarie Léopold Cerf, 1897.
Grossman, Abraham. "A Social Controversy in Biblical Commentaries of Rabbi Joseph Ibn Kaspi," in *Studies in Hebrew Poetry and Jewish Heritage*. Edited by Ephraim Hazan and Joseph Yahalom. Ramat Gan: Bar-Ilan University Press, 2006: 103–24.
———. "Contempt for Women on Philosophical Grounds: Joseph Ibn Kaspi," *Zion* 68 (2003): 41–67.
Gutas, Dimitri. *Avicenna and the Aristotelian Tradition*, 2nd ed. Leiden: Brill, 2004.
Guttmann, Julius. *Philosophies of Judaism: A History of Jewish Philosophy from Biblical Times to Franz Rosenzweig*. New York: Schocken Books, 1973.
Halbertal, Moshe. *Concealment and Revelation: Esotericism in Jewish Thought and its Philosophical Implications*. Princeton, NJ: Princeton University Press, 2007.
———. *People of the Book: Canon, Meaning and Authority*. Cambridge, MA: Harvard University Press, 1997.
Halbertal, Moshe, and Avishai Margalit. *Idolatry*. Translated by Naomi Goldblum. Cambridge, MA: Harvard University Press, 1998.
Halper, Edward. "Maimonides and Nachmanides on Sending Away the Mother Bird," in *Thinking about the Environment: Our Debt to the Classical and Medieval Past*. Edited by Thomas Robinson and Laura Westra. Lanhan, MD: Lexington Books, 2002: 185–202.
Halper, Yehuda. "Da'at Harambam and Da'at Samuel Ibn Tibbon: on the Meanings of the Hebrew Term *Da'at*, and their Relationship to the Central Questions of the *Mishneh Torah* and the *Guide of the Perplexed*," *Daat* 83 (2017), pp. 47–68.
Harris, Jay. *How Do We Know This?: Midrash and the Fragmentation of Modern Judaism*. Albany: State University of New York Press, 1995.
Harvey, Steven. "Did Maimonides' Letter to Samuel Ibn Tibbon Determine Which Philosophers Would Be Studied by Later Jewish Thinkers?" *Jewish Quarterly Review* 83, no. 1/2 (Jul.–Oct., 1992): 51–70.
———. "The Influence of the *Nicomachean Ethics* on Medieval Jewish Thought," *Mélanges de l'Université Saint-Joseph* 55 (2013–2014): 119–42.
———. "The Place of the Philosopher in the City According to Ibn Bājjah," in *The Political Aspects of Islamic Philosophy: Essays in Honor of Muhsin*

S. *Mahdi*. Edited by Charles E. Buttersworth. Cambridge, MA: Harvard University Press, 1992: 199–233.

———. "The Source of Quotations from Aristotle's *Nicomachean Ethics* in Maimonides' *Guide of the Perplexed* and Shem Tov Ibn Falaquera's *The Guide to the Guide*," *Jerusalem Studies in Jewish Thought* 14 (1998): 87–102.

Harvey, Warren Zev. "A Third Approach to Maimonides' Cosmogony-Prophetology Puzzle," *Harvard Theological Review* 74, no. 3 (1981): 287–301.

———. "How to Begin to Study the *Guide of the Perplexed*, 1:1," *Daat* 21 (1988): 5–23.

———. "Spinoza on Ibn Ezra's Secret of the Twelve," in *Spinoza's Theological-Political Treatise: A Critical Guide*. Edited by Yitzhak Melamed and Michael Rosenthal. Cambridge: Cambridge University Press, 2010: 41–55.

———. "Spinoza's Metaphysical Hebraism," in *Jewish Themes in Spinoza's Philosophy*. Edited by Heidi M. Ravven and Lenn E. Goodman. Albany: State University of New York Press, 2002: 107–14.

———. "Two Jewish Approaches to Evil in History," in *Wrestling with God: Jewish Theological Responses during and after the Holocaust*. Edited by Steven Katz, Shlomo Biderman, and Gershon Greenberg. Oxford: Oxford University Press, 2007: 326–31.

Herring, Basil. "Joseph Ibn Kaspi: An Introduction," in *Joseph Ibn Kaspi's Gevia' Kesef: A Study in Medieval Jewish Philosophic Bible Commentary*. Edited and translated by Basil Herring. New York: Ktav Publishing House, 1982: 3–122.

Hollanda de Souza, Igor. "Maimonides for the Masses: A Re-Appraisal of Joseph Ibn Kaspi's Commentaries on the *Guide of the Perplexed*," Association of Jewish Studies Annual Meeting, December 13–15, 2015.

———. *Philosophical Commentaries on the Preface to the Guide of the Perplexed, c. 1250–1362*. Dissertation. University of Chicago, 2014.

Husik, Isaac. *A History of Mediaeval Jewish Philosophy*. New York: Jewish Publication Society of American, 1940.

Idel, Moshe. *Old Worlds, New Mirrors*. Philadelphia: University of Pennsylvania Press, 2010.

Jospe, Rafael. "Rejecting Moral Virtue as the Ultimate Human End," in *Studies in Islamic and Judaic Traditions*. Edited by William Brinner and Stephen Ricks. Denver, CO: University of Denver, 1986: 185–204.

Kahan, Moshe. "Aspects of Medieval Lexicography—Between Jonah ibn Janāḥ's *Kitāb al-'Uṣūl* and Joseph Kaspi's *Šaršot Kesef*," *Revue des Etudes Juives* (Accepted pending revision).

———. "Joseph Ibn Kaspi—New Biographical Data," *Pe'amim* (forthcoming).

———. "The Relationship of Synonyms in Kaspi's *Sharshot Kesef*," *Hebrew Linguistics* 69 (2014): 87–105.

Kaplan, Lawrence. "Maimonides on the Miraculous Element in Prophecy," *Harvard Theological Review* 70, no. 3–4 (1977): 233–56.

Kasher, Hannah. "'How Could the Lord Command Such an Abomination to Be. Done?'—Rabbi Joseph Ibn Kaspi's Critics on the Binding of Isaac," in '*Et Ha-Da'at* 1 (1997): 38–46.

———. "Introduction," in *Shulchan Kesef*. Edited by Hannah Kasher. Jerusalem: Ben-Zvi Institute, 1996: 11–53.

———. "Joseph Ibn Kaspi's Aristotelian Interpretation and Fundamentalist Interpretation of the Book of Job," *Daat* 20 (1988): 117–26.

———. *Joseph Ibn Caspi as a Philosophical Exegete*. PhD Dissertation, Bar-Ilan University, 1982.

———. "Joseph Kaspi." *Stanford Encyclopedia of Philosophy*. October 16, 2013. Web. http://plato.stanford.edu/entries/kaspi-joseph/

———. "On the Book of Esther as an Allegory in the works of Joseph Ibn Kaspi: A Response to Robert Eisen in REJ 160/3–4," *Revue des Études Juives* 161, no. 3–4 (2002): 459–64.

———. "On the Question of the Authorship of the *Explanation of Ibn Ezra's Secrets* attributed to Joseph Ibn Kaspi," in *Alei Shefer: Studies in the Literature of Jewish Thought: Presented to Rabbi Dr. Alexander Shafran*. Edited by Moshe Hallamish. Ramat-Gan: Bar-Ilan. 1990: 97–108.

———. "'Why is the Land in Ruins?' (Jer. 9:11): Religious Transgression versus Natural Historical Process in the Writing of Maimonides and His Disciples," *Hebrew Union College Annual* 69 (1998): 143–56.

Kaufman, Yehezkel. *Exile and Alienation*, vol. 1–2. Tel-Aviv: Dvir, 1929–1930.

Kellner, Menachem. *Dogma in Medieval Jewish Thought*. London: Littman Library of Jewish Civilization, 1986.

———. *Maimonides on the "Decline of the Generations" and the Nature of Rabbinic Authority*. Albany: State University of New York Press 1996.

———. "Rashi and Maimonides on the Relationship of Torah and Cosmos," in *Between Rashi and Maimonides Themes in Medieval Jewish Thought, Literature and Exegesis*. Edited by Ephraim Kanarfogel and Moshe Sokolow. New York: Yeshiva University Press, 2010: 23–58.

Klein-Braslavy, Sara. *Maimonides' Interpretation of the Story of Creation*. Jerusalem: Rubin Mass Ltd., 1987.

Klitsner, Judy. *Subversive Sequels in the Bible: How Biblical Stories Mine and Undermine Each Other*. Jerusalem: Maggid Books, 2011.

Knohl, Israel. *The Divine Symphony: The Bible's Many Voices*. Philadelphia: Jewish Publication Society, 2003.

Koller, Aaron. *Esther in Ancient Jewish Thought*. Cambridge: Cambridge University Press, 2014.

Kreisel, Howard. "From Esotericism to Science: The Account of the Chariot in Maimonidean Philosophy till the End of the Thirteenth Century," in *Judaism as Philosophy: Studies in Maimonides and the Medieval Jewish Philosophers of Provence*. Edited by Howard Kreisel. Boston: Academic Studies Press, 2015: 209–69.

———. *Prophecy: The History of an Idea in Medieval Jewish Philosophy*. Dordrecht: Kluwer Academic Publishers, 2001.

Lasker, Daniel J. *Jewish Philosophical Polemics against Christianity in the Middle Ages*, 2nd ed. Oxford: Littman Library of Jewish Civilization, 2007.

Lebovic, Nitzan. "Finally, This Author Puts the Great Gershom Scholem in Context," *Haaretz* May 2, 2015.

Leibowitz, Nehama. *Commentary on Devarim (Deuteronomy)*. Translated by Aryeh Newman. Jerusalem: World Zionist Organization, Dept. for Torah Education and Culture in the Diaspora, 1993.

Lerner, Ralph. "Introduction," *Averroes on Plato's Republic*. Edited and translated by Ralph Lerner. Ithaca, NY: Cornell University Press, 1974: xiii–xxviii.

Leukam, Mary. *Dignified Animals: How "Non-Kantian" is Nussbaum's Conception of Dignity?* MA Thesis, Georgia State University, 2011.

Levinger, Jacob. "Abstinence from Alcohol in the *Guide of the Perplexed*," *Bar Ilan University Annual: Decennial Volume* 1955–65: 299–305.

Liska, Vivian. *German-Jewish Thought and its Afterlife*. Bloomington: Indiana University Press, 2017.

Lorberbaum, Yair. "On Contradictions, Rationality, Dialectics, and Esotericism in Maimonides' *Guide of the Perplexed*," *The Review of Metaphysics* 55, no. 4 (2002): 711–750.

———. " 'The Seventh Cause': On the Contradictions in Maimonides' *Guide of the. Perplexed*: A Reappraisal," *Tarbitz* 69 (1999–2000): 212–37.

Maccoby, Hyam. *Judaism on Trial: Jewish-Christian Disputations in the Middle Ages*. Rutherford, NJ: Faleigh Dickinson University Press, 1982.

Mahdi, Muhsin. *Alfarabi and the Foundation of Islamic Political Philosophy*. Chicago: University of Chicago Press, 2001.

Manekin, Charles. "Ambiguities of Scriptural Exegesis: Joseph Ibn Kaspi on God's Foreknowledge," in *Philosophers and the Jewish Bible*. Edited by Charles Manekin and Robert Eisen. Baltimore: University of Maryland Press, 2008: 79–111.

———. "Possible Sources of Maimonides' Theological Conservatism in his Later Writings," in *Maimonides After 800 Years: Essays on Maimonides and His Influence*. Edited by Jay M. Harris. Cambridge: Cambridge University Press, 2007: 220–28.

Marmura, Michael. "Some Aspects of Avicenna's Theory of God's Knowledge of Particulars," *Journal of the American Oriental Society* 82, no. 3 (1962): 299–311.

Melamed, Abraham. "Aristotle's *Politics* in Medieval and Renaissance Jewish Thought," *Pear*im 51 (1993): 27–69.

———. *The Myth of the Jewish Origins of Science and Philosophy*. Jerusalem: Magnes Press, 2010.

Melzer, Arthur. *Philosophy Between the Lines: The Lost History of Esoteric Writing*. Chicago: University of Chicago Press, 2014.

Mensch, Barry. *Studies in Joseph ibn Caspi: Fourteenth-Century Philosopher and Exegete*. Leiden Brill, 1975.

Myers, David. "History as Ideology: The Case of Ben-Zion Dinur, Zionist Historial 'Par Excellence,'" *Modern Judaism* 8, no. 2 (1988): 167–93.

Novak, David. "Does Maimonides have a Philosophy of History?" *Proceedings of the Academy for Jewish Philosophy* 4 (1983): 397–420.

Nuriel, Abraham. *Concealed and Revealed in Medieval Jewish Philosophy* Jerusalem: Magnes Press, 2000.

Nussbaum, Martha. 'The Future of Feminist Liberalism," *Proceedings and Addresses of the American Philosophy Association* 74, no. 2 (2000): 47–79.

Parnes, Yehuda. "Torah u-Madda and Freedom of Inquiry," *The Torah U-Madda Journal* 1 (1989): 68–71.

Pines, Shlomo. "Aristotle's *Politics* in Arabic Philosophy," *Israel Oriental Studies* 5 (1975): 150–60.

———. "Jewish Philosophy," in *Studies in the History of Jewish Thought: The Collected Works of Shlomo Pines*, vol. v. Edited by Warren Zev Harvey and Moshe Idel. Jerusalem: Magnes Press, 1997: 1–51.

———. "On the Probability of the Re-Establishment of a Jewish State according to Ibn Kaspi and Spinoza," *Iyyun* 14 (1963): 289–317.

———. "The Philosophical Sources of the *Guide of the Perplexed*," in Moses Maimonides' *Guide of the Perplexed*. Edited and translated by Shlomo Pines. Chicago: University of Chicago Press, 1963: lvii–cxxxiv.

Posnanski, Adolf. *Shiloh: Ein Beitrag zur Geschichte der Messiaslehre*—Downloaded; i. Theil, Die Auslegung von Genesis c. 49, v. 10 im Altertum bis zu Ende des Mittelalters. Leipsig, 1904.

Ravitzky, Aviezer. "Samuel Ibn Tibbon and the Esoteric Character of the *Guide of the Perplexed*," *AJS Review* 6 (1931): 87–123.

———. "The Anthropolgical Theory of Miracles in Medieval Jewish Philosophy," in *Studies in Medieval Jewish History and Literature*, vol. ii. Edited by Isadore Twersky. Cambridge, MA: Harvard University Press, 1984: 231–72.

Raviv, Rivkah. "The Talmudic Formulation of the Prophecies of the Four Kingdoms in the Book of Daniel," *Jewish Studies, an Internet Journal* 5 (2006): 1–20.

Renan, Ernest. *Les Écrivains Juifs Français du XIVe Siècle*. Paris: Imprimerie Nationale, 1893.

Robinson, James T. "Translator's Introduction," in *Samuel ibn Tibbon's Commentary on Ecclesiastes: The Book of the Soul of Man*. Germany: Mohr Siebeck, 2007: 1–142.

Rosenberg, Shalom. "Bible Exegesis in the Guide," *Jerusalem Studies in Jewish Thought* 1 (1981): 85–157.

Ross, J. J. "Maimonides and Progress—Maimonides' Concept of History," in *Hevrah vi-Historia*. Edited by Yehezkel Cohen. Jerusalem: Israel Ministry of Education and Culture, 1980: 529–42.

Rotenstreich, Nathan. "Gershom Scholem's Conception of Jewish Nationalism," in *Gershom Scholem: The Man and His Work*. Edited by Paul Mendes-Flohr. Albany: State University of New York Press, 1994: 104–19.

Sackson, Adrian. *Joseph Ibn Kaspi: Portrait of a Hebrew Philosopher in Medieval Provence*. Leiden: Brill, 2017.

———. "Rationalistic Messianism and the Vicissitudes of History: The Final Chapter of Joseph Ibn Kaspi's *Tam ha-kesef*," *Zutot* 12 (2015): 1–15.

Sadiq, Shalom. "Natural Law and the Law of Moses in the Thought of R. Josef Ibn Kaspi," *Daat* 83 (2017): 161–74.

Sarna, Nahum. *Exploring Exodus: The Origins of Biblical Israel*. New York: Schocken, 1986.

Scholem, Gershom. *Explications and Implications: Writings on Jewish Heritage and Renaissance*. Tel-Aviv: Am Oved, 1989.

———. *Major Trends in Jewish Mysticism*. New York: Schocken Books, 1946.

———. "Against the Myth of the German-Jewish Dialogue," in *On Jews and Judaism in Crisis: Selected Essays*. New York: Schocken Books, 1976: 61–64.

———. "Redemption Through Sin," in *The Messianic Idea and Other Essays in Jewish Spirituality*. New York: Schocken Books, 1971: 78–141.

———. "Reflections on Modern Jewish Studies (1944)," in *On the Possibility of Jewish Mysticism in Our Time and Other Essays*. Edited by Avraham Shapira and translated by Jonathan Chipman. Philadelphia: Jewish Publication Society, 1997: 51–71.

Schweid, Eliezer. *The Classic Jewish Philosophers*. Translated by Leonard Levin. Leiden: Brill, 2010.

———. "The Rejection of the Diaspora in Zionist Thought: Two Approaches," *Studies in Zionism* 5, no. 1 (1984): 43–70.

Seeskin, Kenneth. "Maimonides' Sense of History," *Jewish History* 18, no. 2/3 (2004): 129–45.

———. *Searching for a Distant God: The Legacy of Maimonides*. Oxford: Oxford University Press, 2000.

Shapiro, Marc. *The Limits of Orthodox Theology: Maimonides' Thirteen Principles Reappraised*. London: Littman Library of Jewish Civilization, 2004.

Sirat, Colette. *A History of Jewish Philosophy in the Middle Ages*. Cambridge: Cambridge University Press, 1985.

Smith, Wilfred Cantwell. "The Study of Religion and the Study of the Bible," *Journal of the American Academy of Religion* 39, no. 2 (1971): 131–40.
Socher, Abraham P. "Of Divine Cunning and Prolonged Madness: Amos Funkenstein on Maimonides' Historical Reasoning," *Jewish Social Studies* 6, no. 1 (1999): 6–29.
Steinschneider, Moritz. "Josef Caspi," in *Gesammelte Schriften*. Edited by Heinrich Malter and Alexander Marx. Berlin: Poppelauer, 1925.
Stern, Gregg. "Philosophic Allegory in Medieval Jewish Culture: The Crisis in Languedoc (1304–1306)," in *Interpretation and Allegory: Antiquity to the Modern Period*. Edited by Jon Whitman. Leiden: Brill, 2003: 189–209.
Stern, Josef. *Problems and Parables of Law: Maimonides and Nahmanides on Reasons for the Commandments (Ta'amei Ha-Mitzvot)*. Albany: State University of New York Press, 1998.
Stone, M. W. F. "Augustine and Medieval Philosophy," in *The Cambridge Companion to Augustine*. Edited by Eleonore Stump and Norman Kretzmann. Cambridge: Cambridge University Press, 2006: 253–66.
Strauss, Leo. "How to Begin to Study the *Guide of the Perplexed*," in *Moses Maimonides' Guide of the Perplexed*. Edited and translated by Shlomo Pines. Chicago: University of Chicago Press, 1963: xi–lvi.
———. "On Abravanel's Critique of Monarchy (1937)." Translated by Martin D. Yaffe, in *Reorientation: Leo Strauss in the 1930s*. Edited by Martin D. Yaffe and Richard S. Ruderman. New York: Palgrave Macmillan, 2014: 267–68.
———. "The Literary Character of *The Guide of the Perplexed*," in *Persecution and the Art of Writing*. Chicago: University of Chicago Press, 1952: 60–78.
*The Jewish Political Tradition*, vol. 1: Authority. Edited by Michael Walzer, Menachem Lorberbaum, Noam J. Zohar. New Haven, CT: Yale University Press, 2000.
Touati, Charles. "Le Problème de l'Inerrance Prophetique dans la Théologie Juive du Moyen Age," *Revue de l'Histoire des Religions* 174 (1968): 169–87.
Twersky, Isadore. "Joseph Ibn Kaspi—Portrait of a Medieval Jewish Intellectual," in *Studies in Medieval Jewish History and Literature*. Edited by Isadore Twersky. Cambridge, MA: Harvard University Press, 1979: 231–57.
———. *Introduction to the Code of Maimonides (Mishneh Torah)*. New Haven, CT: Yale University Press, 1980.
Tzeitkin, Yechiel. *The Characteristics of Biblical Exegesis in the Works of Peshat Commentators of the Maimonidean School of Provence in the 13th and 14th Centuries*. PhD Dissertation, Bar-Ilan University, 2011.
Urbach, Ephraim E. *The Sages: Their Concepts and Beliefs*. Jerusalem: Magnes Press, 1975.
Visi, Tamas. "Ibn Ezra, a Maimonidean Authority: The Evidence of the Early Ibn Ezra Supercommentaries," in *The Cultures of Maimonideanism: New*

*Approaches to the History of Jewish Thought.* Edited by James T. Robinson. Leiden: Brill, 2009: 89–132.

———. *The Early Ibn Ezra Supercommentaries: A Chapter in Medieval Jewish Intellectual History.* PhD Dissertation, Central European University, Budapest, 2006.

Walfish, Barry. *Esther in Medieval Garb: Jewish Interpretation of the Book of Esther in the Middle Ages.* Albany: State University of New York Press, 1993.

Weinfeld, Moshe. "Bible Criticism," in *Contemporary Jewish Religious Thought.* Edited by Arthur A. Cohen and Paul Mendes-Flohr. New York: The Free Press, 1972: 35–40.

Wellhausen, Julius. *Prolegomena to the History of Ancient Israel.* New York: The Meridian Library, 1957.

Weiss, Raymond. *Maimonides' Ethics: The Encounter of Philosophic and Religious Morality.* Chicago: University of Chicago Press, 1991.

Weiss, Roslyn. "Maimonides on *Shiluah Ha-Qen,*" *Jewish Quarterly Review* 79 (1989): 345–66.

Wolfson, Harry. "The Veracity of Scripture in Philo, Halevi, Maimonides and Spinoza," in *Alexander Marx Jubilee Volume.* New York: Jewish Theological Seminary of America, 1950: 603–60.

Wright, Alexandra. "Immortality and Resurrection: Maimonides and the Maimonidean Controversy," in *Aspects of Liberal Judaism: Essays in Honour of John D. Rayner.* Edited by David J. Goldberg and Edward Kessler. London: Vallentine Mitchell, 2004: 159–69.

Zunz, Leopold. "On Rabbinical Literature (1818)," in *A Jew in the Modern World.* Edited by Paul Mendes Flohr and Jehuda Reinharz. Oxford: Oxford University Press, 1995: 221–30.

# Index

Aaron, 65, 132, 138–139
Abba Mari ben Moses, 63
Abraham, 8, 21, 27, 45, 47, 55, 62, 63, 64, 66–67, 87–88, 101, 114, 115, 127, 135–136, 138
Active Intellect, 57, 68, 70, 73, 78, 103, 104
Adam, 7, 8, 54, 85, 86, 89–90, 93, 115
Ahasuerus, 5, 24, 28, 33
Al-Farabi, 16, 57, 103, 106, 156n1, 168n3, 180n295, 181n296
Anatoli, Jacob, 10
Aristotle, 3, 7, 10, 12, 13, 14, 19, 20, 21, 27–28, 39, 43, 54–59, 61–62, 63, 64, 65–66, 70–71, 73, 77, 89, 91–92, 94, 95–97, 109–110, 123–124, 135, 136, 156n1, 158n23, 158n29, 163n123, 164n136, 167n192, 173n103, 178n237, 181n10, 181n11, 184n68
  Works:
    *De Animalibus*, 43, 164n136
    *Metaphysics*, 12, 55–58, 62, 63
    *Meteorology*, 136
    *Nicomachean Ethics*, 3, 10, 27–28, 54, 65–66, 89, 156n1, 160n58, 167n192
    *On Interpretation*, 109–110, 158n29, 181n10, 184n68
    *On the Heavens*, 136, 158n31, 173n103
    *Parva Naturalia*, 19, 77–78, 158n23–24, 174n134
    *Physics*, 39–40, 63, 136, 163n123
    *Politics*, 13–14
    *Rhetoric*, 178n237
Averroes (Ibn Rushd), 3, 10, 15–18, 20, 57, 106, 123, 136, 164n136, 167n192
  Aristotle's *Nicomachean Ethics*, 3, 10, 54, 167n192
  Aristotle's *Parva Naturalia*, 19, 77–78, 158n23–24, 174n134
  *De Animalibus*, 164n136
  Plato's *Republic*, 3, 10, 15–18, 157n10, 157n12–14
  *The Book of the Clarification of the Systems of Proof in the Beliefs of the Nation*, 123
Avicenna (Ibn Sina), 31, 77–78, 105–106, 173n118, 173n127, 174n128, 174n130, 174n134, 180n294, 180n295
  God's knowledge of particulars, 31
  Prophecy, 77–78, 173n127, 174n128, 174n130, 174n134

Babylonia, 5, 37, 40, 45–47, 49, 51–52, 134
Babylonian Talmud, x, 6, 33, 37, 39, 40, 49, 65, 66, 70, 97, 108, 117, 119, 120, 129, 131, 140–141, 164n136, 167n193, 172n79
Baron, Salo, 7, 154n39
Benjamin, 3, 39
Binding of Isaac, 64, 87–88, 176n192

Canaan (Land), 6, 21, 22, 27, 41, 45, 47–48, 51–52, 79, 133
Chariot, ix, 2, 5, 11, 12, 30, 55–75, 145
　Abraham, 66–67
　Ezekiel, 2, 12, 30, 55, 70–73
　Isaiah, 2, 12, 30, 55, 68–70
　Jacob, 67
　Moses, 67–68
　Tabernacle, 67–68
　Zechariah, 12, 30, 55, 68, 73–75
Christianity, 1, 23, 32, 36–40, 45, 46, 51–54, 56, 60, 62, 83, 101, 103–106, 107, 112–113, 146
　Christ, 36, 38, 40, 46, 51–54
　Creation, 83
　Translation, 38, 83, 107, 112–113
　Trinity, 103–104
　Virgin birth, 53
Contradictions, 10, 12, 24–25, 36, 75–76, 91–92, 107, 115–126, 146–147
Covenant, 21–22, 26–27, 31, 37–38, 48
Crescas, Hasdai, 6

Daniel, 3, 12, 13, 44–48, 63, 112, 164n145, 165n152–154, 173n106
　Four Animals, 12, 13, 48
David (King), 36–40, 50–51, 101, 118, 133

Deuteronomy, 12–13, 19–20, 22, 31, 32, 40–42, 49, 50, 88, 94–95, 97, 99–100, 104, 108–109, 114, 116, 121, 131, 136, 140, 145, 161n79, 163n118
Dinur, Ben-Zion, xi–xii
Dispersal (in Bible), 10, 12, 107, 126–130

Ecclesiastes, 2, 14–15, 59, 112, 117
Egypt, 1, 4, 8, 15, 21, 22, 56, 79–81, 85–86, 113, 128, 132, 134, 136–137, 140–143, 156n1, 158n38, 189n182, 189n185
　Plagues, 80–81
Eisen, Robert, 24, 159n43–44, 159n49
Empty Spaces (in Bible), 10, 130–134, 147
Esau, 23–24, 65, 165n153
Esther, 2, 5, 24–25, 28, 33, 159n43–44, 159n49, 160n66
Exodus, 4, 15, 21, 50, 60, 63, 67, 79, 109, 112, 114, 115, 116, 121, 127, 132, 135, 136–137, 139, 142–143, 152n17, 161n74, 171n58
Ezekiel, 2, 12, 30, 31, 34–35, 46, 55, 56, 59, 68, 70–73, 90, 118, 120, 121, 133–134, 136

Falaquera, Shem Tov, 174n130, 180n294

Geiger, Abraham, x–xi
Genesis, 2, 15, 21, 34–35, 36–40, 44, 45, 46, 47–48, 81–84, 86–90, 109, 111, 112–114, 119, 125–126, 127, 129, 131, 136, 138–139, 143, 168n10, 170n46, 173n106

Gersonides, Levi, ix, 5–6, 10–11, 155n54
God
   Elohim, 33, 56, 82, 86, 88, 112–113, 115
   First Cause, 33, 35–36, 62, 69, 87, 103, 109, 113, 119, 129, 147, 155n51
   Overflow, 57, 73
   Proximate Cause, 33, 34, 36, 50–51, 129, 147
   YHVH, 33, 56, 82, 86, 88, 112–113, 115
Graetz, Heinrich, x–xi
Greece, 45–46, 56, 62–63, 146, 165n153, 165n157, 169n30
Guttmann, Julius, 5, 152n30

Ham, 47–48, 102, 128
Harvey, Warren Zev, 71, 91
Hebrew (roots), 1, 9–10, 37–38, 43, 53–54, 72–73, 83, 107, 109–113, 146–148
Hegel, Georg Wilhelm Friedrich, x, 15, 153n35, 154n39
Hezekiah, 39, 50, 51, 52, 54, 137
Husik, Isaac, 5, 152n30

Ibn Bajja, 16, 19, 156n1
Ibn Ezra, Abraham, 1, 3, 45, 46, 47, 51, 82, 108, 130, 151n2, 164n145, 165n153, 165n157, 166n160
   Secret of the twelve (sod ha-shneim asar), 108
Ibn Kaspi, Joseph
   'Adnei Kesef, 2, 5, 33–35, 42–44, 46, 50–52, 54, 83–84, 113, 118, 143, 160n69
   Amudei Kesef, 2, 5, 29, 77, 89, 90, 104, 118, 123–124

   Commentary on Ecclesiastes, 14, 117
   Commentary on Job, 65
   Commentary on Proverbs, 44, 49, 64, 79, 122
   Gelilei Kesef, 2, 24, 33
   Gevia Kesef, 2–3, 21, 26, 42–43, 64, 103–104, 160n63, 160n69
   Ḥaṣoṣrot Kesef, 2, 43
   Kapot Kesef, 2, 38
   Maskiyot Kesef, 2, 71, 75–77, 89, 92, 118, 120, 121–122, 124–126
   Maṣref la-Kesef, 2, 18, 34, 37, 38–40, 42, 47–48, 60–61, 82, 88, 94–101, 103, 112–114, 117, 127–129, 131–132, 135–139, 162n100
   Menorat Kesef, 2, 5, 25, 29–31, 32, 33, 36, 61, 62, 66–75, 82, 109, 152n17, 168n3, 170n45
   Mitot Kesef, 2, 52
   Mizraq / Mizraqei Kesef, 2, 115
   Retuqot Kesef, 3, 110–111
   Qe'arot Kesef, 3, 44
   Qevuṣat Kesef, 2, 110
   Sefer ha-Musar, 62, 151n8, 171n51
   Ṣeror ha-Kesef, 3–4
   Sharshot Kesef, 3, 37, 110
   Shulḥan Kesef, 1, 3, 5, 9, 19, 20, 21, 31, 35, 38, 76–77, 81, 112, 126, 130–132, 139–140, 160n69, 163n119
   Tam ha-Kesef, 3–4, 6, 22, 25, 26, 32, 33, 44, 122
   Terumat Kesef, 3, 15–18
   Tirat Kesef, 3, 9, 17, 47, 49, 62, 79–80, 95, 102, 114, 122, 126–128, 136, 139–140, 142
Ibn Tibbon, Moses, 10, 158n23
Ibn Tibbon, Samuel, 10, 58–60, 155n51, 168n13, 170n47, 171n72

Ibn Tibbon, Samuel *(continued)*
  *Ma'amar Yikavu ha-Mayyim*
    (*Treatise of the Gathering of the Waters*), 59–60
Idolatry, 7–8, 51, 85–89, 141, 188n179
Isaiah, 2, 12, 15, 30, 31, 43, 44, 46, 51–54, 55, 56, 59, 68–70, 83, 84, 104, 113, 118, 121, 137, 143
Islam, 45, 46, 56, 62, 143

Jacob, 18, 23, 26–27, 29, 31, 36–37, 46, 55, 64, 65, 67, 101, 103, 115, 128, 129, 131, 137, 142
  Ladder, 29, 65, 67, 128
Jeremiah, 46, 51, 84, 134, 137, 167n179
Job, 64–65
Jonah, 28–29, 33, 35–36, 125–126
Joseph, 3–4, 18, 115, 128, 137, 142
Judah, 12, 13, 36–40, 51, 52, 128–129, 163n114, 163n125, 165n153
  "The Scepter Shall Not Depart from Judah" (Gen 49:8–10), 12, 13, 36–40, 163n114, 163n125, 165n153

Kalonymous ben Kalonymous, 78, 143
Kant, Immanuel, 96
Kasher, Hannah, 5, 151n2, 159n43, 159n44, 159n49, 160n55, 160n66, 164n45, 166n166, 170n35, 174n133, 176n192, 177n229, 180n292
Kimḥi, David, 110–111
Kingship, 12, 13, 14–15, 16–17, 19, 24–25, 28, 36–37, 40–44, 45–46, 48, 51, 62, 69, 70, 72, 78, 112, 129, 145, 189n185

Land of Israel. *See* Canaan (Land)
Lamentations, 2, 38
Leviticus, 94–95, 114, 115, 116

Maimonides, Moses, ix, 1, 5, 6, 7–9, 10, 11, 13, 14–15, 21, 29, 33, 34, 35, 39, 40, 41, 42, 49, 54, 55, 56, 58, 59, 60, 64, 69, 70–71, 72, 74, 75, 76, 79, 83, 85, 88–93, 97–101, 104, 108, 113, 116–117, 119, 123–125, 127–128, 133–134, 140–141, 151n2, 152n30, 153n31, 154n38–39, 154n47, 155n51, 155n56, 156n1, 161n73, 161n77, 162n100, 163n123, 165n152, 166n166, 168n3, 169n24, 169n27, 171n51, 173n120, 173n123, 176n192, 177n228, 178n239, 178n245, 178n256, 179n264, 180n288, 180n295, 180n296, 183n48–49, 184n64, 188n179, 189n182
  Writings:
    *Book of the Commandments,,* 41
    *Commentary on the Mishna*, 108, 119, 154n38, 161n77
    *Guide of the Perplexed*, 1–2, 7–9, 10, 13, 21, 29, 33, 34, 39, 42, 58, 62, 64, 69, 70–71, 72, 74, 75, 76, 83, 85, 88–93, 97–101, 104, 113, 116–117, 119, 123, 124, 127–128, 133–134, 141, 151n8, 153n31, 154n49, 155n51, 155n56, 156n1, 161n73, 161n77, 163n123, 168n3, 173n123, 174n130, 176n211, 178n239, 178n256, 180n294–295, 183n48, 188n179
      Structure, 9, 89–93

*Laws of Character Traits*, 96–97
*Laws of Idolatry*, 7–8, 188n179
*Laws of Kings and their Wars*, 41, 51–52, 100
*Laws of Prayer*, 87
*Laws of Sanhedrin*, 125n163, 188n179
*Laws of the Foundations of the Torah*, 62, 66, 71, 76, 92, 124–125
*Laws of the Temple*, 85
*Letter on Astrology*, 49
*Letter on Resurrection*, 79, 120
Topics:
  God, 6–8, 33, 69
  Hebrew language, 113
  History, 7–9, 11
  Idolatry, 7–8
  Kingship, 40–41
  Messiah, 9, 51–52
  Pious man (*hasid*), 97
  Reasons for the Commandments, 9
  Resurrection of Dead, 119–120
Menorah, 5, 68, 73–74
Messiah, Messianism, xiv, 8, 36, 41, 45, 51–54, 113, 150n19, 159n49, 165n152, 167n193, 175n150
*Midrash Rabba*, 5, 45, 58–59, 73, 83, 105, 115, 137, 171n58
Miracles, 64, 75–81, 124, 139–140, 173n113
Mishna, 8, 14, 43, 58, 59 119
  *Avot*, 14, 43
  *Hagiga*, 58, 59
Moral Virtues, 11, 94–97, 100–101
Moses, 8, 23, 30, 31, 32, 33, 40, 55, 60, 61, 65, 66, 67–69, 79–83, 86, 90, 100–101, 104, 108–109, 112–113, 114, 115, 119, 127, 132, 135–140, 142–143, 152n17, 161n74, 161n77, 161n79, 170n46

Nahmanides, Moses, 45, 85–86, 165n154, 167n193
Nebuchadnezzar, 22, 50–52, 134
Noah, 34, 47–48, 64, 85, 86, 95, 102, 115, 128, 136, 138
Numbers, 21, 50, 100, 116, 121, 133

Pines, Shlomo, 6, 26, 28, 158n29, 158n31
Plato
  *Republic*, 3, 10, 15–18, 157n12–14
  Creation, 91–92, 123–124
  Philosopher-King, 16–17, 19
practical wisdom, 27–28, 49, 54, 62, 167n192
Prayer, 35, 87, 126, 162n100
Prophecy, 19–32, 37–40, 45–49, 51–54, 64, 71, 74, 75, 77, 88, 91–92, 124, 128, 133, 145–146, 159n49, 159n52, 160n69, 174n130, 180n126
  Contingent future (*'atida efsharit*), 20, 23–29, 31, 32, 37–40, 45–46, 47–49, 51–54, 159n52, 160n69
  Experience, 26–29, 88
  Imaginative faculty, 30, 31, 32, 64, 71, 74, 75
  "Intuitive prophecy" (*hads*), 77, 174n130
  Necessary future (*'atida mehuyevet*), 20–22, 25, 29–31, 32, 37, 159n52
Proverbs, 18, 44, 49, 59, 64, 79, 117, 122, 177n229
Providence, 24, 99, 155n51
Psalms, 2, 23, 40, 59, 64, 120

Rachel, 103, 186n111

Rashi, 130, 137, 151n2, 172n79, 186n105
Rebecca, 23, 65, 137
Repetition, 10, 12, 66, 107, 114, 134–137, 147
Rome, 45, 46, 49, 62, 63, 146, 165n152–154, 165n154, 165n157

Sabbatical year, 95, 100
Sacrifices, 4, 42, 85–89, 116
Sarah, 63, 64, 127, 135, 139
Scholem, Gershom, xii–xiv, 149n9
Schweid, Eliezer, 5, 153n31
*Sefer Yosipon*, 46, 118, 165n157
*shiluaḥ ha-ken*, 95, 98–99, 178n256
Sirat, Colette, 5, 153n31
Sodom, 33–36, 125–126

Solomon (King), 4, 36, 58–59, 63, 79, 101, 117
Solomon ibn Aderet (Rashba), 63

Tabernacle, 4–5, 67–68, 114, 152n17
Tamar, 128–129
Temple, xi, 4, 5, 12, 22, 23, 30, 31, 38–40, 45, 48–54, 56, 62, 87, 145, 163n118, 166n166, 170n46
Twersky, Isadore, 6–7, 141, 152n28

Zechariah, 2, 12, 30, 46, 55, 56, 68, 73–75, 81
Zedekiah, 37, 39, 40, 50, 51, 52, 167n179
Zionism, x–xiv, 6 149n9

www.ingramcontent.com/pod-product-compliance
Lightning Source LLC
Chambersburg PA
CBHW020652230426
43665CB00008B/410